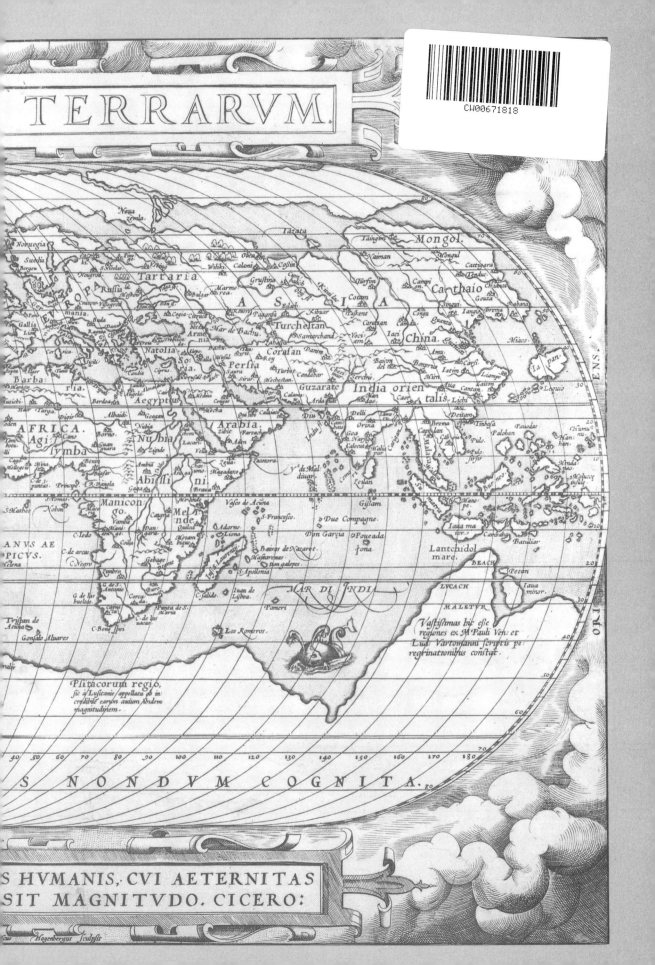

TERRA AUSTRALIS TO AUSTRALIA

Matthew Flinders's first recorded use of the term 'Australia' 1804

The publication of
Terra Australis to Australia
has been assisted by
Esso Australia Ltd.

Terra Australis
TO
AUSTRALIA

Edited by

Glyndwr Williams and Alan Frost

Melbourne
Oxford University Press
in association with the
Australian Academy of the Humanities

OXFORD UNIVERSITY PRESS AUSTRALIA

Oxford New York Toronto
Delhi Bombay Calcutta Madras Karachi
Petaling Jaya Singapore Hong Kong Tokyo
Nairobi Dar es Salaam Cape Town
Melbourne Auckland

and associated companies in
Berlin Ibadan

OXFORD is a trade mark of Oxford University Press

National Library of Australia
Cataloguing-in-Publication data:

Terra Australis to Australia.

  Includes index.
  ISBN 0 19 554908 2.

  1. Australia—Discovery and exploration.
  2. Voyages and travels. I. Williams,
  Glyndwr. II. Frost, Alan, 1943– .

919.4′04

Designed by Derrick I. Stone Design
Typeset by Setrite Typesetters Ltd
Colour separations by Scanagraphix Pty Ltd
Printed by Impact Printing, Melbourne
Published by Oxford University Press,
253 Normanby Road, South Melbourne, Australia

Front endpaper: Abraham Ortelius, World Map ('Typvs Orbis Terrarvm') 1570
Back endpaper: Matthew Flinders 'General Chart of Terra Australis or Australia' 1814

Foreword

This volume is part of The Australian Academy of the Humanities' contribution to the Australian Bicentenary. Like the international conference mounted by the Academy to mark the Bicentenary, it takes its title from the project of the same name, which was one of the first major projects endorsed by the Australian Bicentennial Authority. During 1988 it has seemed fitting to include consideration of the coming of the Europeans to the southern hemisphere, and in particular to this island continent.

The Academy has been fortunate to have as editors of this volume two scholars, working in England and Australia respectively, who are acknowledged experts in eighteenth-century European voyages of discovery and the British settlement of Australia. Professor Glyndwr Williams and Dr Alan Frost are distinguished historians who have not only contributed extensively in their own special areas of expertise, but enlisted two other specialist scholars to contribute to the volume.

None of what follows would have been possible without the generous support of Esso Australia Ltd. which, as sole sponsor of the project 'Terra Australis to Australia', has shown such imagination in participating in this way in the Australian Bicentenary. Esso is a company which obviously takes very seriously its corporate responsibility to the Australian community, and the Academy is very grateful indeed to have been associated with it in this venture.

J. P. Hardy
Director
Terra Australis to Australia Project
The Australian Academy of the Humanities
Canberra

Contents

Acknowledgements

Many individuals and organizations have offered generous help as we have prepared this work.

In particular, we take much pleasure in thanking The Australian Academy of the Humanities and its honorary Secretary, Professor J. P. Hardy, the Australian Studies Centre, University of London and its then director, Professor G. C. Bolton, and Esso Australia Ltd.

It would have been impossible to complete the work without access to the rich collections of the National Library of Australia, Canberra (where Miss Barbara Perry and her colleagues eased our path), and of the Mitchell and Dixson Libraries, The State Library of New South Wales (where we have particularly to thank Miss Shirley Humphries, Ms Elizabeth Imashev, Mr Peter Davis and Mrs Rosemary Block). Staff at libraries and museums in Britain, France, the Netherlands, Austria, Spain, Portugal, and the United States were similarly helpful; and we thank them all most warmly. All illustrations are reproduced by permission of the Directors and/or Trustees of the respective institutions, as indicated in the List of Illustrations.

Ms Sandra McComb, the Managing Director of Oxford University Press Australia, Ms Ev Beissbarth, and their colleagues have enthusiastically supported the production of this work, and aided it. Mr Derrick Stone has shown great skill and expertise in the design. To them, our warmest thanks too.

Ms Shirley Horton, of La Trobe University's History Department, typed successive drafts with great efficiency and cheerfulness; and the University's Reprography Unit helped with a number of the illustrations.

At particular points, we have had help from Professor Elliott Forsyth, Professor Emeritus of French at La Trobe University; Dr Denis Gibbs, of The London Hospital; and Mr Brian Bird, photographer, of Sydney. We thank each of them.

We heartily endorse Professor Hardy's acknowledgement of Esso's very generous and enlightened support of 'Terra Australis to Australia', The Australian Academy of the Humanities' bicentennial project and conference, of which this volume is one reflection.

Preface

In this work, we have sought to indicate how Europeans have conceived of and 'seen' the southern continent, from its classical avatar, through that of 'Terra Australis Nondum Cognita', to the reality revealed to modern view.

In chapter 1, we survey classical, medieval, and renaissance conceptions and knowledge. In chapter 2, Dr Wallis considers the 'Dieppe' maps and charts, striking both for their beauty and for the puzzle of whether the 'Java la Grande' they depict reflects an early Portuguese discovery of the real continent. In chapter 3, Professor Schilder describes the discoveries, both deliberate and accidental, of the actual continent by Dutch navigators in the seventeenth century. In chapters 4, 5 and 6 we look, respectively, at the approaches to the continent of the English and French navigators in the seventeenth and eighteenth centuries; at the European settlement of New South Wales and the often sharp conflict between the expectations that the colonists bore with them and the reality they found; and at the emergence of the modern sense of the continent now known as Australia.

In all this, our stance is explicitly Eurocentric. This is the story of how Europeans first conceived of the southern continent, of how they progressively discovered it, and of how they developed from these discoveries a sense of it which more detailed knowledge then required them to modify. In being so consciously Eurocentric, our stance is the opposite of that found in *Australians to 1988*, for example, which is based on the geological, geographical, biological and botanical history of the continent itself, and on the history of the Aborigines' 40 000 year occupation of it. The two stances complement each other, rather than stand in opposition. Each has a distinctive contribution to make to our modern understanding of 'Australia'.

Glyndwr Williams
Department of History
Queen Mary College
London

Alan Frost
Department of History
La Trobe University
Melbourne

Abbreviations

ARA	Algemeen Rijksarchief, The Hague
BL	British Library, London
BM (NH)	British Museum (Natural History), London
BN	Bibliothèque Nationale, Paris
Dixson	Dixson Library, State Library of New South Wales, Sydney
GC	*The Great Circle* (Perth, 1979—)
Guildhall	Guildhall Library, London
Historical Studies	*Australian Historical Studies* (Melbourne, 1940—)
HRA	*Historical Records of Australia*, series 1 (Sydney, 1914—25)
HRNSW	*Historical Records of New South Wales* (Sydney, 1892—1901)
Huntington	Henry E. Huntington Library, San Marino
JAS	*Journal of Australian Studies* (Melbourne, 1978—)
JRAHS	*Journal* of the Royal Australian Historical Society
Mitchell	Mitchell Library, State Library of New South Wales, Sydney
NLA	National Library of Australia, Canberra
NMM	National Maritime Museum, Greenwich
PMC	*Portugaliae Monumenta Cartographica*, ed. Armando Cortesão and Avelino Teixeira da Mota (Lisbon, 1960)
PRO	Public Record Office, London
La Trobe	La Trobe Library, State Library of Victoria, Melbourne
Sutro	Sutro Library, California State Library, San Francisco
VOC	Dutch East India Company

List of Illustrations,
with Sources and Locations

xi

1.1 Ambrosius Macrobius World Map 1483

Chapter 1

Terra Australis:
Theory and Speculation

Glyndwr Williams and Alan Frost

Knowledge of the earth's sphericity may have developed in what Yeats called the 'Babylonian mathematical twilight', and passed from there to the ancient Greeks.[1] At least by the beginning of the Christian era a second geographical idea of considerable force had become associated with this first one—that there was a great mass of land in the southern hemisphere to counterbalance that of Europe, Asia, and north Africa. Writing about AD 150, the Alexandrine scholar Ptolemy described how

that part of the earth which is inhabited by us is bounded on the east by the unknown land which borders on the eastern races of Greater Asia, namely the 'Sinae' and the 'Seres', and on the south by the likewise unknown land which encloses the Indian sea and which encompasses Ethiopia south of Libya.[2]

Ptolemy's *Geography* was not widely known in Europe during the next thousand years, but his ideas did not entirely disappear. Though the ignorant may have thought that the earth was flat, the learned knew better, and they continued to postulate a southern continent, and to depict it on the elementary maps of the type known as T-O *(Orbis terrarum)*, which they drew to accompany their cosmographies (1.1). In his fifth-century commentary on the *Dream of Scipio*, Macrobius, for example, wrote that the earth

is divided into regions of excessive cold or heat, with two temperate zones between the hot and cold regions. The northern and southern extremities are frozen with perpetual cold ... The belt in the middle and consequently the greatest, scorched by an incessant blast of heat ... is uninhabited because of the raging heat. Between the extremities and the middle zone lie two belts ... tempered by the extremes of the adjoining belts; in these alone has nature permitted the human race to exist.[3]

And in the seventh century Isidore of Seville maintained that

beyond these three parts of the world, on the other side of the ocean is a fourth inland part in the south, which is unknown to us because of the heat of the sun, within the bounds of which the Antipodes are fabulously said to dwell.[4]

Interest in geography grew again during the Renaissance, and Ptolemy's was one of the most popular works as Italian princes vied to patronize lavish examples of the new art of printing. More than fifty editions of the Ptolemaic

1

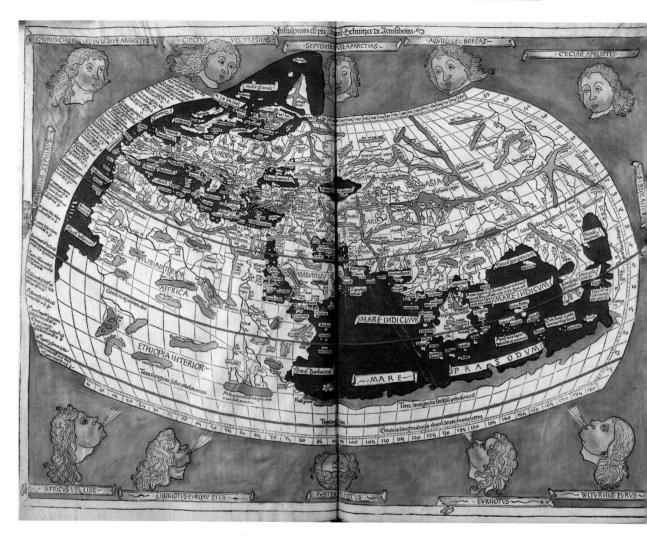

1.2   [Anonymous]   Ptolemaic World Map   1482

1.3   Lopo Homem   World Map   1519

world map (1.2) were published between 1477 and 1730. Showing the Indian Ocean to be enclosed by a vast land mass joined to Asia and Africa, the various versions helped to popularize the idea of a southern continent, for knowledge derived from intervening centuries caused Renaissance geographers to modify ancient notions in certain ways. Medieval travellers had increased Europe's general knowledge of Africa and Asia. At the same time the Arabs, whose works were known in some quarters, had developed a competent understanding of the geography of the fringes of these continents, and of some of the interior regions, and the Portuguese voyages about the turn of the sixteenth century demonstrated that there was a way to India around Africa. By the 1520s, geographers were showing the Indian Ocean connecting with the Atlantic (1.3). Soon after, as a consequence of Magellan's voyage, they began to indicate a southern way from the Atlantic to the Pacific Ocean.

The need for such modifications did not lead the geographers to question the existence of the southern continent, which continued to appear on their maps (1.4). Powerful elements in their world view required them to accept that this continent existed. There was a physical necessity for symmetry, and a religious one. The elder Mercator enunciated the first when he wrote that without a compensating southern land mass the world would fall to destruction among the stars.[5] Juan Luis Arias elaborated the second when, seeking royal sanction for his plan to discover the southern continent and to convert its inhabitants, he reminded Philip III that God's fiat had established the three geophysical levels of land, water, and air, and that if there were not a *Terra Australis* the purposeful symmetry of the fiat would not be satisfied, and articles of scripture would not be true—therefore, 'in the southern hemisphere there is an uncovered surface of land correspondent, or nearly so, to that which has been discovered in the northern hemisphere'.[6]

By the middle of the sixteenth century, those who drew the world were depicting an immense southern continent, *Terra Australis Nondum Cognita*, which occupied almost the whole of the temperate zone, and reached towards the equator below New Guinea (1.5, 1.6). Through reasoning by analogy, and because of such stories as those of Solomon's Ophir,[7] Marco Polo's Lucach or Beach,[8] and the Inca Tupac Yupanqui's islands,[9] the learned had also persuaded themselves that this continent was a region of great wealth. Roger Barlow, for example, represented to Henry VIII that the land to the south-east of China 'be the most richest londes and ilondes in the worlde, for all the golde, spices, aromatikes and pretiose stones, with all other thinges that we have in estimation'.[10] Gerard Mercator characterized Beach as a land of gold, and Maletur as one of spices.[11]

It is difficult to estimate how much authentic information lay behind this fanciful creation. Soon after they reached India, the Portuguese obtained

1.4 Oronce Finé World Map ('Nova, et integra vniversi Orbis Descriptio') 1531

4

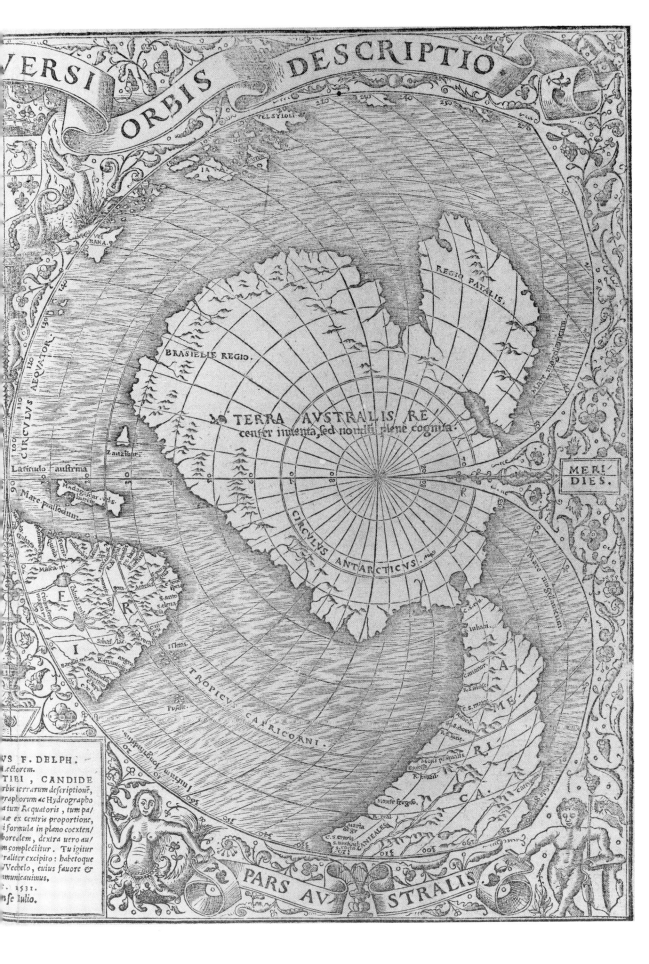

VERSI ORBIS DESCRIPTIO.

PARS AVSTRALIS

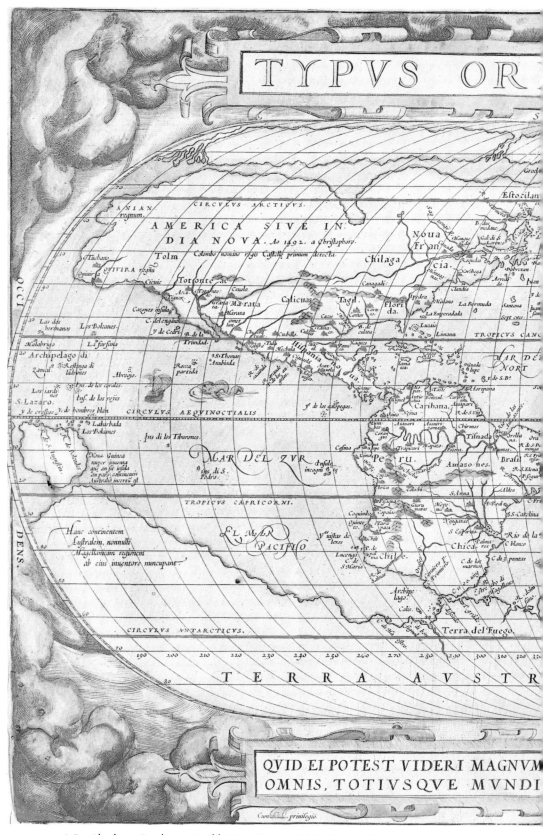

1.5   Abraham Ortelius   World Map ('Typvs Orbis Terrarvm')   1570

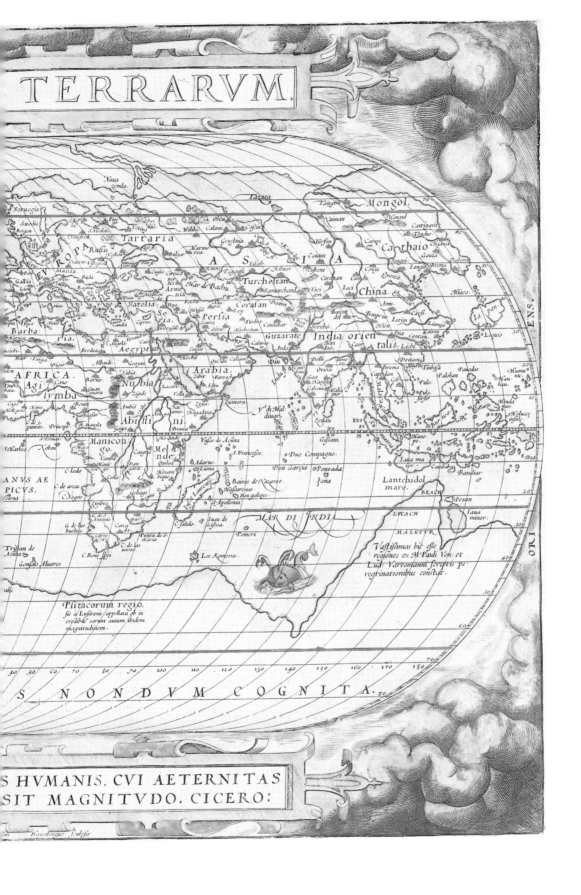

TERRARVM.

S NONDVM COGNITA.

S HVMANIS, CVI AETERNITAS
SIT MAGNITVDO. CICERO:

ENDIOSA DESCRIPTIO

a amatori ac fautori summo, in veteris amicitiæ ac familiaritatis memoriā Rumoldus Mercator fieri curabat A°. M.D.Lxxxvii.

1.6 Gerard Mercator Eastern hemisphere from his World Map ('Orbis Terrae Compendiosa Descriptio') 1587

8

tantalizing details of the geography of the eastern seas, and of the products of the Indonesian islands. They had found Ceylon by 1506, they were at Malacca in 1511, and soon after they reached the Banda Islands, Amboina, and the Moluccas, where they quickly established trading stations. In 1521 Cristóvão de Mendonça left Goa with three ships to search for the 'Isles of Gold' which, the Portuguese had gathered, lay somewhere to the east of Sumatra. Mendonça reached Malacca before the end of the year. Where he went thereafter is unknown, for there is no record of his subsequent progress.[12]

None the less, there has been much discussion of whether Mendonça's voyage, or others by Portuguese navigators in the 1520s, led to the discovery of the continent now known as Australia, and to its imperfect depiction as 'Java la Grande' on the Dieppe maps. Dr Helen Wallis examines this question at length in chapter 2. It is a vexed one, and however it is decided, what is certain is that any Portuguese discovery in the 1520s of the continent now known as Australia had little, if any, bearing on future European contact with it. Buried in the libraries of the wealthy until the end of the eighteenth century, the Dieppe maps offered no stimulus to later explorations; and what personal report lingered into the mid-sixteenth century was quickly subsumed under the much more powerful imaginative entity of *Terra Australis*. Indeed, the later maps of the Dieppe series themselves exhibit the growth of this process. From the Harleian version onwards, each map shows a progressive loss of Jean Rotz's clarity of outline, as the cartographers join Java la Grande to a great land mass stretching across the entire southern hemisphere, and fill its spaces with depictions of people, animals, and birds having no connection with the real Australia. It was the unknown *Terra Australis* as depicted by the Mercators, Ortelius, and their successors (1.5, 1.6) that henceforth held the attention of scholars, dreamers, and sailors, not the sparse country that the Portuguese may have found.

The Spanish were the first Europeans to undertake a sustained quest for the mysterious islands of gold and *Terra Australis*. In 1537, Cortés in Mexico sent two ships out into the Pacific, but the crews mutinied and lost the ships off New Guinea.[13] Thirty years later, after the settlement of the Philippines had resulted in the establishment of a regular route across the northern Pacific, the New World Spanish tried again. Pedro Sarmiento de Gamboa and others persuaded one Viceroy of Peru to mount an expedition to seek out Tupac Yupanqui's islands, only to have a new Viceroy give the command of the two ships to his nephew Alvaro de Mendaña. The vessels sailed in November 1567, and on 7 February 1568 reached Santa Ysabel, in what were soon to be known as Solomon's Islands.

As one Spanish official complained, Mendaña found 'no specimens of spices, nor of gold and silver, nor of merchandise, nor of any other source of profit, and all the people were naked savages'.[14] None the less, the explorer continued to believe that he had found the outliers of the southern continent. After four years

9

of petitioning Philip II, he gained approval to colonize *Terra Australia* and to govern it for two generations. However, mischances in America delayed his sailing until April 1595, when he took out four ships and four hundred persons. The expedition came to the Marquesas Islands in July, where the Spanish wrought much destruction. From there, they sailed west until they reached the Santa Cruz Islands in early September, where they again killed indiscriminately, and made a desultory attempt at settling. Illness and dissension soon afflicted them, and, on Mendaña's death in October, Pedro de Quirós took the survivors to Manila, where they arrived in February 1596.

Quirós ended the voyage convinced that *Terra Australis* extended from near New Guinea to the Straits of Magellan, and was equal in size to Europe and Asia combined (1.7). He also ended it obsessed with the idea of finding this 'Nuevo Mundo' and of converting its inhabitants. After gaining the support of the Spanish king, he sailed from Peru with three ships and three hundred persons at the end of 1605. His aim was to circumnavigate 'the world, returning to Spain by the East Indies, first discovering . . . the unknown lands of the south; thence proceeding via New Guinea to arrive at China, Maluco, and the two Javas, the Great and the Less, and all the other famous islands abounding in silver, gold, gems and spices'.[15] At the beginning of May 1606 they came to the New Hebrides, the size of which persuaded Quirós that his quest was over. The island he stayed at for five weeks and began to settle he termed 'Austrialia del Espiritu Santo'. On their arrival, the Spanish described their situation as though it were Eden, but friction quickly developed with the Melanesians. Abruptly, Quirós gave up the attempt at colonization, and sailed off to realize some obscure dream of greater discovery. He reached Acapulco in November 1606, while Torres took the other vessel to Manila—through the strait that now bears his name—on an altogether more important voyage.

The failures of this expedition did not end Quirós's dreams. He begged his way from Mexico to Spain, arriving in Madrid in October 1607, where he proceeded to bombard the King, the Council of State, and the Council of the Indies with memorials urging the renewal of the quest. He represented the extent of the continent that awaited discovery as being 'as great as all *Europe* & *Asia* the lesse, vnto the Sea of *Bachu, Persia*, and all the Iles, as well of the Ocean, as of the *Mediterranean* sea, taking *England & Island* into this account'. It was the 'fifth part of the Terrestrial Globe, and extended it selfe to such length, that in probabilitie it is twice greater in Kingdoms and Seignories, then all that which at this day doth acknowledge subiection and obedience vnto your Maiestie'. In its geography, its products, and its climate, it was an earthly paradise; it offered such spices as nutmeg, pepper, and cinnamon, and gold and silver; its people were simple, numerous, and awaited the grace of conversion.[16]

Philip III offered Quirós some encouragement, but his councillors were dubious, and procrastinated. Although Quirós did not know it, his cause was

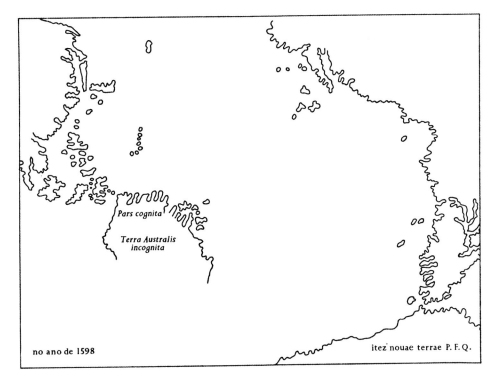

Pars cognita

Terra Australis
incognita

no ano de 1598

itez' nouae terrae P. F. Q.

1.7   Fernando Quirós   Chart of the Pacific Ocean (redrawn)   1598

doomed by the time he died in 1614 on his way back to Mexico. In following years, others took it up, most notably Juan Luis Arias, who represented that the austral land of slightly less 'than one entire half [of the whole globe] ... remains to be discovered, and to have the gospel preached to it'; that it was

greatly stored with metals and rich in precious stones and pearls, fruits and animals; and from the discoveries and investigations which have been already made in this southern hemisphere, there has been found such fertility, so great plenty and abundance of animals, swine, oxen, and other beasts of different kinds fit for the sustenance of man as has never been seen in our Europe; also of birds and fishes of different species, and, amongst them all, those which we most value as wholesome and delicate on the shores of our own ocean; and fruits, some of which we already know, and others of different kinds, all which may well excite the greatest admiration.[17]

But the time was no longer propitious for Spain's would-be discoverers, who found no encouragement from their government.

As the Spanish pursued their quest for *Terra Australis*, so too did the English become interested in this elusive entity. In 1540 Roger Barlow, who fourteen years earlier had sailed with Cabot to look for the 'new spice regions' believed to lie in the southern Pacific,[18] told Henry VIII that a northern way to them and to China should be sought out, adding, 'for such an enterprise no man shuld thinke upon the cost in comparison to the grete profyght that maye therby

11

succede, nor thinke the labour grete where so moche profyt honor and glory maye folow unto this o^r naturall realme and king'.[19]

In the reign of Elizabeth I the remarkable Dr John Dee, mathematician, geographer, astrologer, conjurer and would-be merchant, dreamed of an extensive empire based on the colonization of *Terra Australis*. He advised that 'skilful' sailors and 'discrete' captains be engaged, so that *'this land of Beach* ... and that out of the Scythian Ocean, sailing in manner by shores', might be *'come unto*, [and] *possessed'*.[20] Although Dee's main interest was in voyages in search of a north-west or north-east passage, he also had a hand in planning expeditions through the Straits of Magellan, such as the one proposed by Richard Grenville and his partners in 1574 which showed a distinct interest in *Terra Australis*. Their purpose, the adventurers said, was

the discouerie, traffique and enioyenge for the Quenes Majestie and her subiectes of all or anie landes, islandes and countries southewardes beyonde the aequinoctial, or where the Pole Antartik hath anie elevation above the Horison, and which landes, islandes and countries be not alredie possessed or subdued by or to the vse of anie Christian Prince in Europe.[21]

1.8   Michael Mercator   'Drake' Silver Medal   1589

12

That most celebrated voyage of all in this period, Drake's circumnavigation of 1577–80, increased English interest in the Pacific, and although there is no evidence that he was directed to search for *Terra Australis*,[22] its familiar shape looms large on the silver map of 1589 issued to commemorate the voyage (1.8). Inspired by Drake's voyage, and by reports reaching him from other parts of Europe, the Gascon historian Lancelot Voisin conjured up in his work of 1582, *Les Trois Mondes*, a third, southern world to set alongside the world of the ancients, and the new world of the Americas. In this 'third world', he urged his compatriots, they would find 'a situation wonderful in its pleasures, richesses and other commodities of life'; but in a France torn by religious and political strife this was an appeal which fell on deaf ears.[23]

With none of the sixteenth-century voyages producing reassuring proof of a great southern continent, scepticism about its existence began to grow. Edward Wright's splendid world map of 1599 showed only an unnamed fragment of coastline south of Java (1.9). Offering a suitably sceptical map (1.10), Bishop Joseph Hall asked a pertinent question in *The Discovery of a New World* (1609): 'If they know it for a Continent, and for a Southerne Continent, why then doe

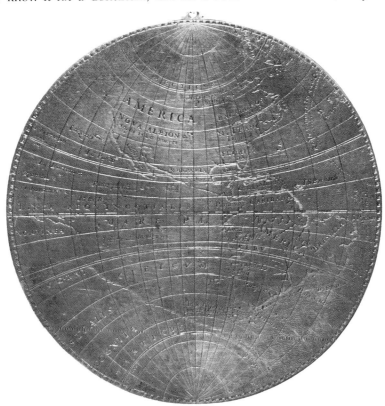

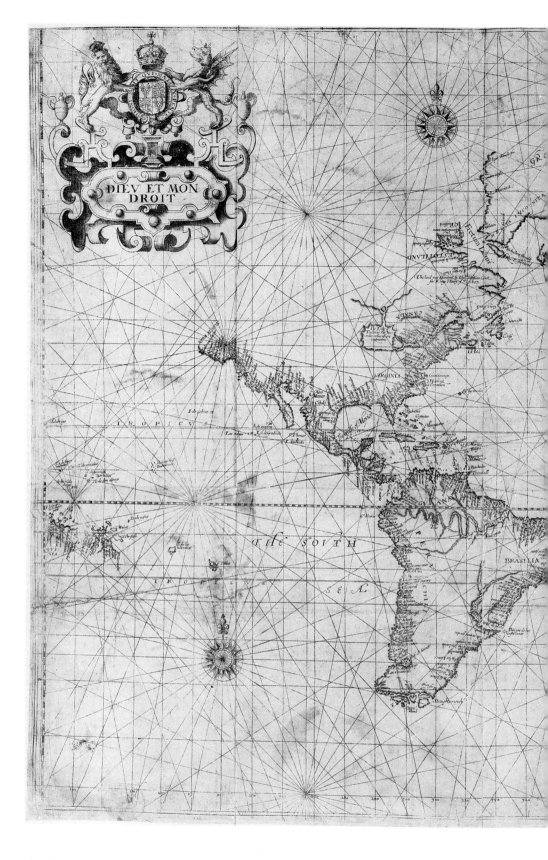

1.9 Edward Wright World Map 1599

It appeareth by the discouerie of Francis Gaulle a Spaniard, in yeare 1584 that the sea betweene the west part of America and the east of Asia which hath bene ordinarily set out as a streight and named in most maps the streight of Anain is aboue 1200 leagues wide at the latitude of 58 degr. And that the distance betweene cape Mendocino and cape California which many maps and seacharts make to be 1200 or 1500 leagues is sarce so much as 600

gentle reader at true hydrographical description of so much of the world as hath therto discouered, and is come to our knowledge, which we haue in such sort performed, haue the same positions and distances that they haue in the globe, being set downe in same longitudes and latitudes which they haue in the chart, which by the ordinarie sea in no wise to be posty used. The way to finde the position or course from any place to described, diffeveth nothing from that which is vsed in the ordinarie sea cha to finde the distance, if both places haue the same latitude, see how many degrees of taken at that latitude are conteyned betweene the two places, for so mane score is the distance. If they differ in latitude, see how many degrees of the meridian the midst of that difference are conteyned betweene them, and so many score leagues is the distance.

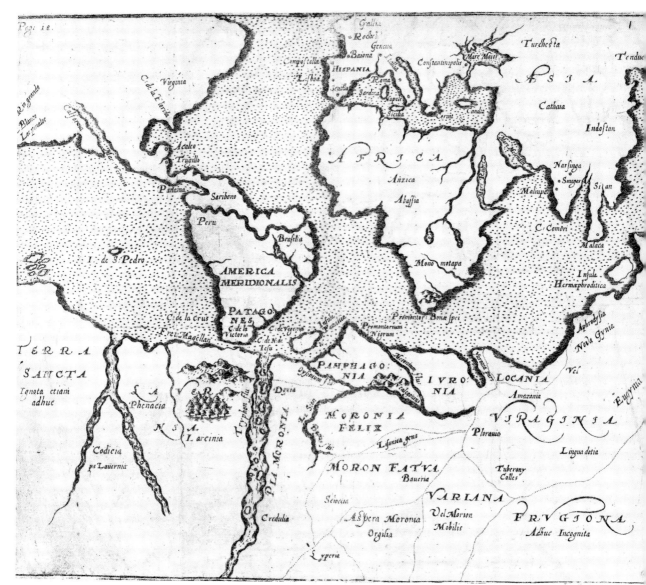

1.10   Joseph Hall   Southern hemisphere   from his World Map   *c.* 1605

1.11   Gerard and Cornelis de Jode   title page   from their *Specvlvm Orbis Terrae*   1597

they call it unknowne?' A few years later Nathaniel Carpenter noted of the 'South Continent': 'we cannot imagine [it] to be so great in quantity, as it is painted in our ordinary Mappes: forasmuch as all places at the first discovery are commonly described greater then they are'.[24]

On the other hand, there were some tantalizing hints which seem to indicate more than a speculative knowledge of what we now know as Australia. There was Cornelis de Jode's odd serpentine marsupial (1.11), for example, and Cornelis Wytfliet's map (1.12) and accompanying comment that

the south-land ... the southernmost of all countries, extends immediately towards the Polar Circle, but also towards the countries of the east beyond the Tropic of the

SPE=
CVLVM
ORBIS
TERRÆ

ANTVERPIÆ.
Sumptibus Viduæ et Heredũ Gerardi de Iudæis

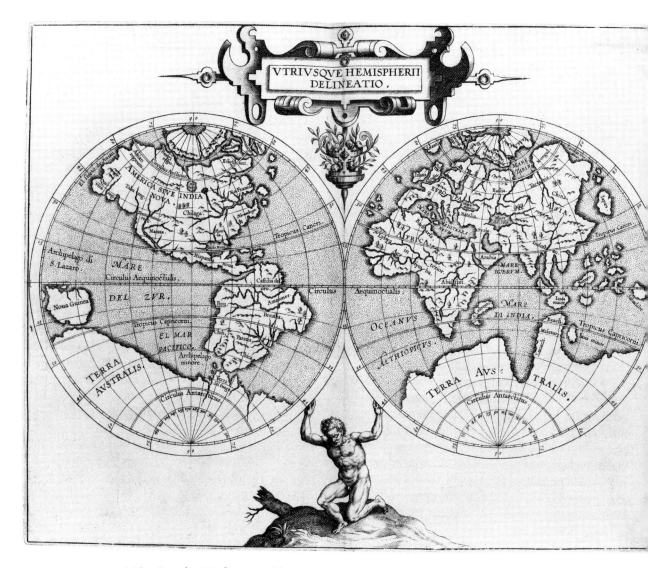

1.12 Cornelis Wytfliet World Map ('Vtrivsqve Hemispherrii Delineatio') 1597

1.13 Mark Ridley Hemispheric World Map 1613

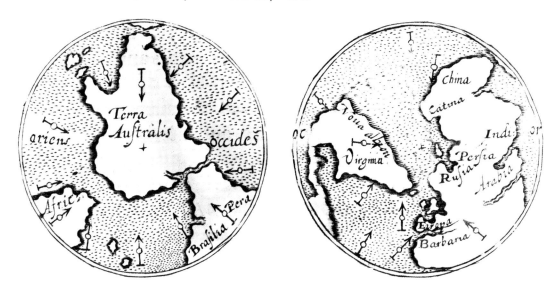

Capricorn and almost at the equator its confines are to be found, and in the east, separated by a narrow strait it lies in front of New Guinea, but is explored only at a few coastal places, because after one and other voyage that route has been discontinued and thence rarely sails are set except that ships are driven off by cyclones. It takes its beginnings two or three degrees under the equator and is assigned such an extension by some that it may well appear to be the fifth continent after having been discovered fully.[25]

In 1625 that determined colonizer Sir William Courteen asked James I for proprietary rights to 'all the lands in ye South parts of ye world called Terra Australis incognita extending Eastwards & Westwards from ye Straights of Le Maire together with all ye adjacent Islands &c., [as] are yet undiscovered or being discovered are not yet traded unto by any of your Maties subjects'.[26] And while writers continued to represent Terra Australis as the seat of Paradise or the site of a possible Utopia, various cartographers continued to depict the continent as filling the greater part of the southern hemisphere—as in the simplified map which accompanied Mark Ridley's *Short Treatise of Magneticall Bodies and Motions*, published in London in 1613 (1.13).[27]

As the seventeenth century developed, however, such cartographers became a minority—if at times a tenacious minority—as the result of actual discovery. In 1602, anxious to share in the wealth of the East, the governing body of the Dutch provinces granted the United East India Company (VOC) a monopoly of Dutch trade in the vast area between the Cape of Good Hope and the Straits of Magellan.[28] As soon as it had established itself in the East Indies, the VOC began seeking further markets. In 1605 officials at Bantam despatched the *Duyfken* 'to discover the great land Nova Guinea and other unknown east and south lands'.[29] Its voyage, and succeeding ones to the northern, western and southern coasts of Australia. are described by Professor Schilder in chapter 3. The Dutch discoveries represent the first major step in the accurate delineation of Australia; and the emergence of this real geographical entity from the shadows of the supposed *Terra Australis* caused cartographers to become a good deal more cautious as to how they represented the regions south-east of Indonesia. In this context Tasman's voyage of 1642−3 was particularly important since it had removed all possibility that the land known by the Dutch as 'New Holland' might be part of the legendary southern continent, and pushed the supposed land mass back at least as far as the stretch of New Zealand coastline he had sighted. For fifty years from the 1620s onwards, Dutch map-makers in general showed only what had been found, not what lay undiscovered, although the time-lag in representing discovery in published form still led to some oddities. Thus, although the Hondius (3.8) and Blaeu maps of 1630 and 1635 (3.9) show Dutch discoveries in New Holland, the impressive world map of the same year by Hondius's partner, Jansz (1.14), is unrepentant in its depiction of a great southern continent.[30] Those narratives of the Dutch voyages that were published conveyed the image of New Holland as a land of barren coasts and backward people, offering small inducement to further exploration.

1.14 Jan Jansz and Pieter van den Keere World Map ('Nova Totius Terrarum Orbis Geographica ac Hydrographica Tabula') 1630

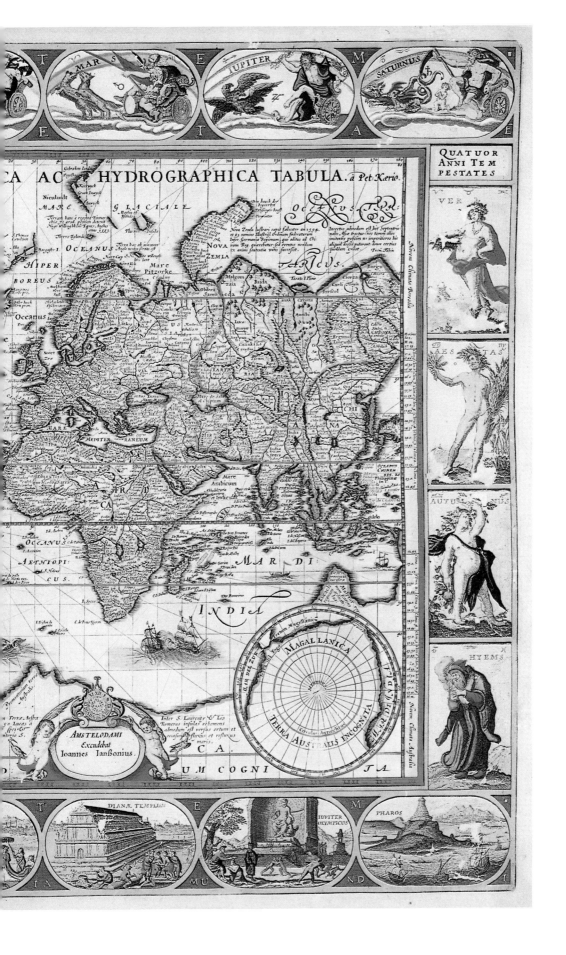

CA AC HYDROGRAPHICA TABULA. *a Pet. Kerio.*

MARE GLACIALE

OCEANVS VARIVS

NOVA ZEMLA

Mare Pitzorke

HIPER BOREVS

OCEANVS

MARE MEDITERRANEVM

AFRICA

ARABIA Felix

Mare Arabicum

OCEANVS CHINEN SIS ad Philippine

CHINA

OCEANVS Æthiop

ÆTHIOPI CVS

MAR DI

INDIA

MAGALLANICA

TERRA AVSTRALIS INCOGNITA

AMSTELODAMI
Excuddbat
Ioannes Ianßonius.

UM COGNI TA

Knowledge of the uninviting New Holland, and the absence of any authentic discovery of *Terra Australis*, did not altogether extinguish the aspirations that the centuries had created about the legendary south land. In the second edition of his *Cosmographie* (1657), Peter Heylyn followed Joseph Hall's satirical line when he wrote that he had often marvelled that no further progress had been made in the discovery of a region 'so large, so free from the Incumbrances of Frosts and Ice, and endless Winters'. 'Without troubling the Vice-royes of *Peru*, and *Mexico*, or taking out *Commission* for a new Discovery', he continued, he would try his fortune and 'make a search into this *Terra Australis* for some other Regions, which must be found either here or no where. The names of which [are] 1. *Mundus alter & idem*, 2. *Utopia*, 3. *New Atlantis*, 4. *Fairy Land*, 5. The *Painters Wives Iland*, 6. The Lands of *Chivalry*, And, 7. The *New World in the Moon'*.[31]

Neither such scorn nor the continuing absence of proven discovery deterred the less cynical from continuing to speculate about the southern continent, and even in the last decades of the seventeenth century it still lingered in some of the geographies. In 1682, for example, the editors of an English compendium gave an 'Antarctique' section to

those vast Countries, which lying under the South Pole, are longly and largely extended through the cold, temperate, and torrid Zone: where not onely *Peter Ferdinand* a *Spaniard* preached; but also are commendable for the constitution of the Ayre and soil; and largenesse of the Countries; equalizing *Europe* and *Africa* taken both together.[32]

In 1692 the Dutchman Luyts similarly offered a short subsection on 'Terra Australis incognita'.[33] Three years later, the author of *A New Body of Geography* indiscriminately grouped the southern lands, known and unknown, real and imaginary, under the twin headings of *New Holland* and *Terra Australis Incognita*. He described the latter as 'a vast tract of Land', and asserted that

the Inhabitants are white, of a large Stature, strong, industrious and couragious: It is very sad to fall into their Hands, as some *Europeans* have found by unhappy Experience. Some modern Relations tell us, That in all that vast Country they have neither King nor Prince, all the People are only combin'd together in several Factions, in the Form of a Commonwealth. They chuse Governours only to make the lazy work, punish Offenders, and render Justice to every Man. They are Idolaters, and have Oratories to pray to their Idols in: They observe certain Fasts, and wash their Bodies on certain Days every Year.[34]

And in 1698, as described in chapter 4, William Dampier told the First Lord of the Admiralty in London that of all the regions of the world remaining unexplored the southern continent most merited attention; and he made his comment in the terms used by Elizabethan predecessors, and animated it with the same concern for trade, empire, and national prestige.[35] Juxtaposed with the actual discoveries, depressing and disheartening, of the seventeenth-century navigators, was a continuing hope that somewhere in the unexplored vastnesses lay lands of unimaginable fruitfulness and wealth. The more Dampier saw of the arid north-west coast, the more convinced he was that further east lay 'some fruitful Lands, Continent or Islands, or both'.[36] The Quirós fantasy shed its glow over the undiscovered regions, while Utopian visionaries persisted in setting extraordinary lands and societies in the area they vaguely identified as Terra Australis.[37] Where imaginative reconstructions failed, a crude environmental geography might be brought into play, so that it could be seriously argued that 'the East Side of Nova Hollandia ... lying North and South as Peru does, and in the same latt[d], I belive ... abounds in Gold and Silver Mines'.[38]

The publication between 1694 and 1705 of narratives of the Dutch and of Dampier's voyages in and about the Pacific Ocean[39] led to a revival of interest in *Terra Australis* in the first half of the eighteenth century. With additional materials available, geographers expanded their accounts, often offering a strange mixture of the real and the imagined. The problem of identifying and categorizing the various lands was faced by the cartographer of Dampier's *Voyages*, Herman Moll, who in 1717 divided *Terra Australis Incognita* into New Holland, Carpentaria, Terra Austral del Spiritu Santo, and Solomon's Islands to the north, and Diemen's Land and New Zealand to the south (4.6, 4.8, 4.9). He suggested in quite traditional terms that the whole mass was 'as large as *Europe, Asia,* and *Africa*' combined, so as to leave the earth 'equally poiz'd'. He offered Quirós's representation of it as a garden of delights:

Here are high Coleworts, and several Sorts of Pot Herbs. The Country abounds with Pigeons, Partridges, Ducks, and other ordinary Fowls, with very good Soals, Salmon, Thornbacks, Sea-Cocks, Eels, and Gurnets, besides other Fishes unknown to us. It also produces Nutmegs, Mastick, Pepper, Ginger, Cinnamon, Gold, Silver, Pearls, Silk, Sugar, Anniseed, Honey, Wax, Ebony-Wood, Turpentine, Lime-Pits, and Marble, with Stones, and other Materials for Building. Here are no snowy Mountains, drown'd Land-Croco-diles, or any other hurtful Creature.

And he repeated information from the *New Body of Geography* about the inhabitants and their mores.[40]

Although geographers refined this general scheme somewhat as a consequence of details from new voyages such as those of Frézier, Roggeveen and Bouvet de Lozier, they retained it into the middle of the century. Recognizing that New Holland was probably of continental extent, but that it could not be the legendary *Terra Australis*, they concluded that there must be *two* southern continents—the one, whose outline was known in general terms, lying between the equator and 44°S latitude, and 122°E and 188°E longitude, comprising New Guinea, Carpentaria, New Holland, Van Diemen's Land, and the countries discovered by Quirós; and the other, lying in the south Pacific between 150°E and 170°E longitude, with New Zealand as the western extremity, which was yet to be substantially discovered, and to which 'the Title of *Terra Australis Incognita* properly belongs'.[41]

The French geographers, in particular, showed considerable cartographical ingenuity in brightening the sombre image of New Holland displayed by the Dutch, and drew on the Quirós discovery of 1606 to suggest the presence of rich

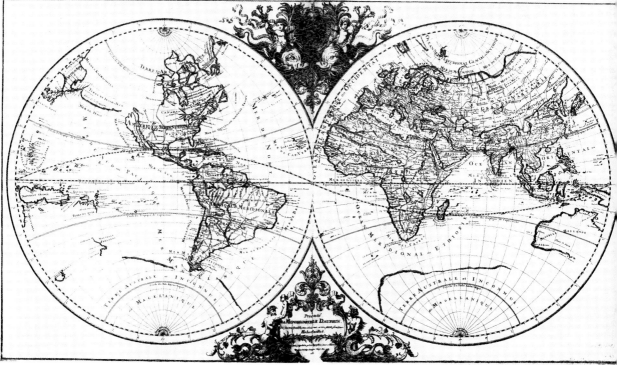

1.15   Nicolas Sanson   World Map ('Mappe-Monde Géo-Hydrographique')   1691

1.16   Guillaume de l'Isle   Southern Hemisphere ('Hémisphère Méridional')   1714

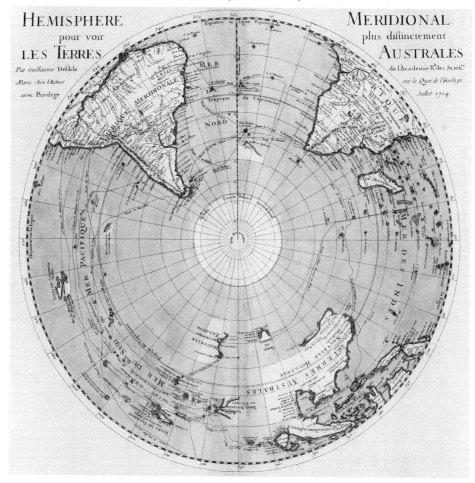

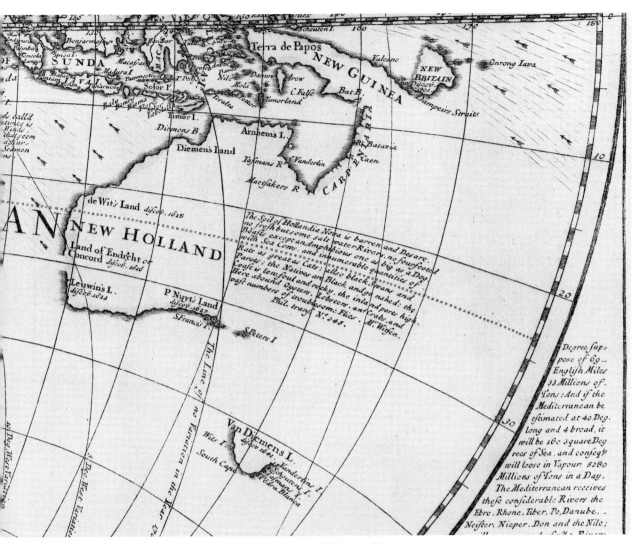

1.17 John Senex New Holland from 'A Map of the World' 1725

countries inside the great oval traced by Tasman on his voyage of 1642–3.
Sanson's *Mappe-Monde Géo-Hydrographique* of 1691 (1.15) showed New
Guinea as a great island set to the northeast of the Gulf of Carpentaria, with a
'Terre de Quir' marked further east, and the elusive Solomon Islands set
between the two. There was no indication on the map as to whether the land
discovered by Quirós was joined in any way to New Holland, but the explorer's
insistence on the continental nature of the land he found made the linking a
predictable if hesitant process. Guillaume de l'Isle, most prestigious of the French
cartographers of the early eighteenth century, produced an influential interpretation in his *Hémisphère Méridional* of 1714 (1.16), a map based on a polar
projection 'in order to see the South Lands more distinctly'. This showed
Dampier's route to the east of New Guinea, and although it left open the
question of the location of the east coast of Australia, it marked a continental-
looking Espiritu Santo in roughly its correct longitude of 168°E. The map was

25

re-issued several times, and was included in Philippe Buache's *Atlas* of 1755, along with Buache's representation of the sighting by Bouvet de Lozier in 1739 of 'Cap de la Circoncision' (Cape Circumcision) in the South Atlantic as part of a great continent. This identification was as fanciful as the supposition which in part inspired the expedition: that the mysterious voyage of the Frenchman, Gonneville, to the 'south Indies' (probably Brazil) in 1503—4 had reached *Terra Australis*.[42]

In England the new focus of attention was demonstrated in the *Complete System of Geography* of 1747, published under Emanuel Bowen's name, and successor to the various editions of Moll's *Complete Geographer*. The reader was told, 'it is very probable, that *New-Guiney, New-Holland, Van Diemen's Land*, and the *Land of the Holy Ghost*, the Country discovered by *De Quiros*, make all together one great Continent, separated from *New-Zealand* by a Streight'. The traditional southern continent, by contrast, was viewed in an altogether more sceptical manner.

What Countries there may be, nearer the South Pole, or round it, is intirely unknown; tho' a large Tract of Land is set down in several Maps of the whole World, under the Name of *Terra Australis incognita*, or *The unknown Southerly Countries*. Well may they be stil'd *unknown*, since we have no manner of Knowledge of them, and it is still uncertain whether there be any Land, or only an open Sea, from the 56th Degree of South Latitude, all round, quite to the Pole.[43]

The concept was graphically illustrated by Bowen's maps drawn for the monumental revised edition of Harris's voyages produced by Dr John Campbell during the 1740s. His 'New & Correct Chart of all the Known World' placed 'Ter. d'St. Esprit' firmly on the east coast of Australia, while a legend attached to his 'Complete Map of the Southern Continent' (1.18) stated in unequivocal terms that 'the Country discovered by *Ferdinand de Quiros* lies according to his description on the east Side of this Continent directly Opposite to *Carpentaria*'. Another legend gave an ecstatic account of the new continent and its potential, in marked contrast to the John Senex map of 1725 (1.17). With references to the silver of Peru, the spices of the Moluccas, and the diamonds of Java, the inscription took readers into a realm of fantasy.

It is impossible to conceive a Country that promises fairer from its Situation, than this of *Terra Australis;* no longer incognita, as this Map demonstrates, but the Southern Continent Discovered. It lies Precisely in the richest Climates of the World . . . and therefore whoever perfectly discovers & settles it will become infallibly possessed of Territories as Rich, as fruitful, & as capable of Improvement, as any that have been hitherto found out, either in the East Indies, or the West.[44]

To substantiate his 'new Indies' Campbell had only the dismal and fragmentary reports of the Dutch and the hallucinations of Quirós. The latter he took at face value, noting that Quirós reported that Espiritu Santo 'abounds with Gold, Silver, Pearls, Nutmegs, Mace, Ginger, and Sugar-canes of an extraordinary Size'. He explained that these reports had not been followed up because of the

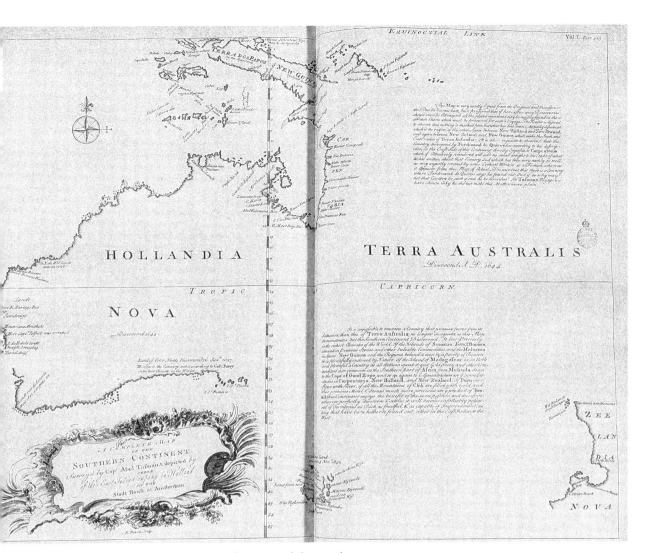

1.18   Emanuel Bowen   'A Complete Map of the Southern Continent'   1744

lethargy of the Spaniards: 'It has been now, for many Years, a settled Maxim in the *Spanish* Politics, not only to lay aside all Thoughts of prosecuting these Discoveries, but even to treat the Relations published of them by their best Authors as absolute Romances.' The more formidable Dutch could hardly be dismissed in the same way; and Campbell saw their reports as being part of a devious plan 'to frighten other Nations from approaching so inhospitable a Coast, every-where beset with Rocks, absolutely void of Water, and inhabited by a Race of Savages more barbarous, and, at the same time, more miserable, than any other Creatures in the World'. For the present, the Dutch were a satiated power, but if driven out of the Spice Islands they would retreat towards New Holland and New Guinea to 'avail themselves effectually of this noble Discovery, which lies open to them, and has been hitherto close shut up to all the World beside'.[45] In hinting thus about Dutch motives, Campbell was repeating a firm tradition which had taken hold in England in the seventeenth century. Sir

27

William Temple, Charles II's ambassador at The Hague, had reported:

I have heard it said among the Dutch, that their East India Company have long since forbidden, and under the greatest penalties, any further attempts of discovering that continent, having already more trade in those parts than they can turn to account, and fearing some more populous nation in Europe might make great establishments of trade in some of those unknown regions, which might ruin or impair what they have already in the Indies.[46]

The main aim of Campbell's work was directed towards 'the Encouragement, Extension, and Protection of Trade, as the surest Means of making us a great, wealthy, powerful and happy People'. To this end, he deliberately erred on the side of credulity. His two huge volumes are studded with optimistic geographical speculations and hopeful 'projects', of which the discovery and exploitation of the true Australia was but one. He recommended an expedition to Van Diemen's Land, and a voyage to New Guinea by which means, he wrote, slipping into more cautious phrasing, 'all the back Coast of *New Holland*, and *New Guiney*, might be thoroughly examined; and we might know as well, and as certainly, as the *Dutch*, how far a Colony settled there might answer our Expectations'.[47]

Campbell wrote in a period of increasing Anglo-French overseas rivalry, and just as he wished his own countrymen to exploit the unknown resources of the southern seas, so too when, in the next decade, de Brosses edited his pioneer compilation of Pacific voyages, *Histoire des Navigations aux Terres Australes*, he looked to French enterprise in the region. The Comte de Buffon, in his *Histoire et Théories de la Terre* (1749) had thrown his considerable scholarly weight in favour of a southern continent as large as Europe, Asia and Africa combined,[48] and de Brosses now set out the implications of the discovery of such a land mass. 'It is not possible', he began,

that there is not, in such a vast sea, some immense continent of solid land south of Asia, capable of keeping the globe in equilibrium in its rotation ... How can we doubt that after its discovery such a vast expanse of land will supply objects of curiosity, opportunities for profit, perhaps as many as America furnished in its novelty? How many peoples different from each other and certainly very dissimilar to us in face, manner, habits, ideas, worship? How many animals ... plants ... medicinal drugs, marbles and metals?[49]

As far as the south land was concerned, de Brosses was not totally convinced by Quirós's description of Espiritu Santo. He suspected that the land might be insular rather than continental, he noted that no European had seen the area since Quirós, and he concluded that a second voyage was necessary before any action could be taken in the way of trade or settlement. The map by Robert de Vaugondy which accompanied this section allowed of little ambiguity, however (1.23). The east coast of Australia was indicated by a broken line, slanting north-north-east from Van Diemen's Land as far as the mainland bulge of the Quirós discoveries. It was a natural development of the trend started by Sanson (1.15) and Guillaume de l'Isle (1.16), and gave the image of an extended Australian continent a greater circulation than ever before. In one form or another it was repeated in many of the atlases of the mid-eighteenth century—a tantalizing union of the known barrenness of the west coast with the expected but still unproven richness of the east.

More was heard of this in the English plagiarism of de Brosses, John Callander's optimistically titled *Terra Australis Cognita,* the last volume of which appeared in the same year as Cook first sailed to the Pacific. Although Callander looked forward, predictably, to British exploitation of the region in the years following the triumphant Treaty of Paris in 1763, there was little in his discussion which was not taken from de Brosses or Campbell. An Anglicized version of Vaugondy's map (1.23) accompanied the book, and although Callander followed the French editor in regarding the Quirós memorials with less than total devotion—'In these, it must be confessed, things appear a little exaggerated, and painted in fairer colours than perhaps the truth will bear'—he had no doubts as to their general reliability. In his introduction explaining 'the Utility of Further Discoveries', Callander departed from the de Brosses text to point out how the discoveries of Quirós, when joined to Dampier's observations on the nearby coast of New Britain, showed that there was 'not the least reason to doubt, that if any part of this country was to be settled, it must be attended with a very rich commerce'.[50]

The 'remarkable discovery' of Quirós, which to many geographers held the key to the location of the northeast coast of New Holland, shuttled around the maps in disconcerting fashion. Bellin, in his map drawn for volume IX of the Prévost *Voyages* (1753) (1.20) showed the Quirós shoreline in longitude 149°E, and removed altogether the familiar eastern bulge of the Australian continent. Vaugondy moved Espiritu Santo to about longitude 158°E and latitude 20°S (1.23). The British geographer John Green showed it farther north and east as an extension of New Guinea (1.19), though he added that 'the published Account of De Quiros is so imperfect, that there is no laying-down any Thing from it with Certainty'.[51] Philippe Buache, taking the earlier Guillaume de l'Isle polar projection map (1.16) as his base, pushed Espiritu Santo almost as far east as the longitude of New Zealand (1.21). If this was correct (and this *was* in fact roughly the longitude of the New Hebrides), and if Quirós's discovery was indeed part of the mainland, then New Holland stretched a thousand miles farther east than Bellin indicated—a mighty land mass indeed. The Buache maps by now were showing New Zealand as the western extremity of the great southern continent, whose misty shapes swirled around his polar projections in imposing if ill-defined fashion. 'We have the impression', a French scholar has written, 'of seeing a new world recently emerged from the oceans.'[52]

If the location of Espiritu Santo was one mystery, the question of whether New Guinea was joined to Australia was another. Torres's discovery of 1606 had long been lost to sight, and there was no agreement between geographers as to the existence of a strait. There was, indeed, often no agreement between maps

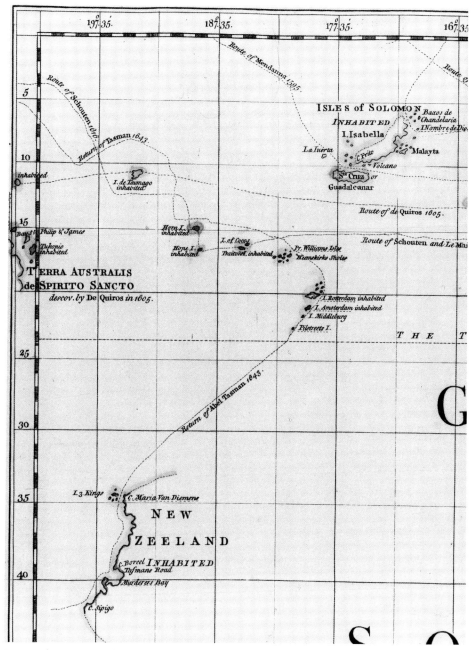

1.19   John Green   Chart of North and South America'   1753

1.20   *Above right* Jacques Nicolas Bellin   New Holland ('Carte réduite des Terres Australes')
       1753

1.21   *Below right* Philippe Buache   New Holland from his World Map ('Mappe par
       Guillaume de l'Isle…augmentée par P.B.')   1755

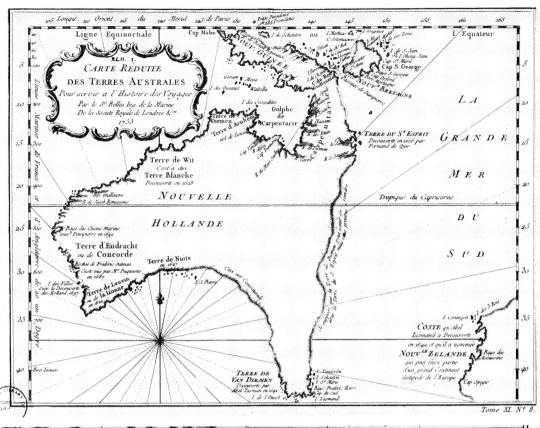

constructed by the same geographer. Bellin was one of those who hedged his bets. In a map of 1755 (1.22) he showed New Guinea joined to the mainland to the south; the following year he indicated a gap where the western entrance of Torres Strait lay, and a dotted line across its eastern entrance (1.24).[53] Bowen's maps in Campbell showed a similar tolerance (1.18). The Vaugondy map in de Brosses (1.25) showed a strait, and this representation was given added credibility by the appearance of Spanish place names along the south coast of New Guinea. Some at least of these also appear on a map of New Holland and New Guinea in the *Neptune François* issued at Amsterdam by Pierre Mortier in 1700 (1.26), and it is a reasonable speculation that these came from a map showing Torres's track, known to have been brought to France from Lisbon in the 1660s. To this particular debate an important contribution was made just before Cook sailed, in the first of many publications on Pacific geography by Alexander Dalrymple, *Discoveries made in the South Pacifick Ocean. Previous to 1764.* Dalrymple had come into possession of an early seventeenth-century memorial by Juan Luis Arias which seemed to refer to a westward passage by Torres south of New Guinea. This Dalrymple showed on an accompanying map (1.27), as also 'Terre del Espiritu Santo' far to the east, though without indicating whether it was part of New Holland.[54] The book was printed in 1767, and although it was not published for another two years, Dalrymple presented a copy of it to Banks before he left on the *Endeavour* in August 1768. There were thus two separate lines of descent from Torres, one through the Mortier map to Vaugondy, the other through the Arias memorial to Dalrymple, though neither was firm enough to carry total conviction. All that we can say is that Cook had with him on the *Endeavour* two maps, Vaugondy's and Dalrymple's, which showed a strait between New Guinea and New Holland.

The insularity or otherwise of New Guinea was only a detail in Dalrymple's grander design for the southern continent, of which he hoped to be the first discoverer. As late as 1770–1 he was arguing that *Terra Australis* extended through one hundred degrees of longitude across the southern Pacific Ocean from Juan Fernández's landfall in the east to Tasman's New Zealand in the west—so that it was of greater extent than 'the whole civilized part of *Asia*, from *Turkey* to the eastern extremity of *China*'. The 'scraps' from its inhabitants' economy, he pronounced, 'would be sufficient to maintain the power, dominion, and sovereignty of *Britain*, by employing all its manufacturers and ships'. All that was needed was an explorer with sufficient '*dauntless* and *perseverant* resolution'.[55] Dalrymple's was the last major speculation about the southern continent, for his and other theories were now to fall under the cold, dispassionate scrutiny of such a 'dauntless' explorer as he conceived—not Dalrymple indeed, but James Cook, who in his first two voyages was to complete the Dutch revelation of the continent now called Australia at the same time as he dispelled the myths surrounding the older concept of *Terra Australis*.

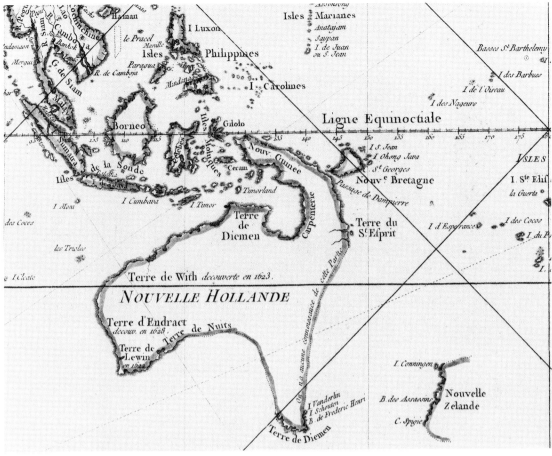

1.22   Jacques Nicolas Bellin   New Guinea and New Holland ('Carte réduite des parties
       connues du Globe Terrestre')   1755

1.23   Robert de Vaugondy   Australasia ('Carte réduite de l'Australasie')   1756

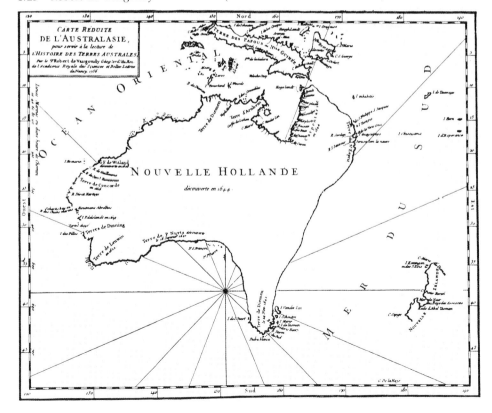

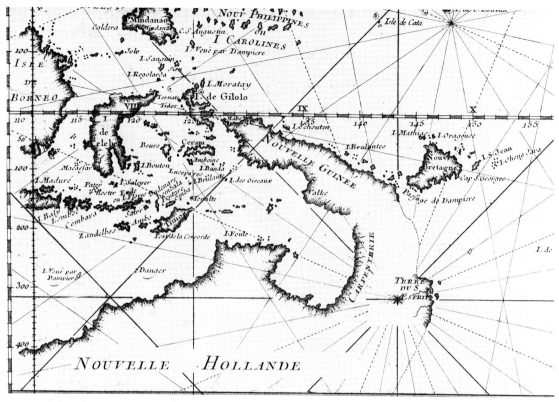

1.24   Jacques Nicolas Bellin   New Guinea and New Holland ('Carte réduite des Mers comprises entre l'Asie et l'Amerique')   1756

1.25   Robert de Vaugondy   New Guinea and New Holland ('Partie de l'Australasie')   1756

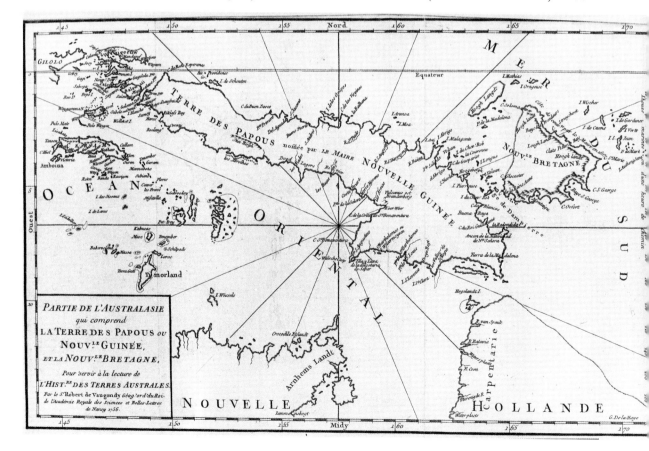

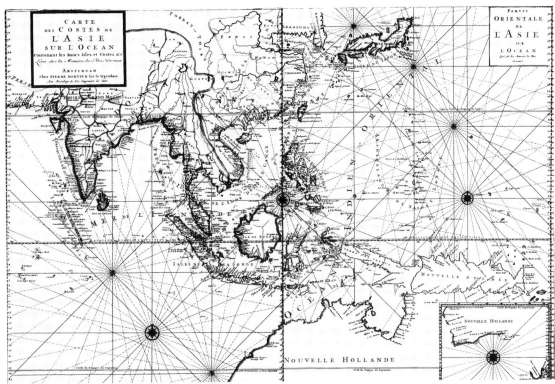

1.26 [Pierre Mortier] South-east Asia ('Carte des Costes de l'Asie') 1700

1.27 Alexander Dalrymple section from his 'Chart of the South Pacifick Ocean' 1767

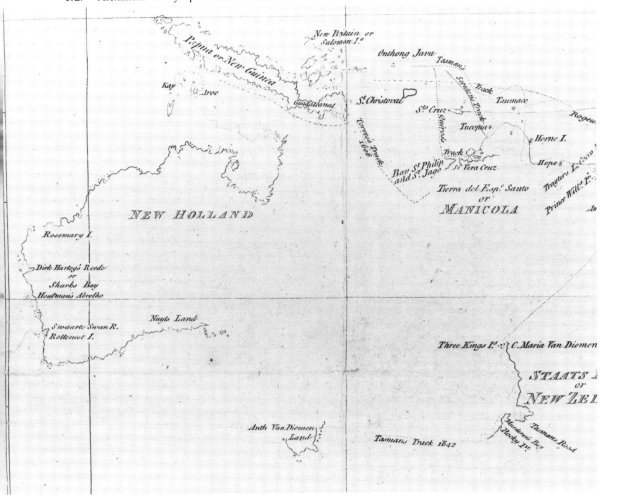

Notes

1. For surveys of classical references to Terra Australis, see: Armand Rainaud, *Le Continent Austral: Hypothèses et Découvertes* (Paris, 1893); Colin Jack-Hinton, *The Search for the Islands of Solomon 1567–1838* (Oxford, 1969); Günter Schilder, *Australia Unveiled* (Amsterdam, 1976); T. M. Perry, *The Discovery of Australia* (Melbourne, 1982); and Numa Broc, 'De L'Antichtone à L'Antarctique', in *Cartes et Figures de la Terre* (Paris, 1980), pp. 136–49.
2. *Geography of Claudius Ptolemy*, trans. and ed. Edward Luther Stevenson (New York, 1932), p. 159.
3. Quoted in Perry, *Discovery of Australia*, p. 11.
4. Quoted *ibid.*
5. Quoted in J. C. Beaglehole, *The Exploration of the Pacific*, 3rd edn (Stanford, 1966), p. 9.
6. Juan Luis Arias, 'A Memorial addressed to His Catholic Majesty Philip the Third, King of Spain', in *Early Voyages to Terra Australis, now called Australia*, ed. R. H. Major (London, 1859), pp. 11–3.
7. 'And King Solomon made a navy of ships in Eziongeber, which is beside Eloth, on the shore of the Red Sea, in the land of Edom. And Hiram sent in the navy his servants, shipmen that had knowledge of the sea, with the servants of Solomon. And they came to Ophir, and fetched thence gold, four hundred and twenty talents, and brought it to King Solomon'—*Third Book of Kings*, ch. IX.
8. Because of misunderstandings and editorial corruptions, by the mid-sixteenth century scholars were taking what Polo wrote of Indochina, Malaya, and the Indonesian archipelago to apply to unknown lands further to the south-east—see, e.g. Jack-Hinton, *Search for the Islands of Solomon*, p. 10.
9. In Miguel Cavello Balboa's version, the Inca Tupac Yupanqui once undertook a western voyage which lasted more than a year, during which he discovered two islands, and returned with slaves, gold, silver, a copper throne and the skins of an animal like a horse—see Clements Markham, 'Introduction', *Narratives of the Voyages of Pedro Sarmiento de Gamboa to the Straits of Magellan* (London, 1895), pp. xii–xiii.
10. Roger Barlow, *A Brief Summe of Geographie*, ed. E. G. R. Taylor (London, 1932), p. 182.
11. Gerard Mercator, Legend on his World Chart of 1569.
12. For an account of what is known about Mendonça's voyage, see Armando Cortesão, 'O descobrimento da Australásia e a "Questão das Molucas"', and 'A Expansão Portuguesa através do Pacifico', in *História da Expansão Portuguesa no Mundo*, ed. A. Baião, et al. (Lisbon, 1939), II, 129–50, 151–73; and O. H. K. Spate, 'Terra Australis—Cognita?', *Historical Studies*, 8 (1957), 1–19.
13. Jack-Hinton, *Search for the Islands of Solomon*, discusses this and the other Spanish voyages in detail. See also O. H. K. Spate, *The Spanish Lake* (Canberra, 1979).
14. Quoted in Jack-Hinton, *Search for the Islands of Solomon*, p. 80.
15. Quoted *ibid*, p. 138.
16. See, for example, '*Terra Australis incognita*', or *A new Southerne Discoverie, containing A fifth part of the World. Lately found out by Ferdinand De Qvir, A Spanish Captaine* (London, 1617). There is a useful collection of facsimile reprints of the version of Quirós's petition No. 8 published between 1609 and 1625 in *Australia: su descubrimiento y denominacion*, ed. Carlos Sanz (Madrid, 1973).
17. Arias, 'A Memorial', in *Early Voyages*, pp. 4, 16.
18. See J. A. Williamson, *The Voyages of the Cabots and the English Discovery of North America under Henry VII and Henry VIII* (London, 1929), p. 262.
19. Barlow, *Brief Summe*, pp. 180–1.
20. John Dee, 'The Great Volume of Famous and Rich Discoveries' (1576), ff. 206r and 248b, as printed in E. G. R. Taylor, *Tudor Geography 1485–1583* (London, 1930), pp. 279–80.
21. Richard Grenville and others, 'A Discovery of Lands beyond the equinoctial', (1574), in *The Three Voyages of Martin Frobisher*, ed. R. Collinson (London, 1867), pp. 4–8.
22. On this interesting question, see Kenneth R. Andrews, 'Drake and South America' in *Sir Francis Drake and the Famous Voyage, 1577–1580*, ed. N. J. W. Thrower (Berkeley and Los Angeles, 1984), pp. 49–59.
23. Voisin's words were 'des choses merveilleuses en plaisirs, richesses et autres commodités de la vie', quoted in Broc, 'De l'Antichtone à L'Antarctique', in *Cartes et Figures*, p. 142.
24. Quoted in W. T. James, 'Nostalgia for Paradise: *Terra Australis* in the Seventeenth Century', in *Australia and the European Imagination* (Canberra, 1982), pp. 65, 68.
25. Cornelis Wytfliet, *Descriptionis Ptolemaicae Augmentum* (1597), quoted in Schilder, *Australia Unveiled*, p. 18.

26 Proposal of William Courteen, printed in *Some Proposals for Establishing Colonies in the South Seas*, ed. George Mackaness (Sydney, 1943), pp. 6–7.

27 We are grateful to Dr Denis Gibbs of The London Hospital for drawing our attention to this map, and for generously supplying a print of it from his own copy of the *Short Treatise*.

28 For a detailed description, see Schilder, *Australia Unveiled*, passim.

29 Quoted *ibid.*, p. 43.

30 See Perry, *Discovery of Australia*, plates 11, 12, 13.

31 Peter Heylyn, *Cosmographie*, 2nd edn (London, 1657), pp. 1091, 1093.

32 [Petavius, et al.], *A Geographicall Description of the World* (London, 1682), pp. 1–2.

33 Joannis Luyts, *Introductio ad Geographiam Novam et Veterem* (Rhenum, 1692), pp. 762–4.

34 [Thesaurus Geographicus], *A New Body of Geography* (London, 1695), pp. 497, 505–6.

35 William Dampier, *Dampier's Voyages*, ed. John Masefield (London, 1906), I, 287–8; and Dampier to Orford, undated but *c.* May/June 1698, *ibid.*, II, 325.

36 William Dampier, *A Voyage to New Holland*, ed. J. A. Williamson (London, 1939), p. 121.

37 For a discussion of this, see the papers by W. T. James, J. W. Johnson, Jean Garagnon, and J. Dunmore in *Australia and the European Imagination*, pp. 41–122; see also Ross Gibson, *The Diminishing Paradise: Changing Literary Perceptions of Australia* (London, 1984), ch. 1.

38 BL Sloane MS 4044, f. 214v. See chapter 4 *infra* for further detail on John Welbe and his projects.

39 Tancred Robinson, comp., *An Account of the Several Late Voyages and Discoveries in the South and North Towards the Streights of Magellan, the South Seas, and the vast Tracts of Land beyond Hollandia Nova* (London, 1694); William Dampier, *A New Voyage Round the World* (London, 1697); [Awnsham Churchill, comp.], *A Collection of the Voyages and Travels*, 4 vols (London, 1704); J. Harris, comp., *Navigantium atque Itinerantium Bibliotheca*, 2 vols (London, 1705).

40 [Herman Moll], *Atlas Geographicus* (London, 1711–17), V, 1–6.

41 J. Harris, comp., rev. John Campbell, *Navigantium atque Itinerantium Bibliotheca* (London, 1744–8), I, 331.

42 For a recent discussion of the voyages of Gonneville and Lozier-Bouvet see Leslie R. Marchant, *France Australe* (Perth, 1982), pp. 15–19, 37–42.

43 Emanuel Bowen, *A Complete System of Geography* (London, 1747), II, 777, 784.

44 The map, with its accompanying legends, was included in John Campbell's edition of *Navigantium atque Itinerantium Bibliotheca*, facing I, 325.

45 *Ibid.*, I, 65, 325, 328.

46 Quoted by R. H. Major, in *Early Voyages*, p. vii.

47 Campbell, *Navigantium atque Itinerantium Bibliotheca*, I, 332.

48 Buffon, *Histoire et Théories de la Terre* (Paris, 1749), Art. VI, pp. 98–9.

49 'il n'est pas possible qu'il n'y ait dans une si vaste plage quelqu'immense continent de terre solide au sud de l'Asie capable de tenir le globe en équilibre dans sa rotation . . .

. . . comment douter qu'une aussi vaste étendue de pays ne fournisse, après la découverte, des objets de curiosité, des occasions de profit, peut-être autant que l'Amérique en procuroit dans sa nouveauté? Que de peuples différens entr'eux & certainement trés-dissemblables à nous, pour la figure, les moeurs, les usages, les idées, le culte religieux. Qued'animaux, d'insectes, de poissons, de plantes, d'arbres, de fruits, de drogues médicinales, de marbres, de pierres précieuses, de fossiles & de métaux'. Charles de Brosses, *Histoire des Navigations aux Terres Australes* (Paris, 1756), I, 13, 16.

50 John Callander, *Terra Australis Cognita* (Edinburgh, 1766–8), II, 143; I, 48.

51 [John Green], *Remarks on a New Chart of North and South America* (London, 1753), p. 44.

52 'On a l'impression d'être en présence d'un monde récemment surgi des ocèans'—Numa Broc, *La Géographie des Philosophes: Géographes et Voyageurs Français au XVIIIe-siècle* (Paris, 1974), p. 180.

53 See J. N. Bellin, *Carte réduite des parties connues du Globe Terrestre* (1755); *Carte réduite des Mers comprises entre l'Asie et l'Amérique* (1742, rev. 1756).

54 Alexander Dalrymple, *Chart of the South Pacifick Ocean* (1767).

55 Alexander Dalrymple, *An Historical Collection of the several Voyages and Discoveries in the South Pacific Ocean* (London, 1770–1), I, xxviii–xxix.

2.1 Jean Mallard World Map *c.* 1540

Chapter 2

Java la Grande:
The Enigma of the Dieppe Maps

Helen Wallis

There are contemporary maps which might tell much if we could read their secrets. These maps are a dangerous type of evidence; too much study of them saps a man's critical faculty. Henry Harrisse knew as much as any man of the Renaissance maps, and one may see from his works that as his learning increased his judgement deteriorated.[1]

When J. A. Williamson in 1937 uttered these words of warning against credulity in the handling of map evidence, he was referring to researches into the voyages of John and Sebastian Cabot to North America, on which topic Henry Harrisse was an established authority. The comment may seem to apply equally well, however, to past and present theories about the early discovery of Australia; and controversialists would no doubt be ready with one name or another to substitute for that of Harrisse. For the belief that the Portuguese reached Australia in the early years of the sixteenth century rests primarily on map evidence. A land of continental proportions named Java la Grande and approximately in the position of Australia is depicted on a number of maps and charts dating mainly from 1540 to 1570. These maps and charts were French in origin and were derived from one main group of chartmakers, the Dieppe school (as it became known); yet the maps marked the discovery of the land as Portuguese. There is no sign of the land mass on Portuguese maps of the period now extant, nor are there any known records of official claims to the discovery by the Portuguese.

EARLY RECORDS OF JAVA LA GRANDE
Such is the enigma of Java la Grande. The lack of Portuguese charts showing the discovery has been attributed to losses in the Lisbon earthquake of 1755, but the selective disappearance of maps marking Java la Grande, as opposed to those which do not, is unlikely. The absence of official reports has been explained by the policy of secrecy which Portugal enforced to protect her empire from intruders. Yet the Portuguese were not otherwise backward in asserting their claims and delineating their discoveries. Between 1482 and 1488 navigators

Diogo Cão and Bartolomeu Dias set up 'padrões' (stone pillars) to mark their acts of possession as they explored the coasts of Africa. Tomé Pires described in a manuscript codex, written in 1512–15, and the pilot Francisco Rodrigues recorded in a rutter illustrated with maps and sketches, *c*. 1513, their explorations in the Eastern Archipelago, from 1511 to 1512. João de Castro, Governor of India, prepared for royal and noble persons three magnificent rutters (1538 to 1542) illustrating navigation routes to India. Portuguese humanists were eloquent in eulogizing their countrymen whose feats of exploration and scientific discovery were claimed to have surpassed those of the Greeks and Romans. António Ferreira (1528–69) in his *Poemas Lusitanos* (Lisbon, 1598) sent greetings from 'old Portugal' through 'new seas, new heavens, new climes', to 'the new Portugal, to famous Goa'.[2]

The discovery of a great land mass beyond 'Little Java' (as the island of Java was sometimes called) would therefore have been a matter of national interest and comment, had it become known in official Portuguese circles. Those who support the theory of the discovery have thus to explain how the French obtained intelligence of a voyage, or voyages, of which the Portuguese apparently remained ignorant. Spies and diplomatic agents in Portugal and *émigré* Portuguese chartmakers in France have been identified as possible sources of the secret information. In 1807 the French geographer Jean Denis Barbié du Bocage suggested that Don Michel Sylva, Bishop of Viseu, who left Portugal in 1542 to travel to Italy by way of France, had passed on news of an expedition from the Moluccas in 1525 by Gomes de Sequeira. Barbié du Bocage named Sequeira as the probable discoverer of Java la Grande.[3]

The navigators and chartmakers of Dieppe were indeed well placed to obtain information about Portuguese discoveries, official and unofficial. Dieppe was the great centre of French maritime activity, with *armateurs* (ship fitters-out) who acted independently of the cautious king and his government in Paris. Charles de la Roncière commented: 'If you are looking for the dominant force in maritime politics in France, don't go to the court of Francis I but to Dieppe.'[4] Under the great *armateur* Jean Ango, Dieppe navigators were crossing the oceans, invading the territories of the Portuguese empire to establish trading posts. Ango's most ambitious plan was to usurp the Portuguese trade with India and the East, so challenging Portugal's right to the monopoly established by the Treaty of Tordesillas, in which Spain and Portugal divided between them those lands not already held by a Christian prince.

In 1529 Jean Parmentier, one of Ango's greatest navigators, made the boldest incursion into the Portuguese sphere, and this voyage was, I suggest, the means by which the French gained their knowledge of the discovery of Java la Grande. Sailing with his brother Raoul and with Pierre Crignon as *astronome* (pilot-navigator), Parmentier led an expedition of two ships to Sumatra, which they reached on 31 October 1529. There the brothers died of fever and, between

February and about July 1530, Crignon brought the ships home by way of the Cape of Good Hope.

This voyage took the French almost to the recorded margins of Java la Grande, and Crignon's journal includes the earliest textual evidence of a possible Portuguese discovery of it. Moreover, Crignon tells of a meeting with a Sumatran named Mocodon, an inhabitant of the old town of Oranchaie, who reported that two ships with men of rank who were white men in the service of a great king had come to trade there.[5] When questioned further by the interpreter Antoine, Mocodon said that he had seen night in the sky. This was presumably an eclipse of the sun, and would date the visit to 12 November 1528.[6] The interest shown by Parmentier's men in sailing on to 'Java', despite their commander's death, suggests that they had special news of the region. A vote was taken and, in the event, by a majority of three or four the company resolved to return to France.

The leading survivor of the Parmentier expedition, Crignon ranks as the key figure in the development of Dieppe hydrography in the 1530s. Despite its total disappearance, his manuscript 'La Perle de Cosmographie' ('The Pearl of Cosmography'), written in 1534 and dedicated to Philippe Chabot, admiral of France,[7] may be considered as one of the earliest items of evidence concerning the discovery of Java la Grande. The French geographer Guillaume de l'Isle, who had it in his hands in 1712, has left a description of this work.[8] It gave the first observation of the variation of the compass known to de l'Isle, namely that for Dieppe, made on 2 March 1534. According to de l'Isle Crignon was the first to devise a 'ligne de direction' ('line of direction'), the line where there is no compass declination. Crignon made this his first meridian,[9] and his claim to have discovered the secret of longitude probably rested on this construction, for the idea that lines of longitude and lines of magnetic variation could be correlated was beginning to take shape.

These are clues to the content and significance of the missing manuscript. They suggest a close relationship between 'La Perle de Cosmographie' and the 'Traicte des differences du compas aymante' ('Treatise on the differences of the magnetic compass')[10] of the Dieppe hydrographer Jean Rotz, who is one of the major authorities for the recording of Java la Grande. Rotz also wrote of a line of no variation, which he called the 'ligne dyametralle' ('diametrical line'). It is therefore probable that Rotz consulted 'La Perle de Cosmographie', and if so, he may have included some of Crignon's material in his own work.

Other writings by Crignon also point to the importance of 'La Perle'. He has been identified as the 'great French sea captain of the town of Dieppe' whose 'molto bello' ('very fine') discourse, written in 1539, was included by G. B. Ramusio in his *Navigationi et Viaggi* (Venice, 1556).[11] This described voyages to New France, Brazil, Madagascar and Sumatra, that to Sumatra being the first published record of Parmentier's voyage. The maps of Giacomo Gastaldi which illustrate the *Discourse*[12] show New France, Brazil, West Africa and Sumatra

41

and must have been obtained from Crignon. Of all the Frenchmen in the 1530s, Crignon was the one best qualified to write a navigational guide to the seas and coasts of the world, which is presumably what 'La Perle' comprised.

This suggests that Crignon's 'La Perle' was the source of three notable works of the same kind, two by Jean Mallard, the third by Jean Alfonse, a Portuguese pilot resident in France. Mallard, who is believed to have been a member of a Norman family which kept bookshops in Rouen and Paris, was 'escriptvain' ('scribe') and court poet to Francis I, and then (from 1539 to 1541) court poet and 'orator in the French tongue' to Henry VIII of England. Mallard's earlier manuscript, entitled 'Premier livre de la description de tous les portz de mer de l'univers' ('Description of all the sea ports in the world: First Book') (c. 1536), is a versified cosmography.[13] It has been described by Georges Musset and most later authorities (including Roger Hervé) as a rendering of Alfonse's *Voyages auantureux* (Poitiers, 1559), of which the manuscript original is believed to have been written about 1536.[14]

The evidence indicates conversely (in my view) that the manuscripts of Mallard and Alfonse were derived from a common source, from Crignon.[15] In his epistle to Francis I Mallard describes himself as a young man who has not made a single voyage to the distant regions which he is describing. Setting out his plan to give an account of all ports, islands and dangers, banks and rocks, the abundance and distribution of resources, and peoples' customs and ways of life, he writes:

> If the task exceeds my knowledge
> I put my trust in your great wealth
> Which will come to the aid of my poverty
> By having this work speedily revised
> By good pilots who know the depths of the waters
> Like those excellent navigators
> Jacques Cartier and Crignon or by Sorin
> Or other men expert in marine lore
> Who have embraced the whole round earth
> Of which the Castellan possesses the whole theory
> In every language and every art in the world.[16]

Mallard thus names as the great navigators of the day Crignon, Jacques Cartier, famous for his two voyages to Canada of 1534 and 1535 to 1536, and the pilot Germain Sorin. Significantly, Mallard does not name Alfonse in this context, but cites him as an authority for two pieces of specific information relating to the West Indies which do indeed appear in Alfonse's *Voyages auantureux*. The implication must be that Mallard's main source was not Alfonse's manuscript, although Mallard knew this work. Mallard was probably personally acquainted with Crignon as a fellow poet, who had won several prizes at the 'puys de la Conception de Rouen', and who composed 'chants royaux' and 'rondeaux', some of which were printed at Paris and Rouen.[17]

This is circumstantial evidence for the suggestion that Mallard's 'First Book' was based on Crignon's 'La Perle'. Mallard's manuscript covers only the coasts of the Atlantic and the west coast of South America. Mallard promised Francis I a second and third volume if the king approved the first, but no other volumes are known. His royal service came to an abrupt end in 1537 when he lost his position at court to a rival poet, Clément Marot. None the less, Mallard's epistle to the king reveals his wide interest in, and knowledge of, those recent French voyages which do not feature in the 'First Book', but which he intended to treat in the promised instalment. He reports that he is making a circular world map showing the results of the French voyages, and criticizes those people who knew longitude but did not wish to reveal it, for France was now at the islands where the Portuguese first had been. These clearly are references to the Portuguese policy of secrecy and to Parmentier's voyage to Sumatra:

> Then you will see on the round map
> That again I make Frenchmen sail the seas
> And make known so many hidden secrets
> That everyone will make his map
> From the book, and without going far away
> Will bring much light to science through experience.
> O what harm and what distress
> Have they caused who know longitude
> But have never wanted to write of their techniques,
> For France would now be in those islands
> Where the Portuguese have first place.
> Oh noble King! Oh sovereign source![18]

Mallard completed the map in time for its inclusion in the 'Cosmographie' which he presented to Henry VIII.[19] This small world map in two hemispheres (2.1) is the earliest of the 'Dieppe school' maps to show the land mass of what appears to be Java la Grande. South of Melacque (Malacca) is a large promontory named 'La Catigare' which is attached to the southern continent, named 'Terre australie'. Catigara appeared as the most south-easterly town on Ptolemy's maps of south-eastern Asia, his 'Ultima thule' of the Far East. When, with the Indian Ocean opened up, and the landbridge from Asia to the southern continent cut, his maps were revised, the name featured on the most easterly peninsula of Asia. On Mallard's map it is now displaced southward and inscribed where the later Dieppe maps give the name 'Java la Grande'. In general the map is crude and suggests that Mallard, a fine miniaturist, was no geographer. This strengthens the presumption that he was copying and versifying another's more expert texts and drafts. Like that for Francis, the 'Cosmographie' written for Henry covers only the Atlantic and America. It may be that the move to England in about 1538 or 1539 prevented Mallard from obtaining the material he needed for providing a second and a third instalment.

The third derivative work (in the light of this interpretation), Alfonse's

Voyages auantureux, was world-wide in compass, and if correctly dated as originally written in about 1536, constitutes the earliest report of Java la Grande, here described as 'la terre de Iaue'. The text reads: 'To the south of Traprobana [Sumatra] is the land of Java, which is a nation of people like those of Brazil. In the land of Java in some places gold is found and there are good rivers. The land is healthy, beyond the line on the Antarctic side.'[20] A reference to the 'diametral line called Estual'[21] at the 'island of white men' ('isle des Hommes blancs'), south-east of the Moluccas, seems an allusion to the 'diametrical line' which Rotz described in his 'Traicte' and Crignon called the 'line of direction', and is thus the antipodean extension of this line. Alfonse also mentions Marco Polo's report that the men of Java worshipped the sun and moon,[22] and this custom is illustrated by Pierre Desceliers on his chart of 1550 (2.9) in a vignette on Java la Grande, with an accompanying legend. Alfonse's comment that the sea between Sumatra (la Tropbonne) and the mainland of Java was so dangerous that ships would not pass that way,[23] has its equivalent on the Dieppe maps in the inscription, to the east of Java: 'anda ne barcha' ('no boats go there').[24] And Alfonse's 'isle des Hommes blancs'[25] reappears as 'Y de los hōbres blancos' ('island of white men') on later works.[26]

The question as to whether Alfonse had ever been to the Far East may be judged from a study of both his *Voyages auantureux* and his manuscript 'Cosmographie' of 1544. Whereas Mallard admitted that he was not a sailor, Alfonse stated in his 'Cosmographie' that he had been a navigator for forty-eight years on all the seas of the world, and had never lost a ship.[27] His *Voyages auantureux* ends with the robust assertion, 'You should not marvel at all these accounts, for things are written as I who have made the voyages have seen them, and those who have made them or read them in books will know if it is true'.[28] Some fifty years later, however, Marc Lescarbot, historian of North American discovery, challenged Alfonse's claims, writing: 'I find little or no truth in the discourses of the man; and well might he call his voyages adventurous, not for himself, who had not been to a hundredth part of the places he describes (at least it is easy to conjecture so) but for those who wish to follow the routes that he recommends for mariners'.[29]

On this evidence, Alfonse appears as a suspect witness, one who was to be accused of plagiarism in due course by his own countrymen. Mallard, in contrast, appears as an honest official, who in copying Crignon (if indeed this is what he did) was merely fulfilling his courtly duties. Yet the words of both men may be seen as offering useful clues to the contents of Crignon's 'La Perle'. The fact that Mallard's texts lack the Far Eastern material makes Alfonse's compilations valuable as comparable derivative works, as the following study of the 'Cosmographie' shows.

Other writings of Crignon besides 'La Perle' point to the importance of his role and that of Parmentier in the development of the Dieppe school, on whose

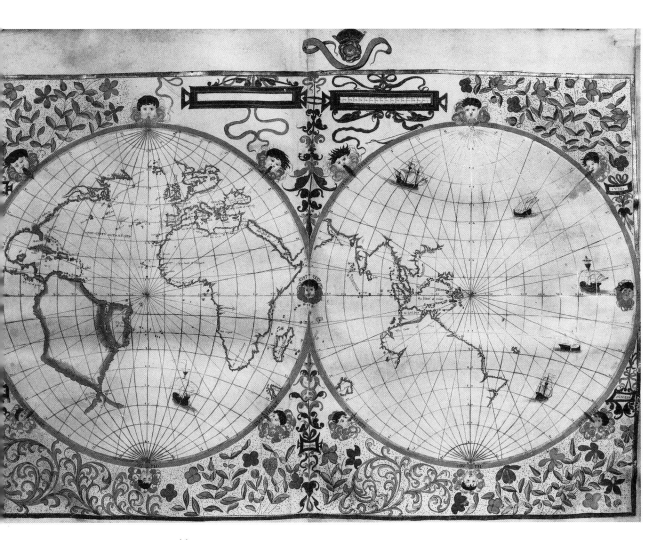

2.2   Jean Rotz   World Map   1542

productions depends the main evidence for the Portuguese discovery of Java la Grande. Crignon writes in his *Plaincte (Lament)* for the death of Parmentier: 'He was a good cosmographer and geographer. By him were many maps of the world prepared as globes or flat sheets, and numerous marine maps by which many have navigated safely.'[30] Thus it appears that many charts and some world maps and globes by Parmentier were available in Dieppe in the 1530s. In his *Mémoires chronologiques pour servir à l'histoire de Dieppe* (1785) Charles Desmarquets wrote that Parmentier 'had produced the first map of the whole earth' (i.e. by a Frenchman).[31] Crignon himself must have added to the collections at Dieppe, and his maps and charts of the 1530s (he died in 1540) would have included the record of Parmentier's voyage to Sumatra and presumably the earliest depictions of Java la Grande.

Through his connections with Paris Crignon secured for Parmentier one other trace on the world map. Parmentier had hoped to circumnavigate the

the fey of the Indis of oriene

Crut Iana

The Indis

2.3   Jean Rotz   Eastern Hemisphere   1542

Trapobana

Zeilon

globe, but his early death at the age of forty had deprived Dieppe of this glory. In the *Plaincte sur le trespas de deffunctz Jan et Raoul Parmentier* (1531), Crignon expressed the wish that if another Frenchman should pass beyond the 'frontiers of the East', he would name the sea after Parmentier.[32]

> And this sea where he tarries
> Must be adorned with both names.
> If any other Frenchman comes to this place,
> He will name this sea 'Parmentière'
> And will commemorate him for ever.[33]

Although Sumatra remained the limit of the Dieppe voyages, Crignon's wish was to be fulfilled by the emigré Portuguese chartmakers Diogo and André Homem, who were probably cousins, and who must have obtained access to Crignon's material. Diogo inscribed the name MARELEPARAMĀTIŪ (Mer de Parmentier) across the North Pacific on the chart of North America in his manuscript atlas made for Queen Mary of England, 1558. André, cosmographer to Charles IX of France, has a legend to the west of Labrador reading 'Mare ynventum per Paramantiee' ('sea discovered by Parmentier') on his manuscript planisphere of 1559.[34] A relic of the name appears in print as 'C. de Paramantia' on the north-west coast of North America on Abraham Ortelius's world map of 1564.

THE DIEPPE MAPS

'The world had enough sea charts of a common kind', remarked the hydrographer Jean Rotz in 1542,[35] with reference particularly to the great working collections at Dieppe. These materials, which would have included the original maps of Parmentier and Crignon, are now lost. They were destroyed when the English fleet blew up the town in 1694. The maps and charts which survive from the Dieppe school and record the discovery of Java la Grande are presumably to a lesser or greater degree derivative of the surveys of Parmentier and Crignon. They are fine presentation pieces made for royal and noble persons and had left Dieppe in the sixteenth century to be scattered in the course of time through various collections and libraries of Europe. They were not all identified as of the Dieppe school until the later years of the nineteenth century, and only recently has it been possible to determine their approximate dates (where they are undated) and their relationship to one another.

The earliest major work of the Dieppe school, and the next cartographic item in date to Mallard's world map, *c.* 1540, is the 'Boke of Idrography' of Jean Rotz.[36] Rotz was a native of Dieppe but of Scots descent through his father David Ross. He prepared the 'Boke' for Francis I, but personal circumstances (probably his failure to secure a post at Court) persuaded him to transfer to England and to Henry VIII's service. He may perhaps have used the good offices of Mallard, whom he presumably knew, and who had similarly changed allegiance.

In London Rotz completed his 'Boke', a magnificent maritime atlas, which he presented to Henry in 1542.

The 'Boke' opens with a navigational treatise, followed by eleven regional charts and a general world map (2.2) in two hemispheres. The regional charts were made from a world chart, and Rotz claimed to be the first to convert a large unmanageable map of the world into the more convenient form of a book containing 'all hydrography or marine science'. (His original must have been thirteen feet wide and seven feet high.) He went on to explain the arrangement of the regional charts, which showed

the lands and sea coasts of the World in so far as by mariners and other sailors it is known; the which description of lands is set by order so that every leaf does begin there where the precedent of it did leave, and so does proceed while all the known parts of the sea coasts be shown in partialities.[37]

Rotz's 'Boke' was thus the first atlas of Dieppe hydrography. That the prototype was derived in part from a Portuguese chart is clear from the many Portuguese place-names on Rotz's chart, and also from the detailed knowledge of Portuguese discoveries in areas where the French had not ventured, such as the eastern part of the East Indian archipelago. The regional chart of the Far East (2.3)[38] shows at the top (all the regional charts are oriented to the south) the northern part of Java la Grande. The name 'Coste dangereuse' ('dangerous coast')—later to be a major source of controversy—appears on the north-east coast and other names on the north-west coast from north to south are 'abaie de', 'abaie a basse' (i.e., 'baye basse'?), 'terra en negade' (i.e., 'terre anegada': 'submerged land'), 'abaie bressille' ('Brazil Bay'), 'Ille Nege' (i.e., 'Ye de Neiges'?). These names show that Rotz's source material included the array of place-names along the coasts which were typical of the later Dieppe charts displaying Java la Grande in detail. Rotz's world map[39] (2.2) reveals the full extent of the land mass in a form similar to that in which it appears on the later larger-scale charts.

Rotz's 'Boke' may be ranked as first class testimony to an actual discovery (that is, of Java la Grande). As a hydrographer and seaman he showed only discovered coasts. As he wrote in his dedicatory letter to Henry: 'All this I have set down exactly and truly as possible, drawing as much from my own experience as from the certain experience of my friends and fellow navigators.'[40]

The prototype which Rotz was copying was mainly Portuguese in nomenclature, hence the description of Rotz's 'Boke' and various other works of Dieppe as Luso-French.[41] On what was a Portuguese base map Rotz (or perhaps his immediate source who may have been Crignon) superimposed a detailed record of the Dieppe voyages made under Ango's auspices. Rotz's charts show French discoveries and trading posts, and vignettes depicting the lives of the people and scenes observed on distant coasts. Rotz thus transformed a seaman's chart into a picture of new worlds of overseas discoveries. Following the example of the Portuguese, the French voyagers carried on board a 'painter' as well as a chartmaker. Rotz himself sailed to Guinea and to Brazil in 1539 and he incorporates eye-witness scenes of these countries in the charts in his 'Boke'.

He also includes vignettes recording the discoveries of Parmentier's expedition to Sumatra in 1529 to 1530 and various incidents of the voyage. There is some evidence to suggest that he had sailed on the voyage himself.[42] The vignettes appear to have been drawn *ad vivum*, and they show several scenes which do not feature on other extant Dieppe charts, such as a fatal encounter with the inhabitants of Madagascar on 24 July 1529, and a portrayal of the Hottentots of southern Africa who were seen at the Cape of Good Hope on the return voyage in 1530.[43] The record for Sumatra is remarkably detailed and accurate. It includes a military procession of the rajah of Ticou and a Sumatran house on stilts. These drawings are placed north of the Malay peninsula, the continental area nearest to Sumatra which has enough space for their depiction. The later Dieppe chartmakers, notably the author of the Vallard atlas of 1546 (2.8), used the more extensive interior of Java la Grande for the Sumatran scenes.

The next work in the sequence is a small world map, Dieppois in style, dated 1543, bearing the initials 'GB' and the arms of Arthur de Cossé, Marshall of France. It is preserved in a portolan atlas now in the Huntington Library, California (2.4).[44] The author has been identified as Guillaume Brouscon, a native of Le Conquet in Brittany who was noted for his nautical guides, tide tables and almanacs. The land mass of Java la Grande is similar to the form in which it appears on Nicolas Desliens's maps of 1567 and 1568. A curious protuberance which deforms the west coast of South America also appears on a world map in a Dieppe style portolan atlas, *c.* 1550, preserved in the Bibliothèque de la Ville de Lyon.[45] Brouscon's map provides a Breton contribution to the history of the recording of Java la Grande. Another link with Brittany is found in the tide tables of the manuscript atlas sometimes named 'La Vallière' after its one-time owner, the Duke de la Vallière, and now preserved in the Koninklijke Bibliotheek, The Hague. This atlas, *c.* 1545 to 1547, does not extend to the Far East.[46]

Like Brouscon's atlas, the 'Cosmographie' of 'Jean Fonteneau dit Alfonse de Saintonge' (Jean Alfonse)[47] does not derive from the Dieppe school, but is notable for providing a graphic and textual record of Java la Grande. The treatise, lacking a title, is signed 'J. Alphonces', and dated May 1544, and includes seventy sketch maps. The map of the Far East (f. 147v) (2.5) is similar to that in Rotz's 'Boke' (2.3) and shows to the south of Sumatra 'Java major' as a land continuing to the edge of the page. The adjoining island 'Java minor' corresponds to Flores. In the text Alfonse describes 'la grande Java', and claims to have been there:

This Java is a land which extends down near to the Antarctic pole; on the western side it is close to the Southern Land, and on the eastern side to the Strait of Magellan. Some say that it is made up of islands. But as regards what I have seen of it, it is a continent... The land called Java Minor is an island. But Great-Java is a continent.[48]

Continuing on a later folio, Alfonse describes his personal experience of the land:

And it is my understanding that [this Java] extends down near to the Antarctic Pole. Nevertheless, I have been in a place where my day lasted three months reckoned by the revolution of the sun, and I did not wish to stay longer for fear that night might overtake me.[49]

The authenticity of this description must be doubtful. Alfonse had sailed to the north of Newfoundland on le Sieur de Roberval's expedition to Canada in 1542 and is believed by some to have discovered Davis Strait. Because of this, Pierre Margry in 1867, followed by Georges Musset in 1904, alleged that he was here writing of an expedition to the Arctic, as opposed to the Antarctic.[50]

The fact that much of Alfonse's 'Cosmographie' was taken from Martin Fernandez de Enciso's *Suma de Geographia,* published at Seville in 1519, with a second edition in 1530, tends to confirm the impression that Alfonse was a skilful compiler rather than a true discoverer of the oriental parts of the world. He could have written his text and drawn his maps from a study of the Dieppe maps and charts then available. Yet his work does supply useful pieces in the jigsaw of clues. Of particular interest is his description of the coast of Java la Grande: 'and in this land there are great quantities of gold, silver and elephants, and there are monkeys like those in Barbary ... and I suspect that it is a continent and that it is joined to the southern land'. Wilma George points out that monkeys are found on both Java and Sumatra, but the pig-tailed macaques, which resemble the Barbary apes, are Sumatran. The combination of elephants and pig-tailed macaques shows that Alfonse was describing Sumatra.[51] This reinforces the impression that Sumatran features had become incorporated in the depiction of Java la Grande.

Pierre Desceliers's world chart of 1546 (2.6),[52] the next dated item, belongs to the main sequence of Dieppe hydrography. Norman historians have regarded Desceliers, priest at Arques, as the 'father' of the Dieppe school. 'As far as sea charts are concerned, I said with Mr Dablon that Mr Pierre des Cheliers, a priest at Arques, has had the honour of being the first to make any in France', David Asseline wrote, referring to the manuscript, now lost, of the earlier chronicler Nicolas Dablon.[53] Desceliers was 'le père de l'hydrographie et de la cartographie française' ('the father of French hydrography and cartography'). He appears to have gained official recognition as a teacher or examiner of pilots, a fact which may explain his reputation as the first of the Dieppe school, whereas he actually belonged to the second group of Dieppe hydrographers, flourishing a decade or so later than Parmentier and Crignon. His charts are the work of a cosmographer using to good effect the abundant material available in Dieppe to which Rotz had alluded when he wrote (in his letter to Henry) that the world was well supplied with the common sort of marine charts.

51

2.4   Guillaume Brouscon
World Map   1543

Desceliers's chart of 1546 is the earliest dated map to show Java la Grande in detail and with a full array of place-names such as (to mention the most notable of the east coast) 'Coste perileuse' (where Rotz had 'coste dangereuse'), 'Baye perdue' ('Bay of the Lost'), 'Coste des herbiages' ('grassy coast'), and 'C. fremose' ('beautiful cape') lying at the tip of the large triangular south-east cape in 46°S. Desceliers's chart is thus the first major piece of evidence permitting elucidation of the enigma by place-name interpretation.

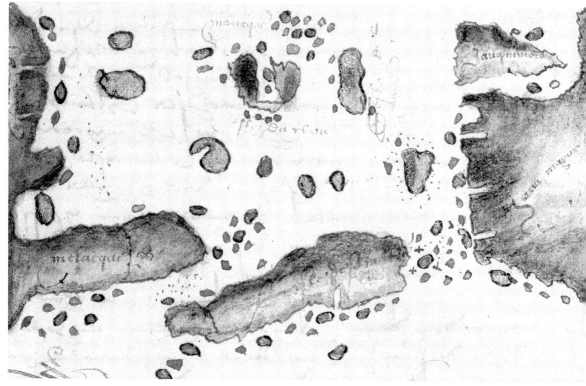

2.5   Jean Alfonse   Sketch Map of the Far East   1544

On the other hand, as on Rotz's chart, the iconography of Java is rather generalized. Pictures of men and animals include four seated monarchs, a group of three people disporting themselves among the rocks and trees, and two lions. In striking contrast to Rotz's portrayal of only known and discovered coasts, the western shoreline of Java la Grande is attached in 19°S to the southern continent, inscribed 'Terre australe non du tout descouverte' ('southern land not completely discovered'). Concerned to incorporate current geographical theory and not to leave loose ends, Desceliers completed the coasts of all the continents and filled in the remote regions of Asia and America with detail from traditional or contemporary sources.

The 'Harleian' map (2.7) (sometimes called the 'Dauphin' map[54]) closely follows in date Desceliers's earliest chart (2.6). It was still being prepared when Henry the Dauphin became Henry II of France in 1547, for the Dauphin's arms have been altered, although this and other decorative work is incomplete. The usual dating of the chart as made between 1537 and 1543 cannot therefore be accepted. This is the most puzzling of the major works of Dieppe hydrography, as its author and provenance remain unknown, and in content it shows deviations from the Dieppe tradition. North America with its narrow waist in 32°N seems

2.6   Pierre Desceliers   World Chart   1546

2.7   [Anonymous]   Harleian or 'Dauphin' World Map   *c.* 1547

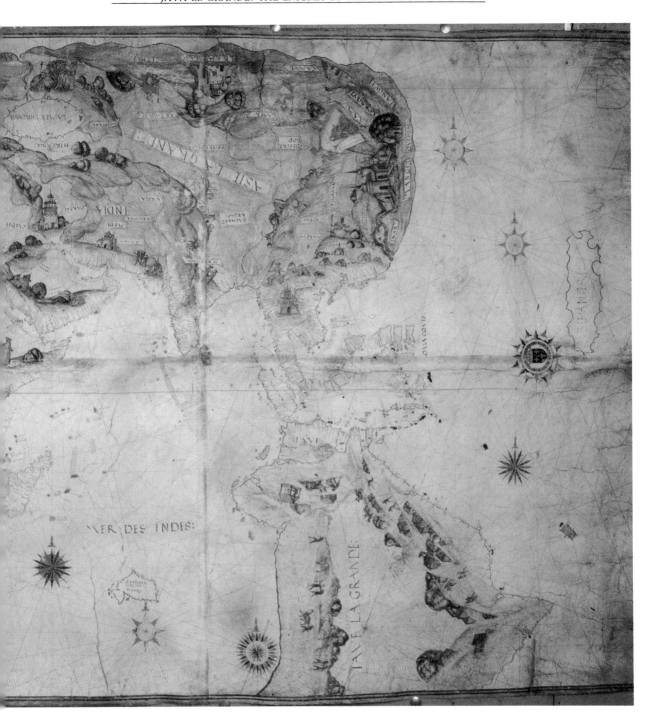

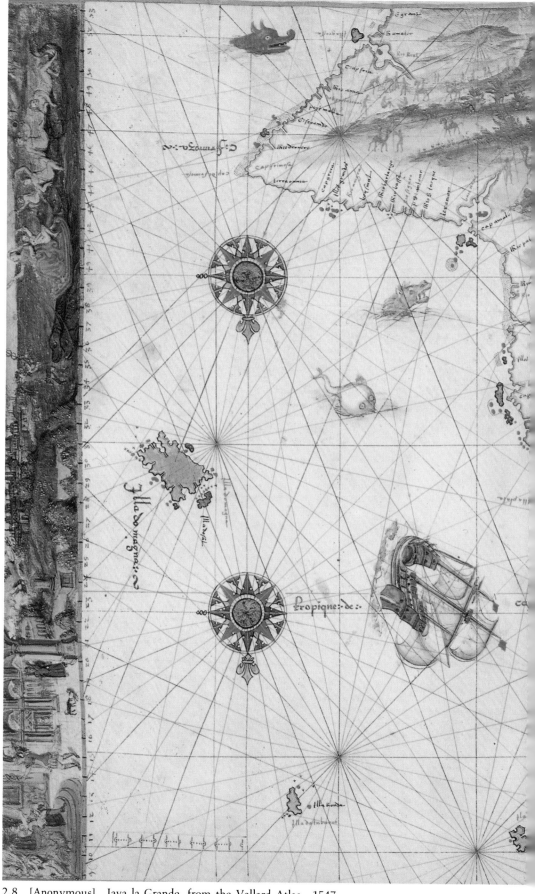

2.8 [Anonymous] Java la Grande, from the Vallard Atlas 1547

to indicate knowledge of Giovanni de Verrazzano's American discoveries of 1524. As Verrazzano ended his voyage at Dieppe in July 1524, a connection of this kind would not be particularly surprising, yet the Harleian map is the only Dieppe work to show the feature. The belief that the map was by Rotz led some authorities such as R. A. Skelton to suggest that the map was made from sources in England.[55] Henry VIII had in his collection a chart which he had received from Giovanni's brother Gerolamo in 1527, and its influence was such that the Verrazzanian concept of North America was popular in England for many years. A detailed comparison of the Harleian map with the charts in Rotz's 'Boke', however, eliminates the possibility of Rotz's authorship. Another oddity of the Harleian map is the archaic form of some of the place-names, such as Cabalu (Cambalu, or China) in South America, and Zipangu (Cipango, or Japan) as a great island off Mangi (South China).

Whatever these features imply, Java la Grande itself is depicted in the Dieppe style. There is the usual river, 'R. Grande', dividing 'Iave' from 'Iave la grande', and place-names are similar to those of Desceliers (2.6). The interior detail is lively, with Sumatran huts, deer, and some camel-like animals which may be guanaco displaced from South America. In contrast to Desceliers's chart of 1546, the land of Java la Grande is not connected to a southern continent but runs off the map in 63°S. A separate land mass named 'La Terre Australle' takes in the south shore of the Strait of Magellan. In this respect the Harleian map is closer to Rotz's world map of 1542 (2.2) and to Brouscon's of 1543 (2.4) than to Desceliers's chart of 1546 (2.6).

The author of the atlas of Nicolas Vallard of Dieppe (1547) is also unknown, as Vallard, named on the frontispiece, is believed to have been the owner.[56] The coastal names appear to be Portuguese and in a Portuguese hand, whereas regional names (in a larger hand) are mainly in French. A notable similarity between the charts in Rotz's 'Boke' and those in the Vallard atlas has been remarked on by various authorities, and both atlases also bear resemblances to The Hague atlas. As Luso-French works all three won a place in an appendix to Armando Cortesão's and Avelino Teixeira da Mota's *Portugaliae Monumenta Cartographica* (Lisbon, 1960).[57] For a time, too, the mistaken dating of The Hague atlas as of about 1538 suggested that it might be the source of the other two atlases.[58] It has become clear, however, that the authors of The Hague atlas and of the Vallard one were copying in the later 1540s some of the source material which Rotz had used (and perhaps had himself provided) in the 1530s and evidently had left in Dieppe when he moved, probably to Paris in 1540 and then to England in 1542.

Java la Grande is portrayed on several maps in the Vallard atlas, with the fullest record on map one (2.8), which has a wealth of ethnographical detail. A lively village scene includes a rajah's procession, houses on stilts, a wattle fence and coconut palms. These features are Sumatran and closely resemble the

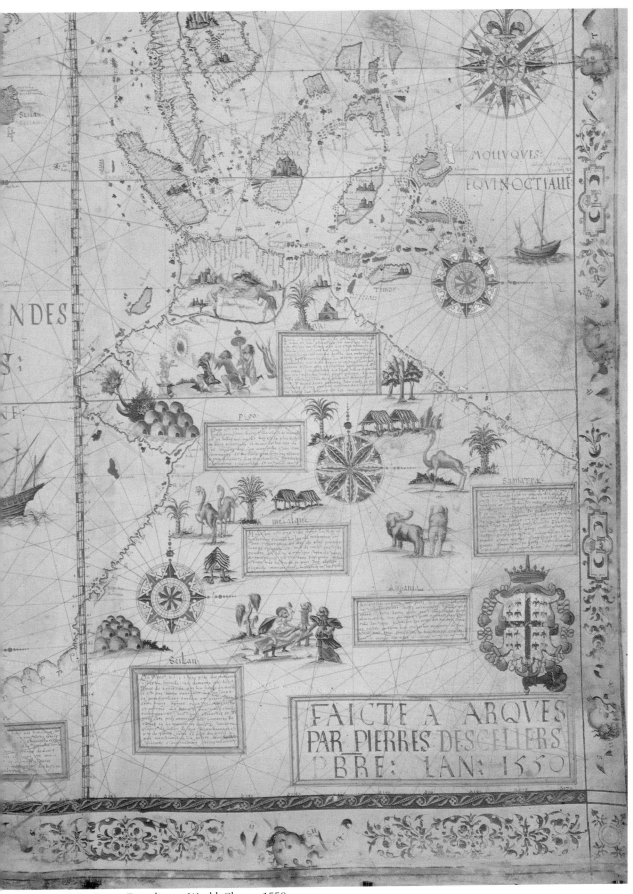

2.9 Pierre Desceliers World Chart 1550

2.10   Pierre Desceliers   Facsimile of his World Map   1553

vignettes on Rotz's chart of south-eastern Asia, as can be seen by comparing the portrayal of the rajah of Ticou's procession. The houses on stilts are well drawn, but the step, a sort of hurdle on the Vallard, is placed some distance away from the entrance, showing that its purpose was misunderstood. The Vallard's depiction

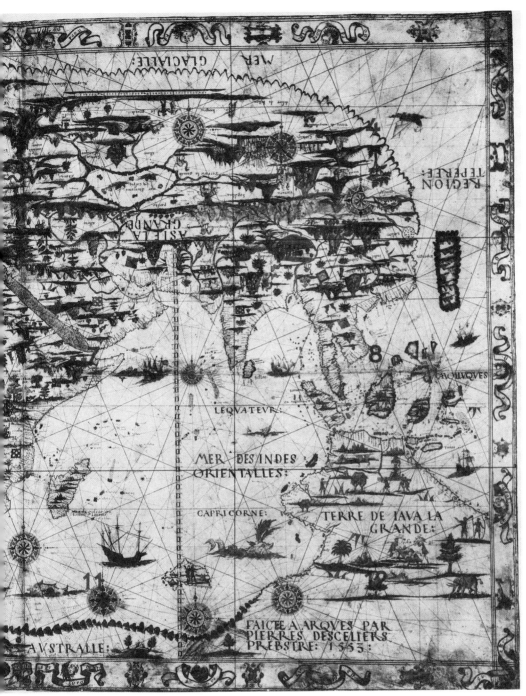

of fauna, which is more extensive than Rotz's, includes turtles on the east coast of Java la Grande. These may represent the smooth-shelled *Platysternum* found in south China or the peculiar snake-necked turtles of northern Australia and New Guinea.[59] In the far distance are scenes of men with horses and camels. The place-names along the coast include some Spanish forms, and the dangerous coast is here named in Portuguese: 'costa dangeroza'.

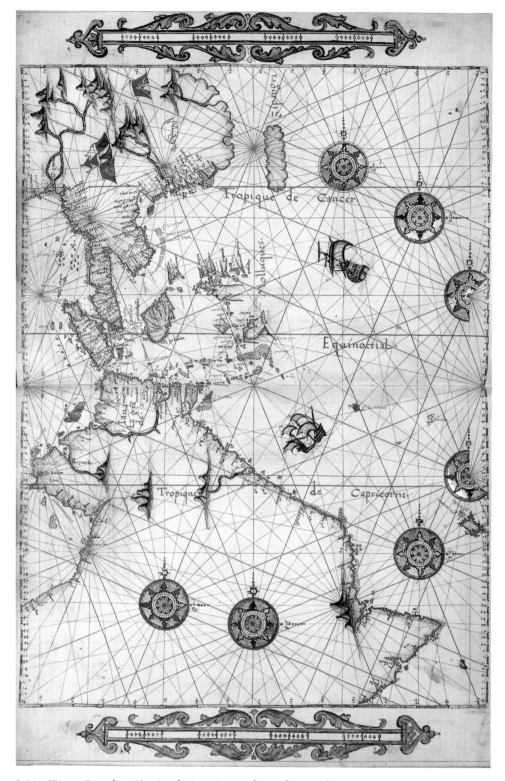

2.11 [Pierre Desceliers ?]   South East Asia and Java la Grande   *c.* 1555

2.12   Guillaume le Testu   Java la Grande   1556

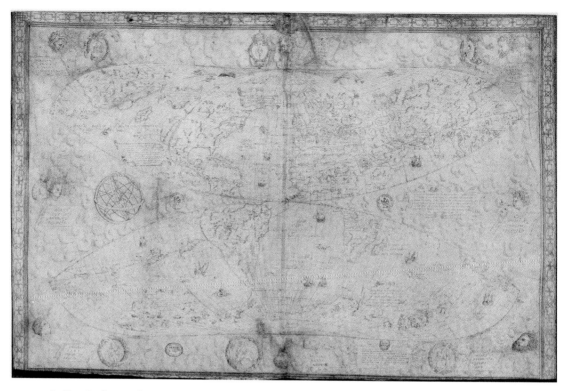

2.13 Guillaume le Testu World Map 1566

Desceliers's chart of 1550 (2.9),[60] like his chart of 1546 (2.6), links the west coast of 'Java' to 'La terre Australle', but its east coast disappears off the map in 29°S, so there is no 'Cap fremose'. The cusps of the southern continent are inscribed 'cap' and 'R' (for Rivière), but closely-written legends can be discerned reading 'Terre non du tout descouverte' ('land not completely discovered'). In contrast to Desceliers's earlier chart (2.6), a wealth of iconographic and textual detail now fills Java la Grande. There are Sumatran huts, and the animals, namely elephants and monkeys, are also Sumatran. There are scenes of idolatry and cannibalism which derive from Marco Polo. A cluster of 'beehive' huts on the west coast resembles the homes of the Nguni-speaking people first encountered by the Portuguese in the fifteenth century on the African coast south-east of the Cape of Good Hope. Desceliers draws two similar villages on the north-west coast of America, with an adjacent legend about pygmies (a reference here to the Eskimos). Legends on Java la Grande describe adjacent regions: Java, Pego (Pegu), Melasqua (Malacca), Samatra (Sumatra), Angani (the Andaman Islands), and Seilan (Ceylon).

The third of Desceliers's charts, dated 1553, formerly in the Geographische Gesellschaft, Vienna, was destroyed and is now known only from the facsimile published in 1924 (2.10).[61] Like the others, it shows 'Terre de Iava la Grande' as part of 'La terre Australle'. Graphic detail includes Sumatran huts on stilts, a Sumatran elephant, a litter, and the familiar cannibal scene. An atlas in the Pierpont Morgan Library, New York, also appears to be by Desceliers and is

66

possibly dated about 1555.[62] Detailed in coastal outline, Java la Grande here (2.11) displays in the interior simplified features comprising two compass roses and four mountain massifs at the heads of rivers.

A more extravagant version of Java la Grande appeared in the 'Cosmographie Universelle' of Guillaume Le Testu 1555 [1556] (2.12).[63] A seaman as well as a cartographer, Le Testu had sailed to Brazil in 1551 with Nicolas Durand, Chevalier de Villegagnon. Java la Grande features on various folios of his 'Cosmographie'. 'Petite Iava' is separated by the 'Riuiere Grande' from 'Grand Iava', also called 'Terre Australe'. The place-names include a Marco Polo allusion with 'Terre de Offir', and a 'Riviere de Cocodrilles [sic]'. The most remarkable feature is the fauna. As Wilma George has observed,[64] Java la Grande here has a curious collection, including an antlered deer, a crocodile, unicorns, dogs, parrots, a flightless bird, a possible swan, a pig and a peculiar looking mammal. George suggests that the flightless bird may have been a cassowary which had already been reported from the 'Australian islands', a term she uses to include some of the easterly islands of the Malay archipelago. The mammal had carnivore feet, long ears, a long nose and goggle eyes. In the light of the apparent mingling of Sumatran and Australian features I asked Wilma George to reassess her verdict on the animal, and she replied that if indeed it was Australian then it would be a dingo. There is no marsupial in the fauna of Le Testu or of any other of the Dieppe maps and atlases.

Le Testu himself seemed to discount the discovery of a southern continent at large, writing 'the land in the south, called "terre australe", which has not yet been discovered ... for this reason is only marked in by the imagination'.[65] It is doubtful, however, that this comment was meant to include the area of Java la Grande. His fauna seems to be based on authentic sources, and although it is mainly tropical (Malaysian), it includes—as we have seen—possible Australian features. Significantly, Le Testu depicted a bird of paradise on the eastern half of his world map of 1566 (2.13). It was the first appearance of this New Guinean bird on a map, although it was already known from drawings in the bestiary of Conrad Gesner (1551), and Pierre Belon's *Portraits d'oyseaux* (1557), as well as from written accounts.

In the 1560s one of the leading Dieppe cartographers was Nicolas Desliens. His large manuscript world chart, formerly in the Königliche Öffentliche Bibliothek, Dresden, was destroyed in the Second World War, and is known through a facsimile of 1903 (2.14).[66] An inscription in a scroll reads 'Faicte a Dieppe par Nicolas Desliens 1541' ('made in Dieppe by Nicolas Desliens 1541'). The penultimate figure of the date appears however to have been altered, and a date of 1561 is suggested from the geographical information supplied, notably that of the East Indies. There is the usual array of place-names of Java la Grande, but no inland detail. Significantly, Portuguese flags mark the discovery as Portuguese. A river, the 'R. Grand', separates the northern part, carrying the name 'Java la grande',

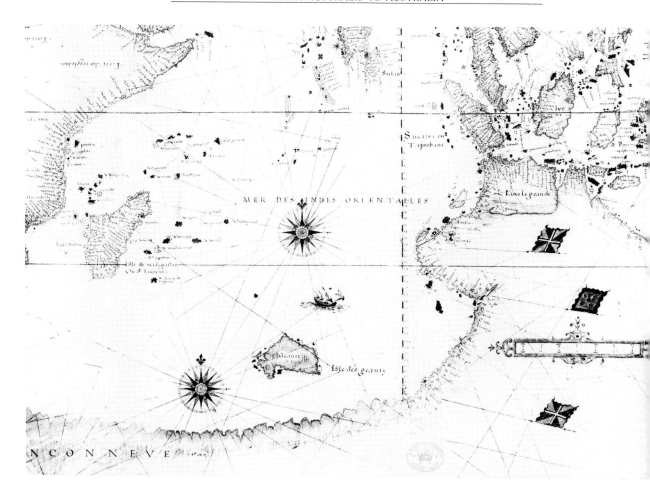

2.14   Nicolas Desliens   southern hemisphere   from a facsimile of his World Map   1561

Right
2.15   Nicolas Desliens   World Map   1566
2.16   Nicolas Desliens   World Map   1567

from the main land mass. Desceliers's chart of about 1550 (2.9) had also shown this configuration of land.

Desliens made smaller manuscript world maps, examples of which are dated 1566 (2.15) and 1567 (2.16).[67] On these, the 'R. Grande' is not marked, and the 'island' of Java as we now know it is incorporated in the mainland of Java la Grande. These later maps have few place-names and are non-pictorial, apart from the Portuguese flags. The fact that Pierre Hamon, the writing master to the young king of France, Charles IX, had a version of the 1567 map in his papers shows that Desliens's maps were circulating in the French capital.

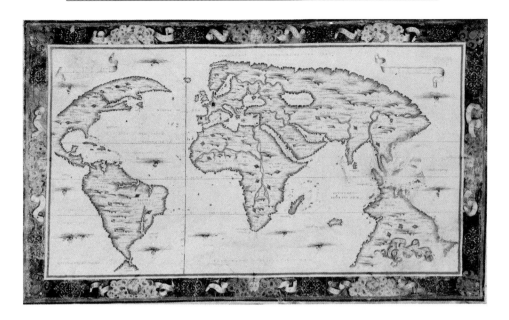

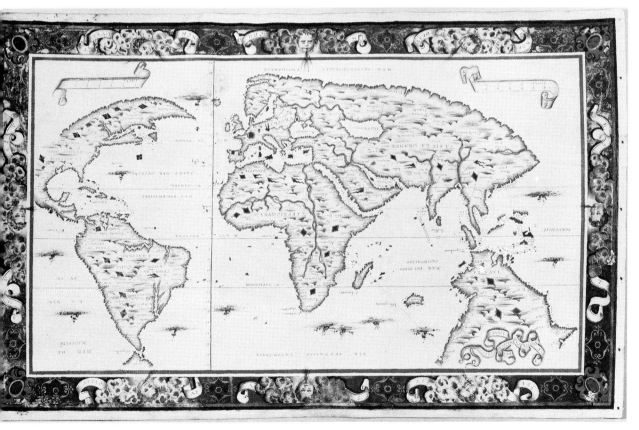

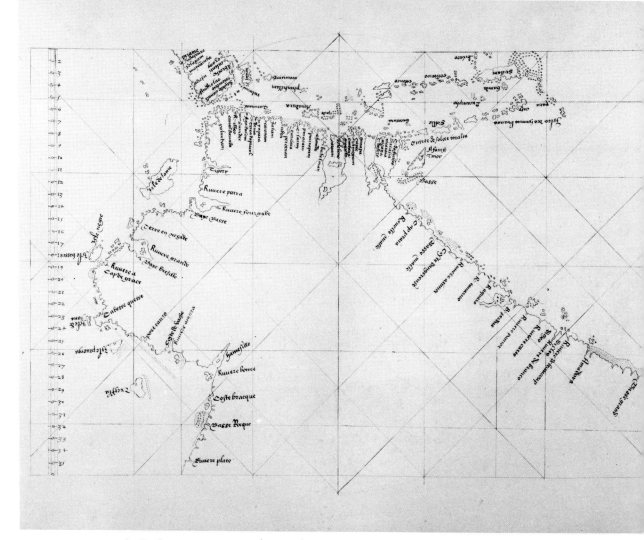

2.17   [Anonymous]   Java la Grande   1587

2.18   [Anonymous]   Section of the East Indies   1587

The last of the Dieppe-style works showing Java la Grande is the manuscript
'Livre de la Marine du Pilote P---t 1587' in the British Library (2.17).[68] The
author's name has been rubbed and is now illegible. It has been read as
'Pasterot', but the space between the 'P' and the 't' allows for only three or four
letters. The work comprises an atlas of maps mostly drawn in pencil or sketched
in pen and ink, while a few are coloured. Many of the maps are unfinished. The
outlines and vignettes suggest that the work is derived from Le Testu's *Cosmographie* or a common source. A swan appears in the 'Australian' region off
the west coast of Java la Grande (2.18) and seems to confirm Le Testu's black
swan (2.13). Wilma George tentatively identifies it with the black swan *Chen-
opsis atrata*—a native of Australia, although with near relatives from other
regions, including South America.

THE HISTORY OF THE DEBATE

These individual works, the showpieces of Dieppe, remained unknown to the world at large although the school of hydrography itself made Dieppe famous throughout Europe. 'Dieppe [is] reputed as the school for good pilots of this Kingdom', Bonaventure d'Aseville wrote to the Governor of Calais, as editor of Lucas Jansz Waghenaer's *Thresorerie ou Cabinet de la Routte Marinesque*, published at Calais in 1601.[69] This was the first well-known reference to the school. The significance of Dieppe hydrography in recording a possible first discovery of Australia was not appreciated until the late eighteenth century.

Only a few works in the intervening period give some hint of knowledge and interest. Indications of a land in the position of Java la Grande appear on a number of printed maps. Gastaldi's large world map 'Cosmographie Universalis' in nine sheets, *c.* 1561, has 'terra incognita meridionale discoperto novamente' ('newly discovered southern [land]') on the southern continent south of the 'Mare di Malucho', while south of Java the land is named 'Terra de Lucahc [sic]'. The continent has more than thirty kinds of fauna, and the connection between Gastaldi and Crignon points to a probable source for the map's rich iconography. Ten years later Benito Arias, called Montano, illustrated the eighth volume of his large Polyglot Bible, published at Antwerp, with a world map. A stretch of land south of Sumatra has raised questions as to whether it should be identified with Australia. A chart of the Indian Ocean by Ghisbert (1593), was evidently based on Portuguese sources, and shows a land mass like Java la Grande south of the Eastern Archipelago. Then there are the strange claims of Manuel Godinho de Erédia, who professed to have discovered 'Nuca Antara' in 1601. The outline he drew on his charts is suggestive of Arnhem Land, and of Java la Grande.[70] Did Erédia, a student at Malacca, obtain some information about Java la Grande from Far Eastern sources to build into his 'Nova India Meridional'? The English mathematician Edward Wright included a curious feature on his second world chart on Mercator's projection (2.19), engraved for his second edition of *Certaine Errors in Navigation* (1610). He inserted a coastline in the area of Java la Grande, with the attached legend: 'The coast of Tartarie and of the South continent we found thus laid forth in a fayre, large anncient sea chart which we referre to the triall of a further discoverie.'[71] The identity of the chart has not been established, but it seems to have been a Dieppe-type map.

However that may be, the subject awaited the indefatigable labours of Alexander Dalrymple (1737—1808), Hydrographer to the East India Company, later the first Hydrographer to the Admiralty. He was also, it is significant, the self-appointed rival to Captain Cook. When the Harleian map came to him on loan from Sir Joseph Banks, he took the first opportunity to bring it to the attention of the learned and maritime world. He described it in his *Memoir concerning the Chagos and Adjacent Islands* (1786), and his declaration that it showed the east coast of New Holland purported to deprive Cook of prior discovery. Dalrymple wrote:

The very curious MS here mentioned is painted on Parchment, with the Dauphin's Arms, it contains *much lost knowledge; Kerguelen's Land* seems plainly denoted; The *East Coast* of *New Holland*, as we name it, is expressed with some curious circumstances of correspondence to Captain Cook's MS, what he names

Bay of *Inlets* is in the MS called	*Baye Perdue*
Bay of *Isles* . . .	R. de beaucoup disles
Where the *Endeavour* struck	Coste dangereuse

So that we may say with Solomon 'There is nothing *new* under the Sun'.[72]

The chart (2.7), which should have come to the British Museum with the Harleian collection in 1753 but which was carried off by the butler, was presented to the Museum by Banks in 1790. Rotz's 'Boke' had come to the Museum in 1757 in the Old Royal Library, but was probably not noticed until Dalrymple publicized the Harleian map. The Keeper of Manuscripts, Joseph Planta, who became Principal Librarian in 1799, showed both items to interested parties, including John Pinkerton, the geographical writer, who visited the museum in about 1800. Pinkerton reported his conclusions in his *Modern Geography* (1802), stating that the Spaniards and the Portuguese had discovered the northern part of New Holland more than a century before 'the pretended Dutch discoveries', and adding patriotically, 'But neither interfere with the discovery of the S.E. part by our immortal Cook'.[73] James Burney (later Admiral Burney), who sailed on Cook's second and third voyages, consulted the two maps at about this time, and wrote in his *Chronological History of the Discoveries in the South Sea* (1803): 'That Rotz, or some of his intimates, visited the "Great Java" appears probable, from the coast being delineated on his chart, with greater resemblance to that of New Holland, than is to be found in the charts of many years later date. All these circumstances justify and support the opinion, that the Northern and Western coasts of New Holland were known, and were the Great Java of the sixteenth century.'[74]

The French, as participants in Australian and Pacific exploration, were also interested in the problem of Java la Grande. Charles Etienne Coquebert de Montbret in a paper to the Société Philomatique in Paris in 1803 added two French works to the corpus for consideration, the Vallard atlas (2.8), and an atlas from the library of the Duke de la Vallière (now in the Koninklijke Bibliotheek, The Hague). This atlas, dated (I suggest) *c.* 1546, and bearing the emblems of the Dauphin and Diane de Poitiers, covers only the Atlantic and Mediterranean. Coquebert de Montbret showed that the 'terre de Java' was entirely different from the 'Terre Australe', and he accompanied his article with four outline sketches which comprise the first attempt to illustrate the history of Java la Grande and to distinguish it from Terra Australis.[75] In 1807 Jean Denis Barbié du Bocage carried the debate a stage further, identifying Rotz's 'Boke' as the earliest work, and drawing attention to the 'Cosmographie Universelle' of Le Testu (2.12). Barbié du Bocage suggested that Gomez de Sequeira on his

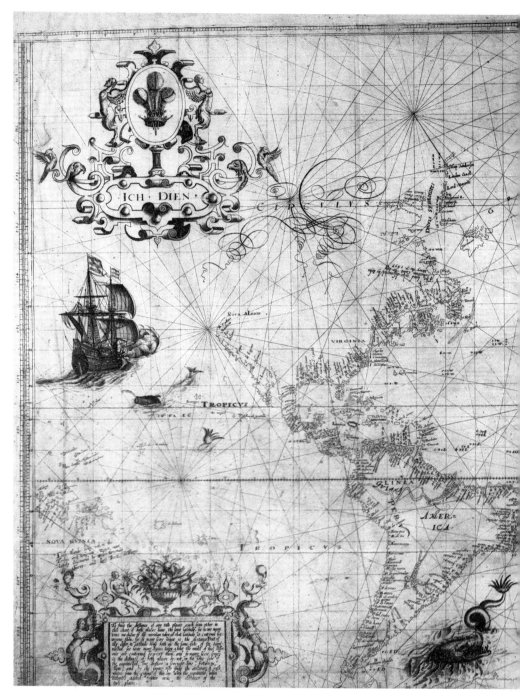

2.19 Edward Wright World Map 1610

expedition from the Moluccas in 1525 might have discovered the land mass, and he proposed Don Michel Sylva, Bishop of Viseu, as the agent of information.[76]

The next stage was the discovery of Desceliers's chart of 1546 (2.6), as yet unidentified, and its reproduction by E. F. Jomard in his *Monuments de la*

74

Géographie, issued in fascicules between 1842 and 1862.[77] When Desceliers's name and the date 1546 were revealed by inspection at the British Museum in 1877, the Dieppe school of hydrography was accepted as the source of most of the charts and atlases which showed Java la Grande. Rotz was identified as a Dieppois by E. T. Hamy in 1889. Henry Harrisse added to the corpus in 1899 the world map of Nicolas Desliens dated 1541 [*c.* 1561] (2.14), and the

'Cosmographie' of Jean Alfonse (alias Jean Fonteneau) (2.5).[78] The most striking of the maps of Java la Grande in the Vallard atlas (2.8), then in the possession of Sir Thomas Phillipps, was reproduced by chromolithography in 1856 with the title 'The First map of Australia', and this work heads the column under 'Australia, General Maps' Australia in the *British Museum Catalogue of Printed Maps* (1967). In August 1895 the three most famous Dieppe charts were put on exhibition in London. These were the Harleian map (2.7), dated erroneously *c.* 1536, and the Desceliers world maps of 1546 (2.6) and 1550 (2.9) (the latter having come to the British Museum in 1861). They were reproduced in *Bibliotheca Lindesiana Collations and Notes*, no. 4, 1898, by Lord Crawford, who had purchased the Desceliers of 1546; and they were described in an introduction by C. H. Coote of the British Museum which also discussed Desceliers's world chart of 1553 (2.10).[79]

The Keeper of the Map Department of the British Museum, Richard Henry Major, meanwhile had added an influential if equivocal voice to the debate. In his *Early Voyages to Terra Australis, now called Australia* (1859), he set out the evidence in favour of an early Portuguese discovery of the continent. He then made a series of conflicting interpretations, asserting in 1861 the claims of Manuel Godinho de Erédia, on the strength of a world map in the British Museum which is now identified as a late copy of a planisphere of João Teixeira (1630).[80] In 1872 Major postulated a French discovery before 1531, on the evidence of Oronce Finé's cordiform map of that year (1.4). In 1873 he denounced Erédia as a charlatan.[81] These reversals illustrate the perils of examining maps in isolation and out of context. After Major's death in 1891 his friend George Collingridge in Australia carried on the work of investigation. In *The Discovery of Australia*, written from the address 'Jave-la-Grande', Hornsby Junction, New South Wales, and published at Sydney in 1895, he set out a detailed history of early European contacts with Australia, pronouncing in favour of a Portuguese discovery. His fellow Australian George Arnold Wood countered with some satirical comments, and characterized as 'geographical romances' the iconographic details of Java la Grande.[82]

In recent years there has been an interpretation 'explosion' on the subject of the Dieppe maps. Theories of considerable interest and great ingenuity have been put forward. The coastlines of Java la Grande have been reworked in the light of what is known about navigational methods and the representation of cartographical data in the early sixteenth century; and links have been sought between the maps and 'lost caravels'. Place-names have also been subjected to close scrutiny, with divergent and some startling results. For example, 'Cape Fremose' has been variously identified as Tasmania (by C. Halls), as Cape Howe (by Ian McKiggan and Kenneth McIntyre), as the East Cape of the north island of New Zealand (by Roger Hervé), and as Cape de Camboja on the coast of Vietnam (by W. A. R. Richardson). It is not my intention in this chapter to attempt an analysis of this continuing debate (though in an extended note[83] I have drawn attention to some of the key books and articles), nor to venture into the drifting sands which obscure the 'mahogany ship' and other relics, real or imagined, of a possible early Portuguese venture to Australia. What I have attempted is to display in sequence the splendid and enigmatic Dieppe maps themselves, with as full a commentary on their provenance and detail as space and the present state of knowledge allow.

In the interpretation advanced here, the voyage of the Parmentiers is seen as the missing link in the chain of evidence. The poet-navigators, hydrographers and cosmographers of Dieppe did not keep their knowledge secret. Their chronicles, poems, charts and pageants described and displayed the coasts of newly discovered lands and their inhabitants. They had no empire to protect, and they challenged and denounced the policy of secrecy maintained by the Portuguese. Moreover, the flora and fauna of Java la Grande were based on discovery and observation. There were no 'geographical romances' in the detail of the Dieppe mapmakers, though some traditional features were added by the cosmographers. My revised dating of the charts (based on heraldic as well as cartographic evidence) shows that the later cartographers were using Rotz's sources which remained in Dieppe, perhaps including some of his own charts and drawings, although of course his successors never saw his 'Boke'.

The presence of Java la Grande on the Dieppe maps thus emerges as the likely result of a local voyage on the edge of a great empire. Paradoxically, it was documented by Portugal's great rivals, interlopers in that empire, the French. Parmentier's verses, translated into English by David Beers Quinn,[84] conjure up the spirit of the Dieppe entrepreneurs and the Portuguese pioneers alike, through whose efforts (dare I say) Australia was discovered and the record preserved for posterity.

> Crossing the vast Ocean of the West,
> Where danger often lies, I may not rest
> Should the winds favour. I'll not stay or fret
> But from the verdant East her secrets wrest,
> And southwards steer. Sterner is the test
> To hold in the mind's eye, not regret,
> But tune a steady heart to my sail's set.
> The spirit in me to this purpose bends,
> Lest time cold contemplations lends.
>
> I often wonder why, for this odd fantasy,
> I Europe leave, and why it lies to me
> To circle Africa so near around,
> Nor can I yet contented be
> Until the coasts of Asia shall be found,
> To such an effort am I tied;
> My head is fired, my spirit has not died.
> So, making ready, I am filled with joy,
> If questioning still the ends of my employ.

Notes

1 J. A. Williamson, *The Voyages of John and Sebastian Cabot* (London, 1937), p. 7.

2 'Do antigo Portugal, da grã Lisboa, / Por novos mares, novos ceos, e climas / Ao novo Portugal, à clara Goa . . .'—António Ferreira, *Poemas Lusitanos*, Carta II, 7, f. 183v. See R. Hooykas, *Humanism and the voyages of discovery in the 16th century. Portuguese science and letters* (Amsterdam, 1979), p. 102.

3 Jean Denis Barbié du Bocage, 'Extrait de la notice d'un manuscrit géographique de S.A.S. Mgr. le Prince de Benevent, lu en séance publique de l'Institut, le 3 juillet 1807', *Magasin encyclopédique, ou journal des sciences, des lettres et des arts*, ed. A. L. Mullin (Paris, 1807), IV, 148–62.

4 'Si vous cherchez en France une idée directrice en fait de politique maritime, n'allez pas a la cour de François I mais à Dieppe'—Charles de la Ronçière, *Histoire de la Marine française* (Paris, 1906), III, 243.

5 BN MS nouv. acq.fr. 7510; *Le Discours de la navigation de Jean et Raoul Parmentier*, ed. Charles Schefer (Paris, 1883), pp. 81–2.

6 See Helen Wallis, ed., *The Maps and Text of the Boke of Idrography presented by Jean Rotz to Henry VIII . . .* (Oxford, 1981), p. 65.

7 Schefer, *Discours de Parmentier*, pp. xxi–xxii. See also Wallis, *Rotz*, p. 7.

8 Guillaume de l'Isle, in *Histoire de l'Academie Royale des Sciences*, Année MDCCXII (Paris, 1714), p. 18.

9 This information is found in a note by Guillaume de l'Isle preserved in the Dépôt des Cartes et Plans de la Marine bearing the title: 'Des auteurs qui ont écrit sur l'aiguille aimantée'—see Schefer, *Discours de Parmentier*, pp. xxi–xxii.

10 BL Royal MS 20.B.VII, f. 21v. See Wallis, *Rotz*, pp. 31, 34.

11 'Discorso d'un Gran capitano di mare Francese del luoco di Dieppa'. Giovanni Baptista, Ramusio, *Navigationi et Viaggi*, 2nd edn (Venice, 1556), III, 423–34.

12 See R. A. Skelton's Introduction to Ramusio's *Navigationi et Viaggi* (Amsterdam, 1970), I, xii–xiii.

13 BN MS français 1382.

14 *La Cosmographie . . . par Jean Fonteneau dit Alfonse de Saintonge*, ed. Georges Musset (Paris, 1904), pp. 21, 42–4.

15 Wallis, *Rotz*, pp. 60–2.

16 Si lentreprise excede le scauoir
Ie me confie a vostre grand auoir
Qui subuiendra a la mienne indigence

Faisant reueoir cest oeuvre en diligence
Par bons pillotz qui scauent les haulteurs
Comme ceulx cy tresbons nauigateurs
Iacques Cartier Crignon ou par Sorin
Du aultres gens expers au faict marin
Qui ont compris dessus le corps sphericque
Dont Castellan a pleine theoricque
En toute langue & en tout art du monde.

BN MS français 1382, ff. 3r–v.

17 Schefer, *Discours de Parmentier*, p. xxi.

18 Lors vous verrez dessus la carte ronde
Quencor ie faiz les francoys nauiguer
Et les secretz cachez tant diuulguer
Que de soy mesme ung chacun faira carte
Dessus le liure & sans que point escarte
Loing de haulteur tant fera la science
Bien acclercye & par experience
O quel meschef & quelle ingratitude
Ont commis ceulx qui scauent longitude
Qui nont voulu descrire oncques leur stilles
Car France feust maintenant a ses isles
Ou portugays ont place primeraine,
O noble Roy O source souueraine

BN MS français 1382, f. 3v.

19 BL Royal MS 20. B. XII.

20 'Au Sud la Tropbonne [Sumatra] est la terre de Iave, qui est une nation de gens comme ceux de Bresil. En la terre de Lave en aucuns lieux lon trouve de l'or, & y ha de bonne riuieres. La terre est saine, au dela de la ligne du costé de l'Antartique.'—[Jean Alfonse], *Les Voyages auantureux du Capitaine Ian Alfonce Sainctongeois* (Poitiers, 1559), f. 65r.

21 'la ligne du diametre, qui ce dit Estual.' Alfonse, *Voyages auantureux*, f. 35r.

22 Ibid., f. 65r.–v.

23 Ibid., f. 35r.

24 The Harleian map of *c*. 1547 has this legend, while Jean Rotz in his 'Boke' has a corrupted version 'au fane bacha'. See George Collingridge, *The Discovery of Australia* (Sydney, 1895), pp. 182–3, who describes this legend as being 'in the Gulf of Carpentaria, or, perhaps, to the east of Java . . .'.

25 Alfonse, *Voyages auantureux*, f. 35v.

26 See also Collingridge, *Discovery of Australia*, p. 189.

27 Musset, *Cosmographie*, p. 88.

28 'L'on ne doit point s'esmerueiller de tous ces discours, car il est escrit comme ie l'ay veu & fait les voyages, ceux qui les ont faits ou leu par liures, sçavent s'il est vray.' Alfonse, *Voyages auantureux*, f. 68v.

78

29 'ie ne reconoy rien, ou bien peu de verité en tous les discours de cet homme ici; & peut-il bien appeller ses voyages aventureux, non pour lui, qui jamais ne fut en la centième partie des lieux qu'il décrit (au moins il est aisé à le conjecturer) mais pour ceux qui voudront suivre les routes qu'il ordonne de suivre aux mariniers?'.—Marc Lescarbot, *Histoire de la nouvelle France* (Paris, 1611), p. 496. See also S. de Champlain, *Les Voyages du Sieur de Champlain* (Paris, 1613), cap V, p. 51 (where there is a reference to the 'marvels' of which others have written).

30 'Il estoit bon cosmographe & geographe. Par luy ont este composez plusieurs mapesmondes en globes et en plat: et maintes cartes marines sur lesquelles plusieurs ont navigé seurement.' In Pierre Crignon's prologue to Jear Parmentier, *Description nouvelle des merueilles de ce monde et de la dignite de l'homme* (Paris, 1531), f. a. iiir.

31 'Il a donné la première mappemonde de la terre entière.'—Charles Desmarquets, *Mémoires chronologiques pour servir à l'histoire de Dieppe, et a celle de la navigation françoise* (Paris, 1785), II, 10. Henry Harrisse records Parmentier's maps and this first French world map in *The Discovery of North America* (London, 1892), p. 568.

32 Desmarquets, *Mémoires*, pp. 10–11.

33 Crignon, *Plaincte sur le trespas de diffunctz Jan et Raoul Parmentier* (Paris, 1531) f. h. iiiir.

34 BL Add MS 5415, A. f. 10; and BN Rés. Ge. AA. 640.

35 'Et apprez auoyr considere le monde estre asez remply de cartes marines selon la maniere vulgaire', from Jean Rotz's dedicatory letter to Henry VIII in his 'Boke of Idrography'—see Wallis, *Rotz*, pp. 79–80.

36 BL Royal MS 20. E. IX.

37 Wallis, *Rotz*, p. 80.

38 BL Royal MS 20. E. IX, ff. 9v–10r.

39 BL Royal MS 20. E. IX, ff. 29v–30r.

40 'Et ce au plus certain et vray quil ma este possible de faire, tant par mon experience propre que par la certaine experience de mes amys et compagnons navigateurs.' See Wallis, *Rotz*, pp. 79–80.

41 They are described by Harrisse, *Discovery of North America*, p. 96 as 'Lusitano-French' and by Armando Cortesão and Avelino Teixeira da Mota, PMC (Lisbon, 1960), V, Appendix II, pp. 132–40, pls 614–25.

42 Wallis, *Rotz*, pp. 6, 33, 43, 44.

43 Ibid., pp. 46–7.

44 Huntington MS HM46. See Louis Dujardin-Troadec, *Les cartographes bretons du Conquet. Les navigation en images 1543–1650* (Brest, 1966), pp. 19–21.

45 Formerly in the Bibliothèque Publique du Collège des Jésuites de Lyon.

46 Koninklijke Bibliotheek, The Hague, MS 129. A. 24. For dating see Wallis, *Rotz*, pp. 41, 84.

47 BN MS français 676. Raulin Sécalart has added his name and at the end an inscription, 'par nous Jehan Allefonsce et Raulin Secalart . . . achevay de par moy Raulin Secalart cosmographe de honnefleur . . . 1545'. The manuscript was edited by Georges Musset and printed in 1904. See note 14 above.

48 'Ceste Jave est une terre qui va jusques dessoubz le polle antartique, et en occident tient à la terre Australle, et du cousté d'oriant à la terre du destroict de Magaillant. Aulcuns dient que ce sont isles. Et quant est de ce que j'en ay veu, c'est terre ferme . . . Celle que l'on appelle Jave Mynore est une isle. Mais la Grand Jave est terre ferme'—Musset, *Cosmographie*, pp. 388–9.

49 'Et selon que j'entens, [ceste Jave] va jusques dessoubz le polle antartique . . . Toutes-foys j'ay esté en ung lieu là où le jour m'a duré trois moys compté pour la révolution du soleil, et n'ay pas voullu attendre davantaige de craincte que la nuict ne me surprint'—Ibid., p. 399.

50 Pierre Margry, *Les navigations francaises* . . . (Paris, 1867), p. 318; Musset, *Cosmographie*, pp. 9–10, 399n.

51 'Et en cette terre y a force d'or et d'argent et elléfans, et y a singes comme en la Barbarye . . . Et je me doubte que soit terre ferme et qu'elle va se joindre à la terre Australle.'—Musset, *Cosmographie*, p. 400. Wilma George, *Animals and Maps* (London, 1969), pp. 175–6. George relates Alfonse's description to the island of Tersye, but its context suggests that he was referring to Java la Grande.

52 The John Rylands University Library of Manchester. Bibliotheca Lindesiana, French ms no. 15.

53 'Pour ce qui est des cartes marines, je disay avec Monsr Dablon que le sieur Pierre des Cheliers, prestre à Arques, a eu la gloire d'avoir esté le premier qui en a fait en France'—David Asseline, *Les Antiquitez et Chroniques de la ville de Dieppe* (Dieppe, 1874), II, 325.

54 BL Add MS 5413. From the collection of Edward Harley, Earl of Oxford.

55 R. A. Skelton, *The influence of Verrazzano on 16th century cartography* (Firenze, 1970), p. 64.

56 Huntington MS HM29. Formerly in the collection of Sir Thomas Phillipps, Bart., no. 13196. From Talleyrand's library, no. 3416. The frontispiece is inscribed 'Nicolas Vallard de Dieppe 1547'.

57 *PMC*, V, Appendix II, pp. 132–40, pls 614–25.

58 *PMC*, V, 140, suggests that a work by the Portuguese author of The Hague atlas, who was allegedly also the author of the Vallard, was Rotz's source.

59 George, *Animals and Maps*, p. 178.

60 BL Add MS 24065.

61 *Die Weltkarte des Pierre Desceliers von 1553* ed. E. Oberhummer (Vienna, 1924).

[62] Pierpont Morgan Library, New York. M. 506.

[63] Ministère des Armées, Pars. D.I.Z. 14.

[64] George, *Animals and Maps*, pp. 176–9.

[65] Le Testu, 'La terre du sud, dite australe, laquelle n'a point encore été découverte ... pour ce n'est marquée que par l'imagination.'

[66] *Kartographische Denkmäler zur Entdeckungsgeschichte von Amerika, Asien, Australien und Afrika*, ed. Viktor Hantzsch and Ludwig Schmidt (Leipzig, 1903), Pl. II–IV.

[67] World chart by Nicolas Desliens. BN Département de Cartes et Plans, Rés. Ge. D. 7895. Inscribed: 'A Dieppe par Nicolas Desliens 1566'. A similar map with the same inscription except for the date 1567 is in NMM, G 201, 1/51. A second at NMM, G 201, 1/52, has some different decorative features and came from the papers of Pierre Hamon, who was hanged on 7 March 1569 in Paris. This latter is reproduced in Maggs Bros, *Biblioteca Brasiliensis* (Catalogue No. 546, London, 1930), item 581.

[68] BL Egerton MS 1513.

[69] 'Diepe reputé comme l'escolle des bons Pilottes de ce Royaulme.' Bonaventure d'Aseville, *Thresorerie ou Cabinett de la Routte Marinesque* (Calais, 1601).

[70] See O. H. K. Spate, 'Manuel Godinho de Erédia: Quest for Australia', in *Let Me Enjoy: Essays, partly geographical* (Canberra, 1965), p. 256.

[71] The chart is only rarely found bound up in Edward Wright, *Certaine Errors in Navigation* (1610).

[72] Alexander Dalrymple, *Memoir concerning the Chagos and Adjacert Islands* (London, 1786), p. 4. Dalrymple issued an engraved version, 'A copy of part of an antient map' (1787), map 4 in a volume of Dalrymple's charts, BL 460, g. 6.

[73] John Pinkerton, *Modern Geography* (London, 1802), II, 468–70.

[74] James Burney, *A Chronological History of the Discoveries in the South Pacific Ocean* (London, 1803), I, 378–93.

[75] See 'Géographie: Extrait d'un Mémoire du C. Coquebert-Montbret ...', *Bulletin des Sciences, par la Société Philomatique*, III, No. 80 (Paris, 1803), pp. 163–4, pl. XX.

[76] Jean Denis Barbié du Bocage, 'Extrait de la notice d'un manuscrit géographique', *Magasin encyclopédique, ou journal des sciences, des lettres et des arts*, ed. A. L. Millin (Paris, 1807), IV, 148–62.

[77] E. F. Jomard, *Les Monuments de la Géographie* (Paris, 1842–62), pp. 1–6 and pl. XIX.

[78] Henry Harrisse, 'The Dieppe World Maps', *Göttingische gelehrte Anzeigen*, 161 Jahrgang no. 6 (1899), pp. 47–9.

[79] C. H. Coote, *Autotype facsimiles of three mappemondes* (Bibliotheca Lindesiana, Collations and Notes, no. 44) ([Aberdeen], 1898), p. 12.

[80] BL Add MS 17647 A. See *PMC*, IV, 43, 116–18, pl. 464.

[81] See articles by R. H. Major in *Archaeologia*, 38 (London, 1860), 453–9; 44 (1873), 237–41 and 242–58.

[82] Collingridge, *Discovery of Australia*, pp. 166–75; G. A. Wood, *The Discovery of Australia* (London, 1922), p. 129.

[83] Books and articles relating to the debate are, in chronological order:

Roger Hervé, 'Australia in French Geographical Documents of the Renaissance', JRAHS 41 (1955), 23–38.

O. H. K. Spate, 'Terra Australis—Cognita?', *Historical Studies*, 8 (1957), 1–19; reprinted in *Let Me Enjoy*, pp. 267–95.

Andrew Sharp, *The Discovery of Australia* (Oxford, 1963)

Marcel Chicoteau, *Australie Terre Légendaire* (Brisbane, 1965).

K. G. McIntyre, *The Secret Discovery of Australia: Portuguese Ventures 200 Years before Captain Cook* (Medindie, 1977).

Ian McKiggan, 'The Portuguese Expedition to Bass Strait in AD 1522', JAS, No. 1 (1977), 2–32.

B. C. Rennie, 'The Dauphin Map', JAS, No. 3 (1978), 75–8.

Ian McKiggan, 'The Dauphin Map—A Reply', JAS, ibid., 78–80.

Helen Wallis, ed., *The Maps and Text of the Boke of Idrography presented by Jean Rotz to Henry VIII* (Oxford, 1981).

J. L. Anderson, 'The Mahogany Ship: History and Legend', GC, 3 (1981), 46–8.

Jeremy Green, 'The Carronade Island Guns and Australia's Early Visitors', GC, 4 (1982), 73–83.

T. M. Perry, *The Discovery of Australia: The Charts and Maps of the Navigators and Explorers* (Melbourne, 1982).

Roger Hervé, *Découverte fortuite de l'Australie et de la Nouvelle-Zélande par des Navigateurs Portugais et Espagnols entre 1521 et 1528* (Paris, 1982). Translated by John Dunmore as *Chance Discovery of Australia and New Zealand by Portuguese and Spanish Navigators between 1521 and 1528* (Palmerston North, 1983).

C. C. Macknight, 'On the non-"discovery" of "Australia"', *Canberra Historical Journal*, No. 12 (1983), 34–6.

Lawrence Fitzgerald, *Java La Grande. The Portuguese discovery of Australia* (Hobart, [1984]).

W. A. R. Richardson, 'Jave-la-Grande: A Place Name Chart of its East Coast', GC, 6 (1984), 1–23.

O. H. K. Spate, 'Jave-la-Grande: The Great Whodunnit', GC, 6 (1984), 132–4.

A. Ariel, 'Navigating with Kenneth McIntyre: A Professional Critique', GC, 6 (1984) 135–9.

Helen Wallis, 'Did the Portuguese discover Australia? The Map Evidence', W. A. R. Richardson, 'Jave-la-Grande: A Case Study in Place-Name Corruption', and Lawrence Fitzgerald, 'Jave la Grande. The Portuguese discovery of Australia circa 1521', in *Technical Papers of the 12th Conference of the International Cartographic Association* (Perth, 1984), II, pp. 203–20, 221–49, 341–57.

Helen Wallis, 'Terra Australis, Australia and New Zealand: voyages, discoveries and concepts', in *British Library Occasional Papers*, 4: *Australia and New Zealand Studies*, ed.

Patricia McLaren-Turner (London, 1985), pp. 184–93.

W. A. R. Richardson, 'Jave-la-Grande: Latitude and Longitude versus Toponymy', JAS, No. 18 (1986), 74–91.

I. F. McKiggan, 'Jave-la-Grande: an Apologia', JAS, No. 19 (1986), 96–101.

J. L. Anderson, 'The Mahogany Ship: History and Science', GC, 8 (1986), 122–6.

P. L. Coleman, 'Is *Java La Grande* Australia?', JRAHS, 72 (1986), 190–203.

[84] Private communication.

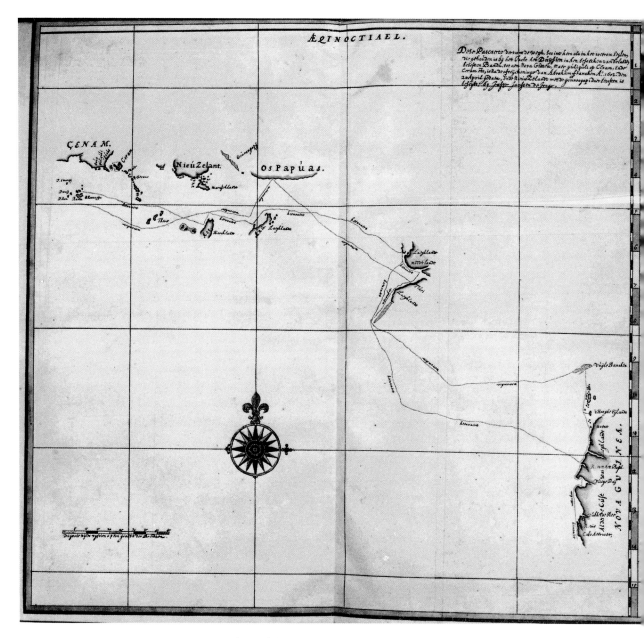

3.1 [Anonymous] Chart of the *Duyfken*'s route 1605/6

82

Chapter 3

New Holland:
The Dutch Discoveries

Günter Schilder

In 1602 the States General granted the newly-formed United East India Company (VOC) a monopoly of Dutch navigation in the vast area between the Cape of Good Hope and the Straits of Magellan. At once the Company centred its operations on the Malay archipelago, and in a remarkably short time established a trading empire that extended from Southern Africa to East Asia. Voyages of exploration to seek out new commercial possibilities were an integral part of the Company's activity, with the direction of the voyages often determined by stories heard in the east of countries and islands that offered great riches.

This desire to open new trade led the merchants to undertake a number of voyages to the south land shortly to be named 'Nova Hollandia', but not all Dutch discoveries of its coasts reflect this conscious purpose. Much of the knowledge of its western and southern regions came from accidental discovery, made as a consequence of captains following the VOC's instruction in 1616 to sail 1000 'mijlen' directly east after passing the Cape of Good Hope before turning north for Bantam. Given the prevailing difficulties in measuring longitude accurately and therefore knowing the exact distance sailed, this injunction led to a series of unintended sightings which also played an important part in the 'unveiling' of the southern continent.[1]

Dutch sightings, both deliberate and unintended, led to the discovery of the entire coastline of the Gulf of Carpentaria, much of the north-west coast of the continent, all of the western coast and much of the southern coast in the seventeenth century. Because its concern was always at heart commercial, while the VOC preserved records of the voyages in its closed archives, it followed no policy of announcing them to the world.[2] None the less, too many persons had access to these archives or opportunities to talk to the captains for the discoveries to remain entirely secret, and general results soon appeared on maps and globes available commercially. In this way, geographers at home were able to convey to the public some information about the continent which slowly emerged from the mirage of Terra Australis.

THE FIRST SIGHTING

The first discovery of the real southern continent came as a consequence of conscious intent. In 1605, Jan Willemsz Verschoor, the director of the Bantam factory, took the initiative in discovering 'the vast land of Nova Guinea and other east- and south-lands'. On his orders, Willem Jansz was given the command of the *Duyfken*, a small yacht of 20 to 30 lasts (40 to 60 tons) whose small draught and manoeuvrability made her very well suited to making landfalls in unknown waters. Jan Lodewijcksz also sailed on this voyage to promote the commercial interests of the VOC. While the original logs of the voyage are lost, there are sufficient sources to give some sense of the geographical results.[3]

Initially, the expedition sailed along the south coast of New Guinea, looking for places offering commercial possibilities. At one of the landings, eight of the crew were killed in an encounter with the Papuans. Despite this setback, Willem Jansz continued along the coast. Misled by the many shoals and small islands situated in front of the western entrance of Torres Strait, he thought himself against an extremely low section of coast running south. Passing Torres Strait unawares, he sailed south for 200 miles along the west coast of Cape York Peninsula. Here, their first encounter with the Aborigines was also hostile. During a reconnaissance to collect more data about the land and its inhabitants, the crew was attacked, and one mortally speared. Short of water and food, and with half of his crew dead, Willem Jansz was forced to turn for home. Though he and Jan Lodewijckz still thought themselves off the coast of New Guinea, they must be given the credit for being the first known European discoverers of the fifth continent.

This discovery was not included in any contemporary printed cartographic source, map or globe. However, its results are well recorded on an invaluable manuscript chart, which is a copy of that made on board the *Duyfken* during the voyage (3.1).[4] This chart marks the beginning of the period of Dutch discovery of Australia, and is a milestone in the history of the cartography of the continent. Willem Jansz's mistake about the identity of the coast he sailed south along is shown by its being named 'Nova Guinea'. His first landfall on Cape York Peninsula is recorded at 11°45'S, where 'R met het Bosch' ('river with bush') indicates what is now Pennefather River. Also shown is 'Vliege Baij' ('Fly Bay'—now Albatross Bay), while the southernmost point is recorded as 'Cabo Kerweer' ('Cape Turn-again'). Curiously, the mouth of the Batavia River, the scene of the conflict with the Aborigines, is not shown. The results of the *Duyfken*'s voyage also appear on a chart of the Pacific made in 1622 by Hessel Gerritsz, cartographer of the VOC in Amsterdam.[5] Here, the coast of New Guinea is called 'Custe van de Papouas' ('Coast of the Papuans') and bears the name 'Duyfkenslandt' ('Land of the little dove'). However, Willem Jansz's discovery of Cape York Peninsula is shown as a separate coastline, with the name 'Nueva Guinea', and the voyage is mentioned in two long legends.

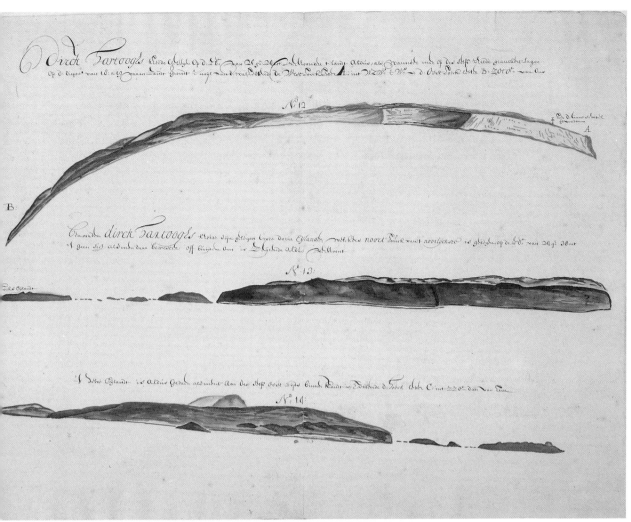

3.2 Victor Victorsz   Dirk Hartog Island and other coastal profiles   1697

3.3 Dirck Hartochsz   Pewter Plate   1616

From a commercial point of view, the voyage of the *Duyfken* did not yield any worthwhile results, for the only discoveries were of barren coasts lacking water and inhabited by hostile natives. None the less, the voyage confirmed the rumours of a large land to the south-east of the archipelago, which might repay further investigation. It was to be some time, though, before the voc became interested enough in its possibilities to undertake further conscious exploration. In the meantime, the Company's resources were fully absorbed in the struggle with the Portuguese, Spanish and English for dominance of the East Indies; and it was only after it had won this struggle, and a good deal of additional information had accumulated from accidental sightings, that the voc once more turned to Australian exploration.

ACCIDENTAL SIGHTINGS

The first stone in the mosaic of accidental discovery was laid in 1616, when Dirck Hartochsz in the *Eendracht*, following the new southern route, spotted 'different islands, but uninhabited' in October (3.2).[6] Dirck Hartochsz anchored at one, exploring it for two days. To mark his landing, he had a pewter plate fixed to a pole (3.3), offering the information that the ship arrived there on 25 October and left for Bantam on 27 October 1616.[7] A second stone followed in 1618, when the *Mauritius*, on which Willem Jansz sailed as supercargo, reached the west coast at approximately 22°S. No log of either voyage has survived, but the *Eendracht*'s discovery is recorded in several contemporary letters, and Willem Jansz reported that of the *Mauritius* from Bantam, including the detail that he had named a river 'Willems' after his own Christian name.

Though the VOC as usual did not publicize them, these sightings were soon reflected in Amsterdam cartography. In 1622, Hessel Gerritsz presented the results of them on his manuscript chart of the Indian Ocean,[8] showing the 'landt van d'Eendracht' ('Land of Eendracht') and 'Dirck Hartogs ree' ('Dirck Hartog's roadstead') (cf. 3.7). Hessel Gerritsz's charts were kept secret, but others soon managed to learn their import. Jodocus Hondius (1594/5–1629) drew on that of the Indian Ocean for his world map of about 1625.[9] This extremely rare work is the first engraved example on which the representation of the mythical Terra Australis has been deliberately omitted, with instead only the authentic recent Dutch discoveries shown. Nor was Jodocus Hondius the only one (cf. 3.8). Arnold Florent van Langren also showed the south-west coast of western Australia in a globe dating from about 1625, the oldest one known to exist (3.4).[10]

Although the results of these accidental sightings quickly appeared on commercial works, not a single report of them was printed. The written records went into the VOC archives, and the logs are now lost. Only a few letters remain to show the impression gained by the Dutch in these years of the western coasts of the south land. Two of these letters were written by Frederik

3.4 Arnold Florent van Langren   Eendracht Land ('Het Land't van Eendracht')   1625

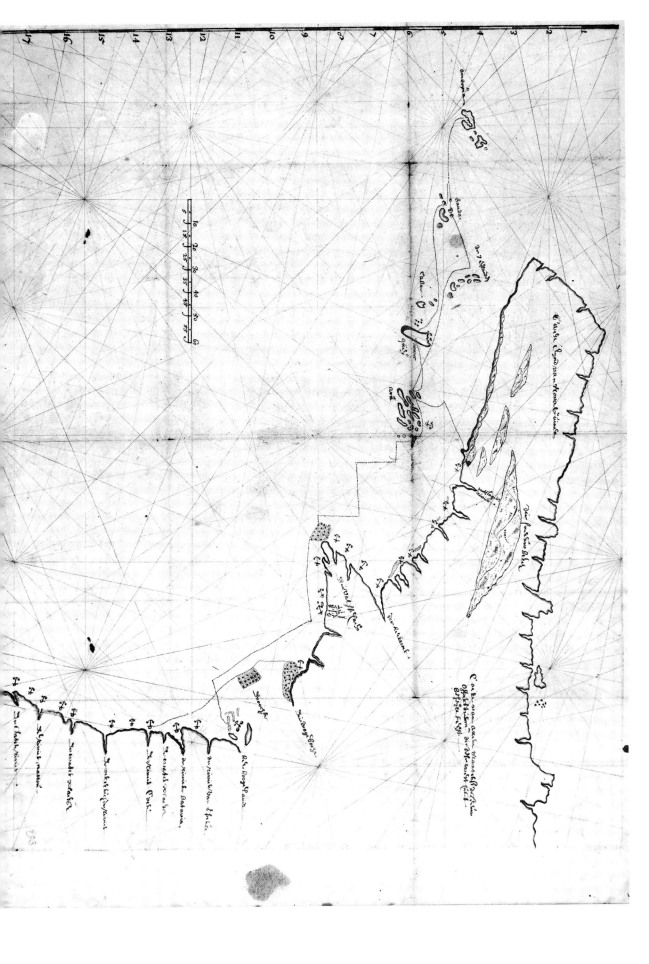

de Houtman and Jacob Dedel who, sailing on the *Dordrecht* and *Amsterdam*, found land looming before them in July and August 1619. On their arrival at Batavia, the pair reported to the company's directors in Amsterdam how, on 29 July, they saw 'a level, broken country with reefs all round it. We saw no high land or mainland, so that this shoal is to be carefully avoided as very dangerous to ships that wish to touch at this coast. It is fully ten miles in length, lying in 28°46'S'. On 2 August they again came to land, in 27°S, 'a red, muddy coast, which according to the surmises of some of us might not unlikely prove to be gold-bearing, a point which may be cleared up in time'.[11] They followed this coast south:

We are all assured that this is the land which the ship *Eendracht* discovered . . . and noways doubt that all the land they saw in 22°, 23°, 25° and which we sighted down to 33°S, is one uninterrupted mainland coast . . . This South land, as far as we could judge, seems to be a very fair coast, but we found it impossible to land on it, nor have we seen any smoke or signs of inhabitants there, but further investigation is wanted on this point.[12]

They called the land at 27°S 'Dedelsland', after the highest ranking person on the ships, and 'Houtman's Abrolhos' remains the name of the shoal.

DELIBERATE EXPLORATION

These accidental sightings of the western coasts of Australia revived the VOC's interest in exploring the south land further. The directors' concern was twofold. First, there was the danger that uncharted coasts posed to their shipping and therefore to their revenues, a danger pointed out by de Houtman and vividly stressed by the wreck of the English ship *Trial* off the north-west coast of Australia in 1622.[13] Second, there was the ever-present desire to find new commercial prospects, prospects to be buttressed where possible by the acquisition of territory. Trade and territorial expansion were then the pillars of the VOC's colonial policy, and they remained so until the time of Tasman's voyages.

The instructions issued by officials in Batavia to the commanders of the ships *de Haringh* and *Hasewint* on 29 September 1622 reflected both these purposes:

The main object for which you are dispatched on this occasion is, that for 45° or 50°S, or from the farthest point to which the land shall be found to extend southwards within these latitudes, up to the northernmost extremity of the South land you will have to discover and survey all capes, forelands, bights, lands, islands, rocks, sandbanks, depths, shallows, roads, winds, currents and all that appertains to the same, so as to be able to map out and duly mark everything in its true latitude, longitude, bearings and confor- mation. You will moreover go ashore in various places and diligently examine the coast in order to ascertain whether or not it is inhabited, the nature of the land and the people, their towns and inhabited villages, the divisions of their kingdoms, their religion and polity, their wars, their rivers, the shape of their vessels, their fisheries, commodities and manufactures, but especially to inform yourselves what minerals, such as gold, silver, tin, iron, lead, and copper, what precious stones, pearls, vegetables, animals and fruits, these lands yield and produce.[14]

Iacob Remmen riuier

HET LANDT VAN EENDRACHT
id est
CONCORDIAE REGIO
Sic dicta ab Hollandis, qui eandem
nomine Ordinum confœderatorum
Inferioris Germaniæ primum detexerunt.

Dierck barrochs Rade

F. Holtmans eylanden

Deelalis landt

MARE

3.5 Arent Martensz de Leeuw   Chart of the *Pera*'s discoveries   1623

The need to assist two of the Company's ships found in difficulty in the Straits of Sunda quickly aborted the expedition, however; and when it was taken up again the next year, it was by the ships *Pera* and *Arnhem* under the command of Jan Carstensz. Fortunately, a good deal of information about this voyage is available. Jan Carstensz's journal has survived,[15] and there are important cartographic records which show detailed coastlines.[16] The ships sailed on 21 January 1623. On 11 February the captain of the *Arnhem*, Dirk Melisz, and nine crew members were killed in an encounter with Papuans at 'Dootslager Rivier' ('Murderers' River'), which led Willem Joosten van Colster, the second mate of the *Pera*, to become commander of the *Arnhem*.

The expedition continued, with the ships skirting the south coast of New Guinea (3.5). By the end of March they had reached the western entrance to

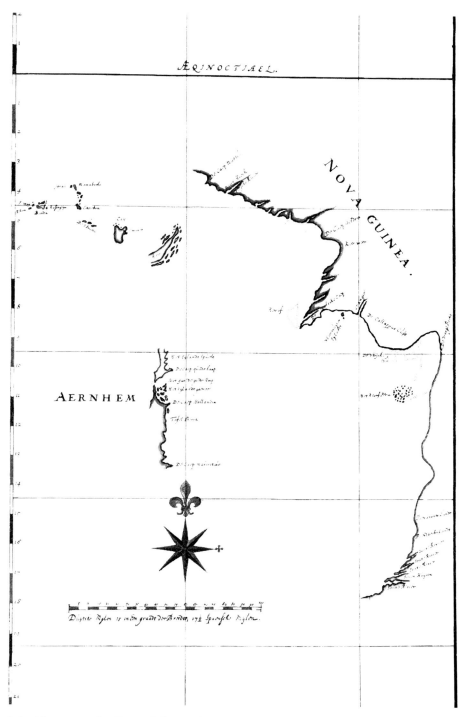

3.6 [Anonymous] Chart of the *Arnhem*'s discoveries 1623

Torres Strait. Probes by the ships' boats showed shallows everywhere, 'so that the space between us and Nova Guinea seems to be a bight to which on account of its shallows we have given the name of "drooge bocht" ("shallow bight") in the new chart'. As with Willem Jansz before him, these shoals prevented Jan Carstensz from finding the strait between New Guinea and Cape York Peninsula. Proceeding south, the expedition reached the west coast of Cape York, which the explorers took for a continuation of New Guinea. They made a number of reconnoitres to obtain knowledge of the land and its inhabitants. On 17 April Jan Carstensz investigated a considerable distance inland, finding 'a flat, fine country with few trees, and a good soil for planting and sowing, but so far as we could observe utterly destitute of fresh water'. The most southerly landfall was at 17°8'S, which revealed a salty river ('Staten rivier') and country

submerged in many places, thus somewhat resembling Waterland in Holland, from which it may be concluded that there must be large lakes farther inland ... and since by resolution it has been determined to begin the return voyage at this point, we have, in default of stone caused a wooden tablet to be nailed to a tree, the said tablet having the following words carved into it: 'Anno 1623 den 24n April sijn hier aen gecomen twee jachten wegen de Hooge Mogende Heren Staten Genl. [AD 1623, on 24 April there arrived here two yachts dispatched by their High Mightinesses the States General.]

The ships turned for home on 26 April, with the commanders intending to take the same route so as to check the accuracy of their charts. Soon after, however, van Colster diverged to take the leaky *Arnhem* to Batavia by the most direct route. Though he sailed without intending to make discoveries, this route took him across the Gulf of Carpentaria to north-eastern Arnhem Land and the Wessels Islands. A chart made during the voyage recording these discoveries survives (3.6), although the ship's log is lost. Jan Carstensz recorded in his journal:

The land between 13°S and 17°S is an arid and poor tract without any fruit tree or anything useful to man; it is low and monotonous without mountain or hill, wooded in some places with bush and little oily trees; there is little fresh water and what there is can only be collected from pits specially dug; there are also no points or inlets except some bays which are, however, not sheltered against winds from the sea and it extends mainly northeast and southwest all along with muddy and sandy bottoms, with many and different salt rivers which extend inland where their tributaries are overgrown by the dry boughs and foliage of the trees. In general the men are barbarians all much alike in build and features, pitch-black and entirely naked, with a knotted net on head and neck for keeping their food in and what they mainly live on (as far as we have seen) were certain roots which they dig out from the earth ... Their house or abode we observed in the east monsoon on the beach, here we saw many and different huts made of dry hay; also a great number of dogs, herons and waterfowl and other wild fowl as also very excellent fish which can easily be caught in a net, they have no knowledge at all of gold, silver, tin, iron, lead and copper; even nutmegs, cloves and paper which had been shown to them several times on the voyage made no impression on them.[17]

This is the first extended description of Cape York Peninsula and its Aboriginal inhabitants, and its details parallel those in Captain James Cook's descriptions of New South Wales 150 years later.[18]

3.7 Hessel Gerritsz   Chart of the Malay Archipelago and of the Dutch Discoveries of Australia 1618/1628

3.8 *Right* Henricus Hondius   Eastern hemisphere from his World Map ('Nova Totivs Terrarvm Orbis Geographica ac Hydrographica Tabula')   1630

92

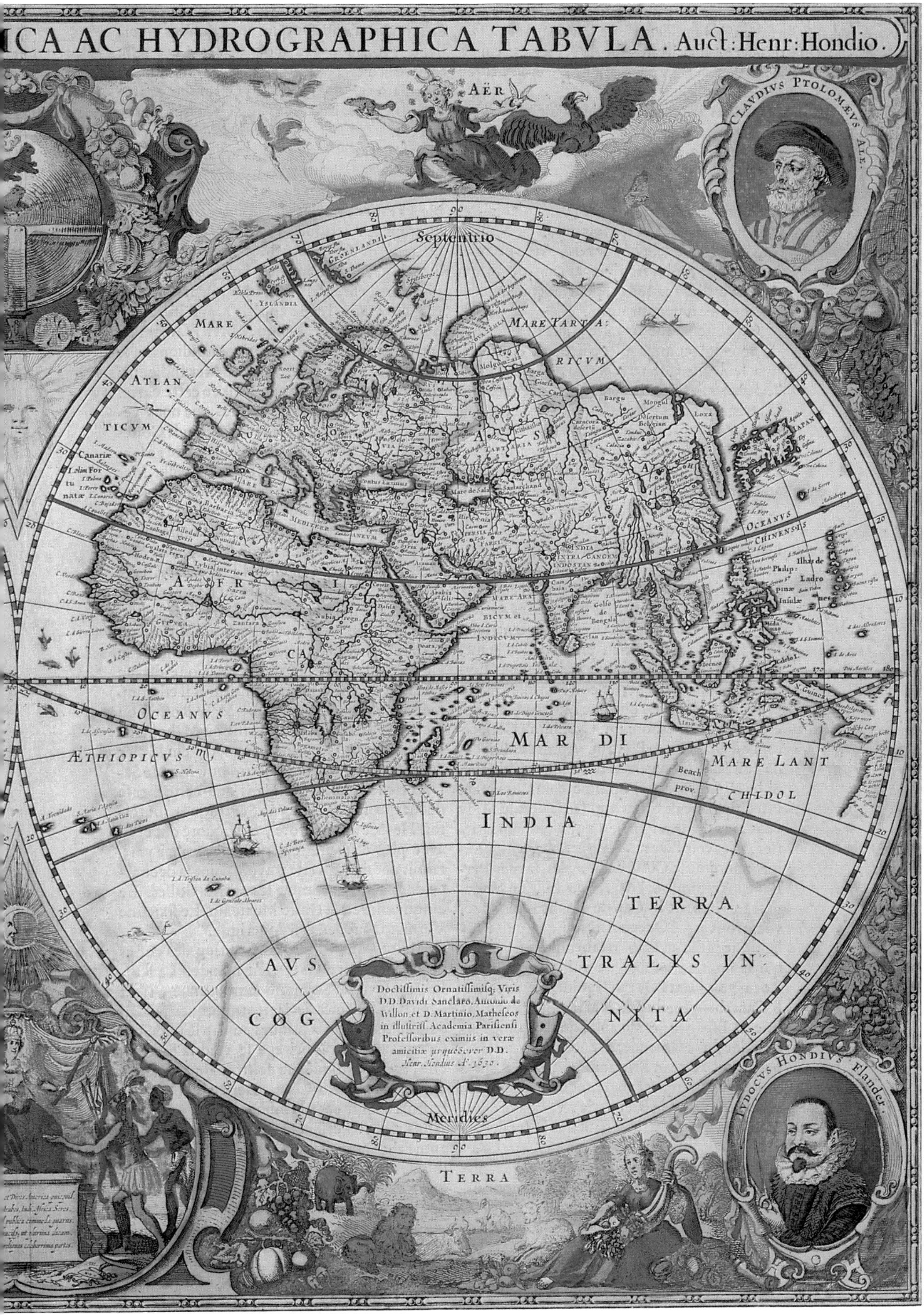

ICA AC HYDROGRAPHICA TABVLA. Auct: Henr: Hondio.

AËR

Septentrio

GROENLANDIA

MARE TARTA:

RICVM

MARE

YSLANDIA

ATLAN

TICVM

Canariæ

natæ

MEDITER

ANEVM

AFRI

CA

MARE ARA

BICVM

INDICVM

OCEANVS CHINENSIS

INSTRA-GANGEM

INDOSTAN

Golfo

de

Bengala

Ilhas de

Ladro

Pinæ

Insulæ

OCEANVS

ÆTHIOPICVS

MAR DI

MARE LANT

Beach

Prov. CHIDOL

INDIA

TERRA

AVS

TRALIS IN

COG

NITA

Doctissimis Ornatissimisq; Viris
D.D. Davidi Sanclaro, Antonio de
Willon et D. Martinio, Matheseos
in illustriss. Academia Parisiensi
Professoribus eximiis in veræ
amicitiæ ụᵴᵹụễẽʋʋ D.D.
Henr. Hondius A° 1630.

Meridies

TERRA

Two years later, Nicolaes van Wassenaar published a short notice of the expedition in his *Historisch Verhaal,* which is one of the earliest printed descriptions of any part of Australia.[19] A little later, commercial cartographers began to show the results of the *Pera*'s voyage, with Cornelis Danckerts and Melchior Tavernier

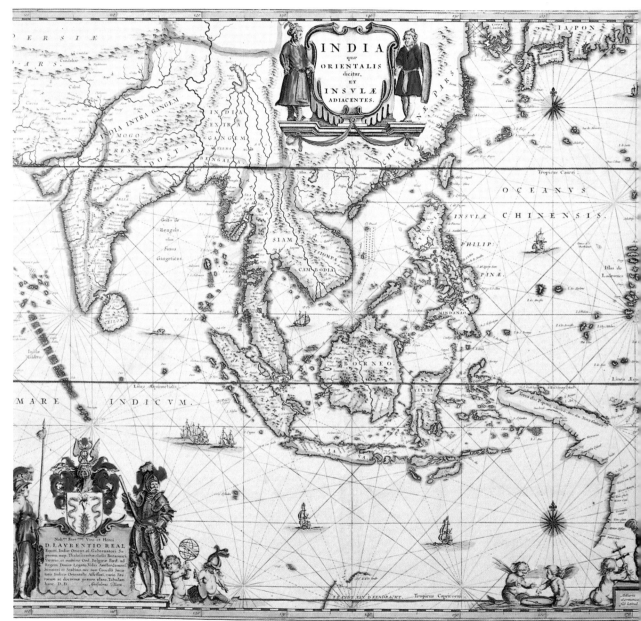

3.9   Willem Jansz Blaeu   India and the East Indies ('India quae Orientalis dicitur et Insvlae Adjacentes')   1635

presenting the west coast of Cape York on their world map of 1628,[20] Henricus Hondius on his world map of 1630 (3.8),[21] and Willem Jansz Blaeu on his map of the East Indies of 1635 (3.9).[22] The results of the *Arnhem's* voyage, however, did not appear on any map until Tasman drew attention to them by his second voyage in 1644.

FURTHER ACCIDENTAL SIGHTINGS

Very little is known about the first of further accidental sightings in the 1620s, by the *Leeuwin*, the best source being Hessel Gerritsz's map of 1627.[23] This shows the outline of the south-west corner of Australia, and identifies the region as the 'Landt van de *Leeuwin*, beseylt A° 1622, in Maart' ('the land of the *Leeuwin*, sailed to in March 1622'). In front of the coast Hessel Gerritsz depicted a strip of small islands, which he described as 'laegh ghelijck verdroncken landt' ('low land that might be flooded'). To one part of the coast, he gave the name 'laegh duynich landt' ('low land with dunes'), and to another 'duynich landt boven met boomen ende boscage' ('land with dunes and above trees and bush'). From this, we may gather that in March 1622 the *Leeuwin* sailed along the coast north and south of the present Cape Leeuwin, between Hamelin Bay and Point d'Entrecasteaux or Point Nuyts.

More explicit is the description left by Claes Hermansz, captain of the *Leyden*, which coasted from 27° up to 25°30'S in July 1623:

On 21 [July] in the morning we sighted Eendrachtsland in latitude 27°S at about 6 miles distance . . . the land showing outwardly like Robben Island in the Table Bay . . . On 22 [July] in the latitude 26°30'S . . . we sighted everywhere a hilly coast with large bays, with low-lying land in between, the whole covered with dunes . . . On 26 [July] in latitude 25°48'S . . . the land looked like the west coast of England with many reddish rocks.[24]

In 1624 the yacht *Tortelduyff* ('Turtledove') discovered the small island now known by its name. In 1627 *'t Gulden Zeepaard* ('Golden Seahorse') under the command of François Thijssen struck the south coast, in January and February exploring a large section of the coast including the present Recherche Archipelago, the Great Australian Bight and the Nuyts Archipelago. In 1628 a Company ship returning to Europe made an unexpected landfall on the north-west coast at 21°S, including the section between the present Port Hedland and the Monte Bello Islands and Barrow Islands. While the tragic story of the shipwreck of the *Batavia* on Morning Reef on 4 June 1629 created a sensation in the Netherlands, it did not contribute much to the elucidation of the coastline.[25]

Hessel Gerritsz reflected these accidental sightings in his charts of the later 1620s, which he stressed he had 'composed with the help of journals and drawings by seamen'. Showing the pre-Tasman discoveries, these charts are the oldest special ones of Australia to be preserved. One (3.7) is particularly noteworthy. Dated 1618, this none the less shows discoveries up to 1628, so that we must suppose the date is that of its origin only.[26] The bottom part of this chart

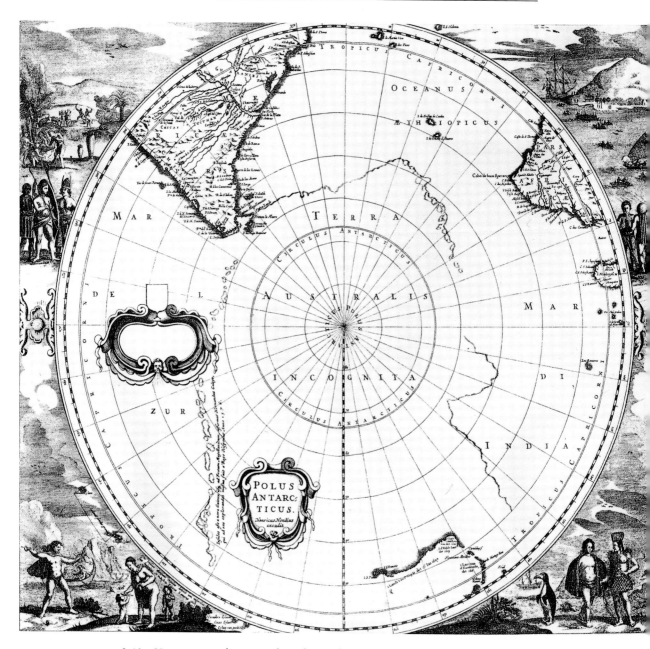

3.10 Henricus Hondius   Southern hemisphere ('Polus Antarcticus')   1639

chart shows the coasts of western and southern Australia from 21°S down to 35°S, with every discovery drawn separately and hypothetical coasts deliberately omitted. Taking into account the difficulties of accurately calculating latitude and, more particularly, longitude in those days, it is amazing to see how close Hessel Gerritsz came to the real coastline when he combined the various discoveries.

This sectional work strongly influenced Dutch cartography and globemaking in the 1630s. It was the basis of a map on parchment printed by Jacob Aertsz Colom (1630–40), which also showed the results of the *Pera's* voyage[27] (which Hessel Gerritsz did not include). A globe manufactured in the workshop of the Colom family likewise shows all Dutch discoveries up to 1627,[28] as does a map on parchment printed by Theunis Jacobsz, who named the whole continent ''t Land van de Eendracht'.[29] The pre-Tasman discoveries appeared too on the many editions of the maps of the *Polus Antarticus* by Henricus Hondius (3.10),[30] as well as on those of the *Mar di India* by Joannes Janssonius,[31] all of which together mark the considerable advance in Dutch knowledge of the southern continent.

TASMAN'S VOYAGES, 1642–4

Tasman's voyages of deliberate exploration were prefaced by the expedition of the *Cleen Amsterdam* and the *Wesel* in 1636, which produced little in the way of new information.[32] Governor General Anthonie van Diemen (3.11) was not discouraged by these disappointing results. Continued speculation about rich lands to the south and the east had fuelled his interest in solving the problem of the south land once and for all. However, the obtaining of authentic geographical information and the exploitation of whatever commercial possibilities the mysterious continent might present were not van Diemen's only motives. He also hoped to find a passage to the Pacific that would offer convenient access to Chile, in which the VOC was then very interested, from the point of view both of licit trade and piracy. The governor told Abel Jansz Tasman (3.13, 3.17), to whom he gave the command of the projected expedition, that he was to 'sail to the partly known as well as the undiscovered South and East lands, to discover them and find some important lands, or at the very least some practicable passages to well known rich places, to be used eventually to enhance and enlarge the general welfare of the company'.[33]

Van Diemen equipped two vessels, the *Heemskerck* (3.12), a yacht of 60 lasts (120 tons) carrying a crew of sixty, and the *Zeehaen* (3.12), a flute of 100 lasts (200 tons) with a crew of fifty. As commander, Tasman sailed on the *Heemskerck*. François Jacobsz Visscher, who had distinguished himself with his charting of several areas in Indonesian waters, sailed at van Diemen's wish to compose a memorial on 'the discovery of the South land'. Visscher was the scientific leader of the expedition, while Gerrit Jansz was captain of the *Zeehaen*.

Also on board the *Zeehaen* was Isaack Gilsemans, who had orders to map the coast, and as well to inspect with a commercial eye. He was to 'map out and describe very accurately all the lands, islands, angles, bights, inlets, bays, rivers, shallows, banks, beaches, rivers, crags and rocks that would be encountered and passed, as well as to draw their exact positions and forms'. Fortunately, the surviving records—resolutions, instructions, letters, and particularly journals and charts—offer abundant information about this, the most important of all the voyages of deliberate discovery made by the Dutch towards Australia.[34]

Amply provided with trading goods, the ships left Batavia for Mauritius on 14 August 1642. Beginning the voyage of discovery proper, they left Mauritius on 8 October, and headed for 49°S latitude, where they turned east. In the face of bad weather and 'very tempestuous' seas, Visscher advised Tasman to take a more northerly course. This was a fortunate change (3.16), for had he continued on his first course, Tasman would have found nothing but sea and sky until the south island of New Zealand. Sailing along 42°S latitude, he sighted 'very high-lying land' at a distance of ten miles on 24 November 1642. It was the west coast of the present Tasmania. Its discoverer recorded: 'This land was the first land in

3.11   Matthijs Balen   Anthonie van Diemen   *c.* 1720

98

the South Sea we encountered not hitherto known to any European nation; we have given this land the name Anthoonij van Diemens landt in honour of our Governor General who sent us to make this discovery.' For ten days, the explorers sailed along its south coast and east coasts, anchoring and landing from time to time, but having no contact with the Aborigines. On the shore of the present Prince of Wales Bay Tasman fixed a flag to a pole, as a 'memorial' for 'posterity and the inhabitants of the land' of their discovery.[35]

Since prevailing winds made it impossible for the ships to swing back so as to trace the coast westwards, Tasman decided to proceed east. Leaving the coast on 5 December 1642, he headed into what is now known as the Tasman Sea. By 12 December the continuous swelling of great waves from the south-west had convinced him that there was no large land mass in that direction, but the next day, when in 42°10'S latitude, they saw another 'large high land' loom before them. This was the west coast of the south island of the present New Zealand, against which they turned north. Thinking that it might possibly be the western extension of the Staten Land discovered by Jacob le Maire in 1616, Tasman gave it the same name. After a hostile encounter with Maoris on 18 December at

3.12 *Heemskerck* and *Zeehaen*

3.13 Tasman's signature

'Murderers' Bay', Tasman continued north, 'because one could not judge [whether it was possible] to befriend these people there or obtain water and refreshments'.

Tasman next paused in the mouth of a wide inlet, the present Admiralty Bay which debouches into Cook Strait. This was such a passage to the eastern Pacific as he had been sent to find, but winds and currents setting from the east discouraged him from probing it. It is interesting that while Visscher left a gap on his chart at this 'Zeehaens bight', Tasman drew an uninterrupted coastline as he continued north.[36] The explorers reached the northernmost point of the north island of New Zealand, which they named Cape Maria van Diemen after the Governor General's wife, on 6 January 1643, and faced the vastness of the south Pacific. The prevailing easterly swell persuaded Tasman, as it was to persuade Cook 130 years later, that 'in the east no sizable land is to be expected', and that 'this course from Batavia to Chile is a good fairway for nothing obstructs the way . . . on that route'. Again sailing north, they discovered the Tongan and Fijian islands where, in distinct contrast to New Zealand, they were warmly welcomed. Rounding north of New Guinea, they reached Batavia again on 15 June 1643, after a voyage of ten months (3.19).

Though Tasman conducted the voyage skilfully enough, it failed to realize van Diemen's hopes. It did not result in the discovery of any regions whose riches the VOC might exploit; and while it showed that the south land was not connected with the antarctic regions and indicated that Chile might be reached by sailing east in southerly latitudes, it gave rise to very little fresh information about the south land itself, whose main coast Tasman had not actually seen. As van Diemen reported in a letter to his superiors in the Netherlands, '[Tasman] has not made many investigations regarding the situations nor form and nature of the discovered lands and peoples, but has in principle left everything to a more inquisitive successor'.[37]

The determined van Diemen was not however deterred by these disappointing results, organizing another expedition in 1644 consisting of the yachts *Limmen* and *Zeemeeuw*, with crews of 56 and 41 respectively, and the galliot *de Bracq*, with a crew of 14. Despite his reservations about Tasman's lack of initiative, the Governor General again gave him the command, instructing him to 'take up seriously the further discovery of these South lands in the hope of achieving something profitable'. Van Diemen looked for elucidation of two points in particular. First, was there a passage between New Guinea and the south land? It was for this purpose that he sent the *de Bracq*, which was shallow draughted enough for Tasman to sail into the bight for two or three days, to find out whether within '[it] is a passage to the South Sea'.[38] Second, Tasman was to investigate whether his newly-discovered Van Diemen's Land (Tasmania) could be reached by way of a short cut from the 'Staten rivier' found by Jan Carstenz in 1623.

Unfortunately, we have only fragmentary records of this voyage. No log

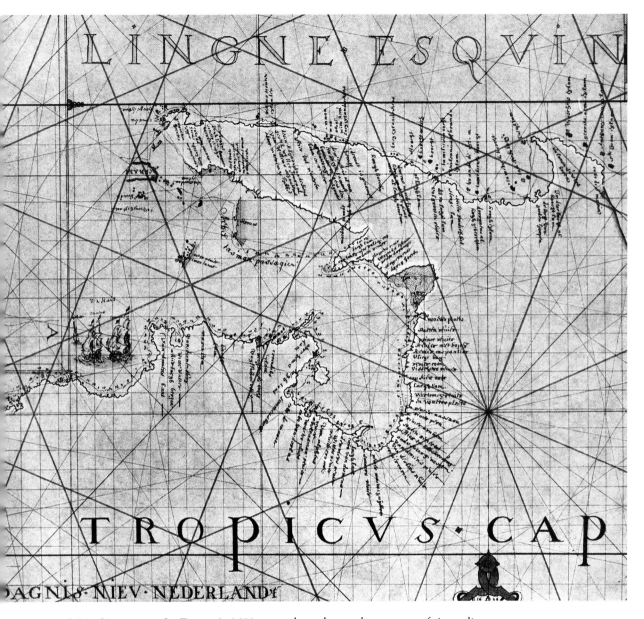

3.14 [Anonymous] Tasman's 1644 route along the northern coasts of Australia

3.15   Joan Blaeu   New Holland   ('Hollandia Nova')   1645–6

has survived, and in its absence the so-called 'Bonaparte Map' becomes an extremely important source of information, for it shows Tasman's route from Banda along the south coast of New Guinea and the north coast of Australia (3.14).[39] As Willem Jansz and Jan Carstensz had done before him, Tasman mistook the western entrance of Torres Strait for a bay. Then, sailing south in search of a short way to Van Diemen's Land, he found instead a 'big and wide bight or gulf' (the Gulf of Carpentaria). After coasting it west and then north, evidently he rounded Arnhem Land and sailed west along the entire northern coast of the continent (3.18).

In the Netherlands, the results of these voyages first became known to those outside the VOC by way of maps. The first to show them was Joan Blaeu, whose position as cartographer to the company's Chamber at Amsterdam gave him access to the latest information. In 1645 or 1646 Blaeu revised the large world map made by his father in 1619, beating out from the copperplates the outline of the great Terra Australis, and replacing it with that of Australia so far as was then revealed (3.15).[40] A second point of major significance is that Blaeu gave the now half-unveiled continent the name of 'NOVA HOLLANDIA', evidently the first usage of the name. Then, in 1648 on the occasion of the Peace of Munster, Blaeu published a completely newly-drawn world map on twenty copperplates (4.1).[41] Widely circulated, this map contributed greatly to the spread of information about Tasman's voyages, which now appeared, together with the earlier Dutch discoveries, on most Dutch charts, maps, and atlases. Conversely, the representation of Terra Australis disappeared. None the less, it was not until 1671 that Montanus published the first condensed report of Tasman's first voyage.[42] He was followed three years later by Dirck Rembrandtsz van Nierop.[43] Because he had access to a copy of Tasman's log, van Nierop's account in *Eenige Oefeningen* greatly influenced following ones. Two of the most noteworthy of these were that of Nicolaes Witsen, whose second edition of *Noord en Oost Tartarie* (1705) shows that he too had access to the records in the VOC archives,[44] and that of François Valentijn, whose famous *Oud en Nieuw Oost Indien* included the first full account of the first voyage, together with accurate maps.[45]

The results of Tasman's voyages were clearly disappointing, with van Diemen reporting to the directors of the VOC after the second that the expedition 'found nothing profitable, only poor, naked people walking along the beaches; without rice or many fruits, very poor and bad-tempered in many places'.[46] These results caused officials in both Batavia and the Netherlands to lose interest in exploring further the emergent New Holland. For fifty years, knowledge of the fifth continent remained essentially as it was after Tasman's second voyage, with only a few accidental additional landfalls such as that of the shipwrecked *Vergulde Draeck* (Gilt Dragon).[47] Then, in 1696, the VOC's interest rekindled once more with the despatch of an expedition strikingly scientific in its orientation, under the command of Willem Hesselsz de Vlamingh.[48]

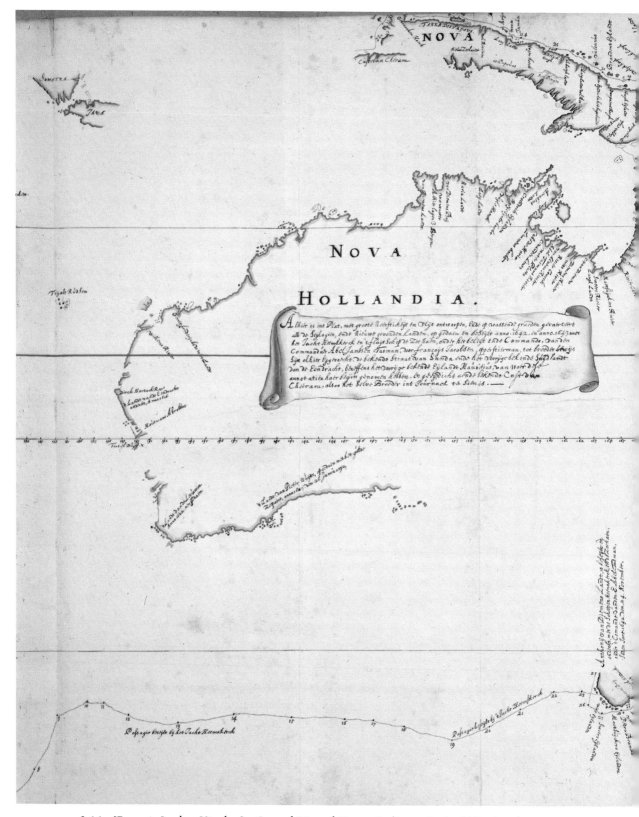

3.16 [Francois Jacobsz Visscher] General Map of Tasman's discoveries in 1642–3 and 1644 *c.* 1670

3.17 Jacob Gerritsz Cuyp Detail from his portrait of Abel Tasman with his second wife and daughter *?c.* 1640

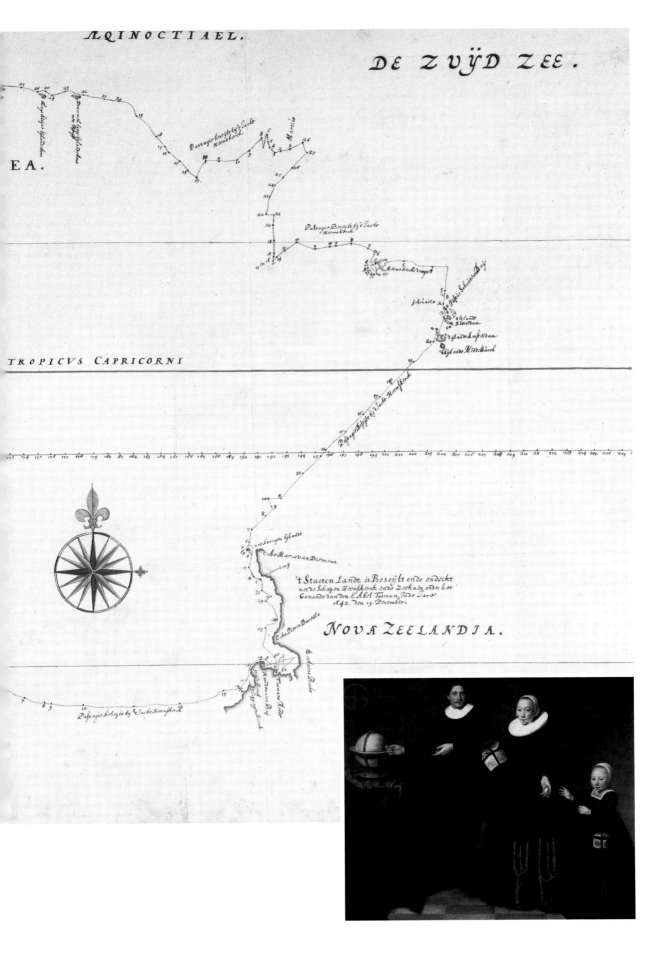

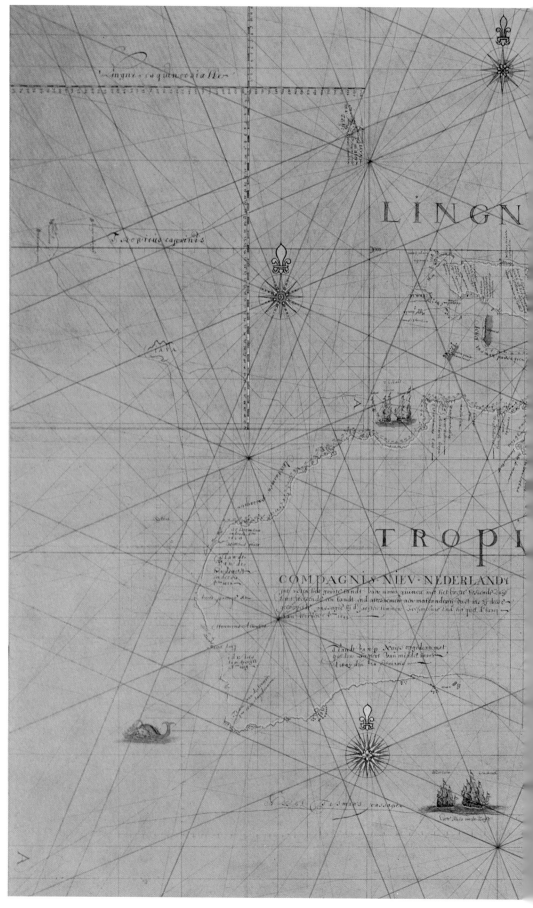

3.18 [Anonymous] 'Bonaparte' Map *c.* 1695

ÆQVINOCSIALLIS

CAPRICORNVS

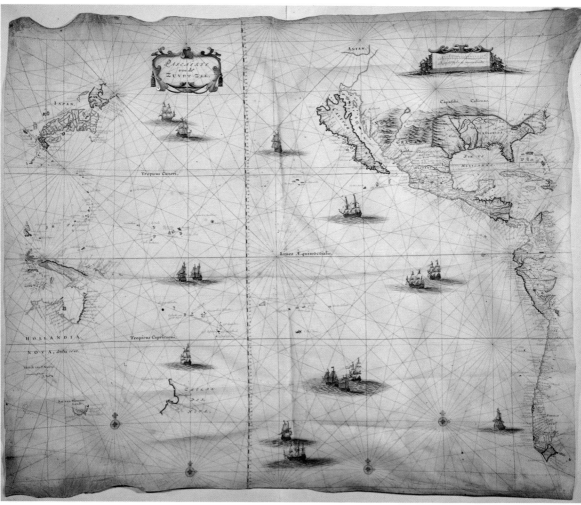

3.19   [Joan Blaeu]   Chart of the Pacific Ocean   *c.* 1650

3.20   [Anonymous]   Black Swans drifting at Rottnest Island ('Swarte Swanne drift op het
        Eyland Rottenest')   1724−6

DE VLAMINGH'S EXPLORATION OF THE WEST COAST

De Vlamingh's expedition consisted of the frigate *Geelvinck* with a crew of 134, the hooker *Nijptangh* with a crew of 50, and the galliot *'t Weseltje*, with a crew of 14. Uniquely among the Dutch expeditions to New Holland in the seventeenth century, he sailed from the Netherlands not Batavia. The Company's instructions to him concerning New Holland were quite explicit. He was to 'investigate whether there were any people or remains of either of the ships *Ridderschap* or *Vergulde Draeck*, or of any other VOC ships wrecked on its western coast. He was also to investigate further 'the coast as well as the inland, as far as possible'. He was to anchor the ships as often as feasible, explore surrounds in barges and map them out. He was to examine 'inlets, creeks or rivers, . . . sailing up-country as far as they would judge necessary to make discoveries of the land'. Reflecting past sad experience, the directors warned him against the 'very violent barbarian and cruel' inhabitants, and told him to undertake probes of the land with the 'utmost care and circumspection' so as not to be surprised and murdered. With the expedition went Victor Victorsz, with orders to chart every coast sighted between Texel and Batavia with absolute accuracy.

The expedition sailed on 3 May 1696. As it went, Victor Victorsz followed his orders faithfully, making a number of beautiful water-colour coastal profiles of Tristan da Cunha and Amsterdam and St Paul islands.[49] The ships reached Rottnest Island, off the present Fremantle, at the end of 1696 (3.21). The party who examined it were greatly puzzled by the marsupial quokkas they found in great numbers: '[there are] a multitude of wood-rats, approximately as big as cats, which [have] bags below their throats in which one could put one's hand, while no evidence exist[s] as to the purpose for which Nature had created the animal'. De Vlamingh added that the wood was 'the most beautiful in the world, the entire island was filled with the smell of it'. He cut a sample, which was afterwards pressed for its oil, much to the satisfaction of company officials.

The next day the party explored the Swan River. Then, on 13 January 1697, de Vlamingh decided to turn north, and for the next five weeks the ships coasted up to North West Cape. Victor Victorsz kept a careful chart (3.21), now in the Algemeen Rijksarchief, which provides a detailed record of this section of the voyage. From time to time, de Vlamingh landed parties in attempts to contact the Aborigines, but these failed. At Dirk Hartog Island (3.2), they found the pewter plate left in 1616 (3.3), which was recovered by de Vlamingh, who was astonished at how it had 'survived there so many years, despite the effects of air, rain and sun', and who left another in its place. On 21 February 1697, when at North West Cape, the commander decided to abandon further exploration. The captain of the *Nijptangh* recorded how, as they turned for Batavia, they fired volleys 'in farewell of the wretched South land'.

De Vlamingh's voyage went off without incident, but also without the hoped-for results. What distinguishes it, however, from all its Dutch predecessors

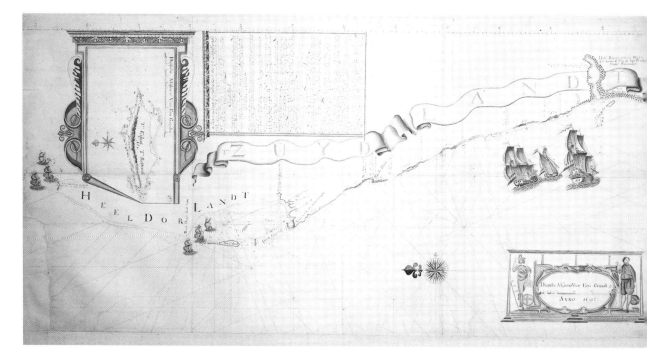

3.21   Victor Victorsz   Outline chart of the western coast of 'the Southland'   1697

are Victor Victorsz's delicate water-colours. Found by this author in the 'Prins Hendrik' Maritime Museum in Rotterdam in 1970, they are the oldest complete set of coastal views of Australia, and constitute a striking record of the monotonous and inhospitable coast the explorers found. Particularly noteworthy is that of 'Dirck Hartogs Reede', which shows a pole in the western corner with the accompanying legend: 'hier de tinne schotel gevonden' ('here was found the pewter plate').

The Dutch public were informed of this, the last major Dutch voyage of exploration to the south land, by a brief report by Mandrop Torst, the surgeon of the *Nijptangh*, published in 1701.[50] Curiously, though, its cartographical results were not then published, being represented on only a few manuscript maps and charts. Evidently, the disappointing results led people to be content with the outline of New Holland established up to Tasman's time. Only in the sixth volume of the *Zee-fakkel*, published by Jan de Marre and Joannes van Keulen in 1753, did the results of de Vlamingh's voyage appear fully.[51] This work presented in comprehensive detail the coastlines, islands, and harbours of the VOC's area of operations and its map of New Holland reflects de Vlamingh's discoveries.[52]

De Vlamingh's expedition was followed by two later ones to the northern shores of New Holland, by van Delft in 1705 and by Gonzal in 1756, which produced similarly disappointing results.[53] Though they could not have known it, the Dutch navigators saw some of the most desolate and barren of Australia's coasts, and it is hardly surprising that their findings led the directors of the VOC to lose interest in the south land. New Holland, as the Dutch came to know it, evidently offered nothing that might be advantageous to the Company's commerce—no spices, no precious metals, no minerals, no fertile regions that might be settled and cultivated, no inhabitants with whom the company might trade. Where there is explicit comment, almost all the extant records refer to sterile strips of rocky or sandy coast, without water, sometimes without vegetation. Similarly, the accounts speak of wild and savage native inhabitants, rendered conspicuous by their nakedness, their incomprehensible language, and their lack of interest in things European. As officials in Batavia reported to the Company after the 1705 expedition, the Aborigines went 'stark naked, without any regard to age or sex', with the exception that women caring for children wore 'a slight covering of leaves or such-like over their middle'. They possessed 'nothing which is of value ... and have neither iron nor anything like mineral ore or metal, but only a stone which is ground and made to serve as a hatchet'. Furthermore, they had 'no habitations, either houses or huts'. They seemed 'foul and treacherous' by nature, and 'no one was able to understand their language'.[54] The general image differed nothing in essence from that offered contemporaneously by Dampier.

Occasionally the explorers did find the environment more promising. In 1756, for example, Gonzal described a section of the Cape York Peninsula as being 'overgrown with tall grass', and as exhibiting 'a number of fine dells or valleys, through which flowed various small rills of fresh water', with some 'trees very tall and straight, of regular growth', and with the soil 'rich'.[55] But this was not the notion of the south land which prevailed. Jan Carstensz conveyed that which did prevail when he reported in 1623 that the land he had seen was 'an arid and poor tract without any fruit tree or anything useful to man'.[56] Only in its natural history did New Holland offer anything of interest. Befitting its scientific orientation, de Vlamingh's expedition found the curious quokka, which observers mistook for a kind of rat, on Rottnest Island; and then at Swan River the even more curious black swan (3.20). Long postulated as the antithesis of regular creation, this marvel created resonances both with older ideas of antipodean inversion, and with subsequent responses—particularly those of the English—to the flora and fauna of New South Wales.

Notes

1 The share of the Dutch in the discovery of Australia has been treated by various author: R. H. Major, *Early voyages to Terra Australis, now called Australia* (London, 1859); J. E. Heeres, *Het aandeel der Nederlanders in de ontdekking van Australië, 1606–1756* (Leiden, 1899) and *The part borne by the Dutch in the discovery of Australia 1606–1756* (Leiden, 1899); E. Scott, *Australian discovery: By sea* (London, 1929); F. W. Stapel, *De Oostindische Compagnie en Australië* (Patria 4, Amsterdam, 1937); A. Sharp, *The Discovery of Australia* (Oxford, 1963); G. Schilder, *Australia Unveiled. The share of the Dutch navigators in the discovery of Australia* (Amsterdam, 1976).

2 G. Schilder, 'Organisation and evolution of the Dutch East India Company's Hydrographic Office in the seventeenth century', *Imago Mundi*, 28 (1976), 61–78.

3 P. Murdoch, *Duyfken and the first discoveries of Australia* (Artamon, 1974).

4 *Dese Pascaerte vertoont de wegh, soo int heen als in het weerom seylen, die gehouden is bij het Jacht het Duijfien in het besoecken van de landen beoosten Banda, tot aen Nova Guinea, Maer Guli-guli op Cenam, ende Ceram etc. is na de afteijckeninge van Abraham Francken A°. 1602. den 20 April gedaen, Ende Nieuw Zelandt met de Gounongapi daer beoosten is beseijlt, bij Jaspaer Janssen de Jonge.* Ms on paper, coloured, 560 × 615 mm. Österreichische Nationalbibliothek, Wien, *Atlas Van der Hem* (389030-FK, XLI, 31). There is a full-size fascimile in F. C. Wieder, *Monumenta Cartographica* (The Hague, 1933), V, pl. 125.

5 (*Mar del Sur. Mar Pacifico*) *Hessel Gerritsz. met Octroy vande E. H. M. Heeren de Staten Generael der Vereenichde Nederlanden M.DC.(X)XXII(II)* (1622). Ms on vellum, coloured, 1070 × 1410 mm, BN, Archives du Service hydrographique de la Marine, no. 30. There are reproductions in M. Destombes, *Catalogue des cartes nautiques manuscrites sur parchemin 1300–1700 ... Cartes hollandaises* (Saigon, 1941), pl. I; J. Keuning, 'Hessel Gerritsz!, *Imago Mundi*, 6 (1949), 58; *Cataloque Exposition* (Paris, 1960), IX; Schilder, *Australia Unveiled*, map 23 and pl. IV.

6 ARA VOC 313, ff. 58–61.

7 C. Halls, 'Two plates. Being an account of the Dirk Hartog and Vlamingh plates their loss and subsequent recovery', *Westerly* (March 1964), 30–40.

8 [Map of the Indian Ocean.] *'t Amsterdam/by hessel gerritsz/met octroy/Vande E:h:m°. heeren de staten/generael der vereenichde/nederlanden A°. 1622'*. MS on vellum, 855 × 1020 mm, Staatsbibliothek Preussischer Kulturbesitz, Berlin, T 7165. This is reproduced in Schilder, *Australia Unveiled*, map 29.

9 *NOVA TOTIUS TERRARUM ORBIS GEOGRAPHICA AC HYDROGRAPHICA TABULA; Amstelodami apud Judocum Hondium*. Copper engraving, 390 × 570 mm. There is a copy in a private collection in Vienna. It is reproduced in Schilder, *Australia unveiled*, map 32. A second edition was published by Francois van den Hoeye in 1630. The only known copy is preserved in the Sächsische Landesbibliothek, Dresden. A third unchanged edition was again published by Clement de Jonghe in 1664. There are copies in the Bayerische Staatsbibliothek, München; Maritiem Museum 'Prins Hendrik', Rotterdam; Rijksmuseum 'Nederlands Scheepvaart Museum', Amsterdam; and Library of Congress, Washington.

10 Terrestrial globe by Arnold Florent van Langren of 1612, brought up to date about 1625, BN. The globe bears the following address: 'auctore Arnoldo Florentio á Langre Reg: Cat: Matis Cosmographo et Pensionaris'. See fig. 32 in Schilder, *Australia Unveiled*.

11 ARA VOC 1070, ff. 1139–40.

22 ARA VOC 1070, ff. 147–51.

13 *Australia's Oldest Wreck: the historical background and archaeological analysis of the wreck of the English East India Company's Ship 'Trial'*, ed. J. N. Green (British Archaeological Reports, Supplementary Series 27, Oxford, 1977).

14 ARA VOC 850, ff. 26–27v.

15 ARA VOC 1080, ff. 56–73.

16 See, for example, *Caerte van Arent Martensz. de Leeuw, Opperstierm". die dese westcust beseijlt heeft*. On the back of the chart the following note: 'Caerte vande ontdecte custe ende plaetsen van Nova Guinea 1623'. Ms on paper, 440 × 560 mm. Algemeen Rijksarchief, Den Haag (VEL 493). There is a full-size facsimile in *Remarkable Maps* (Amsterdam, 1895). V, pl. 5. There is also Anonymous, Copy of the chart of the ship *Arnhem*, Ms on paper, coloured, 535 × 330 mm, Österreichische Nationalbibliothek, Wien, *Atlas Van der Hem* (389030-FK, XLI, 34). There is a full-size facsimile in F. C. Wieder, *Monumenta Cartographica* (The Hague, 1933), V, pl. 126.

17 ARA VOC 1080, f. 67r.

18 See below, pp. 162–74.

19 *T'Neghenste Deel of 't Vervolgh van het Historisch Verhael aller gedenkwaardighe geschiede-
nissen, die in Europa . . . in Asia . . . in America
. . . van April des jaers 1623, tot October toe,
voorgevallen syn. Beschreven door Nicolaus a
Wassenaer Amsterdammer Medicijn* (Amsterdam, 1625), pp. 67–8.

20 *CHARTE VNIUERSELLE DE TOVT LE MONDE . . . PAR
CORNEILLE DANCKERTZ ET MELCHIOR TAVERNIER. A
PARIS chez Melchior Tauernier, graveur et La-
primeur du Roy pour les Tailles douces deme en
l'Isle du Palais A° 1628.* Copper engraving, 510
× 910 mm (2 sheets). Four copies are known to
me: Library of Congress, Washington (vault),
BN (Ge C 8462) and Ge (8463), BL London (Maps
184i 1[2]).

21 *NOVA TOTIVS TERRARUM ORBIS GEOGRAPHICA AC
HYDROGRAPHICA TABVLA: AUCT: HENR: HONDIO.*
Copper engraving, 380 × 540 mm. This ap-
peared for the first time in *Appendice de L'Atlas.
L'Appendice De L'Atlas De Gerard Mercator et
Iudocus Hondius . . . A Amsterdam chez Henry
Hondius . . . 1633.* There is a full-size facsimile
in *Remarkable Maps* (Amsterdam, 1895), II,
pl. 6.

22 *INDIA quae ORIENTALIS dicitur ET INSVLAE ADIACENTES.*
Copper engraving, 410 × 500 mm. Appears for
the first time in Blaeu's atlas *Toonel des Aerdri-
icx, Ofte Nievwe Atlas, Dat is Beschryving van
alle landen; Nu nieulyckz uitgegeven. Door
Wilhelm: en Iohannem Blaeu* (Amsterdam,
1635). There is a full-size facsimile in *Remarkable
Maps* (Amsterdam, 1895), II, pl. 10.

23 *Caert van't Landt van d'Eendracht / uyt de
Iournalen ende afteykeningen / der Stierluyden
t'samengestelt. / A°. 1627 / Bij Hessel Gerritsz.
/ Met Octroy vande H. M. H. de Staten Generael
/ der vereenighde Nederlanden.* Copper engraving, 285 × 1610 mm. There are copies in
Universiteitsbibliotheek, Leiden; Algemeen Rijksarchief, Den Haag (2 copies); Badische Landesbibliothek, Karlsruhe; BN; and NLA. There
is a full-size facsimile in *Remarkable Maps*
(Amsterdam, 1895), II pl.4.

24 ARA VOC 1079, f. 156r.

25 For the loss of the ship *Batavia* see *Ongeluckige
Voyagie, Van 't Schip Batavia, Nae de Oost-
Indien. Gebleven op de Abrolhos van Frederick
Houtman, op de hooghte van 28 1/3 graet by
Zuyden de Linie Aequinoctiael. Vuytgevaren
onder den E. Froncoys Pelsert. Vervatende Soo 't
verongelucken des Schips als de grouwelijcke
Moorderijen onder 't gebergde Scheepsvolck op
't Eylant Bataviaes Kerck-hof voorgevallen;
nevens de Straffe de Hantadigers overkomen.
Geschiet in de jaren 1628, en 1629,* (Amsterdam
1647). In 1648 another edition was published by
Joost Hartgers, followed by another six. For
detailed discussion see the excellent study by H.
Drake-Brockman, *Voyage to disaster. The life of*

Fransisco Pelsaert. Covering his Indian report to
the Dutch East India Company and the wreck of
the ship 'Batavia', in 1629 off the coast of western
Australia together with full text of his journals
concerning the rescue voyages, the mutiny on
the Abrolhos Islands and the subsequent trials of
the mutineers (London, 1963).

26 (Chart of the Malay Archipelago and the Dutch
discoveries in Australia), '*A° 1618 / t' Amsterdam /
by Hessel Gerrtiz. / met Octroy / Van de HM
Heeren de Staten Generael / der Vereenichde
Neerlanden'.* Copper engraving, 510 × 330 mm.
There are copies in Universiteitsbibliotheek,
Leiden; Badische Landesbibliothek, Karlsruhe;
NLA; Mitchell (Huydecoper Ms). There is a full
size facsimile in Heeres, *Het aandeel der Neder-
landers*, no. 5.

27 *OOST-INDISCHE Pas Caart Nieulycks Beschreven
Door IACOB AERTSZ. COLOM.* Copper engraving
printed on vellum, 705 × 920 mm. The following
copies are known to me: Bibliothèque de l'Institut de France, Paris (2 copies: Ms 1288, nos 5
and 7); Koninklijke Bibliotheek 'Albert I',
Brussels (III 9396); and Mitchell. It is reproduced
in Schilder, *Australia Unveiled*, map 42.

28 National Maritime Museum, Greenwich (G.170),
Ø 336 mm. The nomenclature on the globe is
more restricted than the chart of the East Indies
mentioned in note 29, due to its small circumference.

29 *Pascaerte van OOST-INDIEN, En de Omgelegen
Eylanden, als Madagascar, Seylon, Sumatra,
Iava, Borneo, Celebes, Molucco, en Banda C. de
Bona Speranca tot Iapan. 't Amsterdam, By
Theunis Iacobsz. op 't water inde Lootsman.*
Copper engraving, printed on vellum, 720 × 900
mm. The only known copy is in the Badische
Landesbibliothek, Karlsruhe (West Germany),
sign. D. 41 (R). It is reproduced in Schilder,
Australia Unveiled, map 43.

30 *POLUS ANTARCTICUS. Henricus Hondius excudit.*
Copper engraving, 440 × 495 mm. Appears for
the first time in *Gerardi Mercatoris Et I. Hondij.
Appendix Novi Atlantis . . . Amstelodami,
Sumptibus Johannis Janssonii, Anno Domini
1637.* There is a full-size facsimile in *Remarkable
Maps* (Amsterdam, 1895), II, pl. II.

31 *MAR DI INDIA.* Copper engraving, 435 × 550 mm.
This appeared for the first time in *Het vijfde Deel
des Grooten Atlas, Vervatende de Water-
wereld . . . Amstelodami. Apud Ioannem Ians-
sonium. 1650.* There is a full-size facsimile in
Remarkable Maps (Amsterdam, 1895), II pl. 12.

32 See Schilder, *Australia Unveiled*, pp. 129–83.

33 ARA VOC 866, f. 490–500.

34 *Abel Janszoon Tasman's Journal of his discovery
of Van Diemens Land and New Zealand in 1642
with documents relating to his exploration of
Australia in 1644 being photographic facsimiles
of the original manuscript in the Colonial Ar-*

113

chives at *The Hague with an English translation and facsimiles of original maps to which are added life and labours of Abel Janszoon Tasman*, ed. J. E. Heeres (Amsterdam, 1898); A. Sharp, *The voyages of Abel Janszoon Tasman* (Oxford, 1968).

35 Three large-scale charts relate to the discovery of the Van Diemens Land. One by Isaac Gilsemans, supercargo on the *Zeehaen* entitled *Anthonio van Diemens Landt beseijlt bij de Schepen Hemskercken Ende Zeehaen Adij 24en November Anno 1642*. The signature reads: *Isaac Gilsemans Fecit*. Ms on paper, coloured, 445 × 350 mm, Österreichische Nationalbibliothek, Wien, *Atlas Stosch* (313/1). There is a full-size facsimile in F. C. Wieder, *Monumenta Cartographica* (The Hague), IV, pl. 97. Another chart is copied from an unknown original chart and preserved in the *Atlas Stosch*. It is entitled *Anthonie van Diemens Landt is Beseijlt en Ondeckt met de Scheepen Heemskerck ende Zeehaen onder 't Commando Vande Command' Abel Tasman. Inde Iaeren 1642 den 24. novem.* Ms on paper, coloured, 425 × 520 mm, Österreichische Nationalbibliothek, Wien, *Atlas Stosch* (313). There is a full-size facsimile in F. C. Wieder, *Monumenta Cartographica*, III, pl. 98. The third chart is to be found in Tasman's own journal. This is entitled *Anthony van Diemens Landt. Dit is beseijlt ende ontdeck met de Scheepen Heemskerck ende Zeehaen. Onder het Commando Vanden E. Abel Tasmans Inden Jare 1642 Den 24 Nouuember.* Ms on paper, coloured, 235 × 355 mm, ARA (aanwinsten, le afdeling 1867 A III, f. 23v). There is a full-size facsimile in Heeres, *Tasman's journal*, f. 23v.

36 Three charts extant relate to the discovery of New Zealand. The first chart is by Franchoys Jacobsen Visscher, the chief pilot of the expedition. This is entitled *Staeten lant beseijlt en ontdekt anno 1642 den 13 Decemb' met Het Jacht heemskerck en de zeehaen, ende met groot vlijt seer naerstich ontworpen door Francoijs Jacobse Stierman.* Ms on paper, 350 × 455 mm, Mitchell. It is reproduced in Sharp, *Voyages of Tasman*, pl. 14. A copy of this chart is preserved in the Österreichische Nationalbibliothek, Wien, *Atlas Stosch* (311). There is a full-size facsimile in F. C. Wieder, *Monumenta Cartographica*, IV, pl. 99. A third chart is in Tasman's own journal. This is entitled *Staete Landt dit is Beseijlt ende ontdeckt met de Scheepen Heemskerck ende Zeehaen onder het Commando vanden E. Abel Tasman Inden Jaere 1642 Den 13 December.* Ms on paper, coloured, 350 × 455 mm, ARA (Aanwinsten, le afdeling 1867 A III, ff. 38v-39r). There is a full-size facsimile in Heeres, *Tasman's Journal*, ff. 38v-39r.

37 ARA VOC 1142, ff. 7v.

38 ARA VOC 868, ff. 39-50. These instructions of 29 January 1644 are also an important source for the Dutch voyages to Australia before 1644.

39 Anonymous, the so-called 'Bonaparte' map. Ms on vellum, coloured, 715 × 945 mm, Mitchell. There is a full-size facsimile by F. C. Wieder, *Tasman's kaart van zijne Australische ontdekkingen 1644*, 'De Bonapartekaart' ('s-Gravenhage, 1942).

40 *NOVA ACCVRATA TOTIUS TERRARVM ORBIS TABVLA ex optimis quibusq. in hoc genere auctorib⁵ desumpta, et duob⁵ planisphaerijs delineata, auct. Gul: lanssonio.* CICICCXVIIII [1619]. Copper engraving, 1730 × 2760 mm. The only known copy is preserved in the Maritiem Museum 'Prins Hendrik', Rotterdam. It is reproduced in Schilder, *Australia Unveiled*, maps 61-3.

41 (Joan Blaeu), *NOVA TOTIUS TERRARUM ORBIS TABULA.* Copper engraving, 1710 × 3030 mm. There is a full-size facsimile in F. C. Wieder, *Monumenta Cartographica*, III, pls 51-71.

42 *De Nieuwe en Onbekende Weereld: of beschryving van America en 't Zuid-Land, Vervaetende d'Oorsprong der Americaenen en Zuidlanders, gedenkwaaerdige togten derwaerds ... Door Arnoldus Montanus* (Amsterdam, 1671) Derde Boek, Elfde Hoofd-Stuk, pp. 578-85. An English version by John Ogilby appeared in the same year as the Dutch original and a German edition by O. Dapper came out two years later.

43 *Eenige Oefeningen, in God-lijcke, Wis-konstige en Natuerlijcke dingen ... By een gestelt door Dirck Rembrantsz. Van Nierop, Liefhebber der Mathmatise Konsten* (Amsterdam, 1674). The third part includes 'een kort Verhael uyt het Journael van den Kommandeur Abel Jansen Tasman, int ontdekken van 't onbekende Suit-Lant', pp. 55-64. Robert Hooke's English translation of 1682, and later editions by John Narborough (1694) and John Harris (1705) attracted the attention of a large number of English readers.

44 N. Witsen, *Noord en Oost Tartarye, ofte Bondig Ontwerp Van eenige dier Landen en Volken, Welke voormaels bekent zijn geweest* (Amsterdam, 1705), pp. 173-85.

45 F. Valentyn, *Oud- en Nieuw Oost-Indien, vervattende Een Naaukeurige en Uitvoerige Verhandelinge van Nederlandse Mogentheyd In die Gewesten ... Derde Deels Tweede Stuk* (Amsterdam, 1726), pp. 47-58. See also Schilder, *Australia Unveiled*, pp. 197-205.

46 ARA VOC 1147, ff. 36-37r.

47 For the voyages in connection with the shipwreck of the *Vergulde Draeck*, see J. N. Green, 'The Jacht *Vergulde Draeck* wrecked', *British Archaeological Reports*, *Supplementary Series*, 36 (1977), 2 vols; and *Catalogue of Dutch Relics*, compiled by M. Stanbury (Department of Maritime Archaeology, Western Australian Museum, Fremantle, WA, 1979).

114

[48] G. Schilder, *Voyage to the Great South Land. Willem de Vlamingh 1696–1697* (Sydney, 1985).

[49] Maritiem Museum 'Prins Hendrik', Rotterdam. There is a description and full-size facsimile in G. Schilder, *The Southland explored. The voyage by Willem Hesselsz. de Vlamingh in 1696–97, with the coastal profiles and a chart of Western Australia in full-size colour reproduction* (Alphen a.d. Rijn, 1984).

[50] *Journaal wegens een voyagie gedaan op order der Hollandsche Oost-Indische Maatschappy in de jaaren 1696 en 1697 door het hoekerscheepje de Nyptangh, het schip de Geelvink, en het galjoot de Wezel, na het Onbekende Zuid-Land, en wyders na Batavia* (Amsterdam, 1701). This is translated into English *in extensio* in Schilder, *Voyage to the Great South land*, pp. 146–62.

[51] *De nieuwe Groot Lichtende Zee-Fakkel, Het Ses-de Deel, Vertoonende de Zee-Kusten, Eylanden en Havens van Oost-Indien . . . door Jan de Marre . . . en Joannes van Keulen* (Amsterdam, 1753).

[52] *Het Westelykste Gedeelte van 'T LAND VANDE EENDRAGT, of NOVA HOLLANDIA, Strekkende van het Eyland Rottenest, tot voorby de Willems Rivier. te AMSTERDAM by JOANNES VAN KEULEN, Boek-en Zee-Caart verkooper op de hoek van de Nieuwe-brug-steeg*. Copper engraving, 588 × 988 mm.

[53] Heeres, *Het aandeel de Nederlanders/Part borne by the Dutch*, pp. 87–100.

[54] Major, *Early Voyages*, pp. 168–9.

[55] Heeres, *Het aandeel de Nederlanders/Part borne by the Dutch*, p. 92.

[56] See note 17.

4.1   Joan Blaeu   New Holland   from his World Map ('Nova Totius Terrarum Orbis Tabula')   1648

116

Chapter 4

New Holland to New South Wales: The English Approaches

Glyndwr Williams

KNOWLEDGE OF THE DUTCH DISCOVERIES

In an England which became an overseas power of some consequence during the seventeenth century, the oceanic explorations of the Dutch in the distant reaches south of Java were of only marginal importance. The commercial expansion of the nation stopped short at the East Indies, and not until the last years of the century was there any inclination to contemplate enterprise in far southern latitudes. The English East India Company held the dubious distinction of losing a vessel, the *Trial*, and a hundred men off the north-west coast of Australia as early as 1622; but the ship was in that area as the result of a gross navigational error by the master as he attempted to follow the new Dutch route in latitude 20°S to Java.[1] The curiosity of English traders about the activities of their powerful Dutch rivals did lead, however, to news of Tasman's discoveries reaching England at a surprisingly early date. The India Office archives in London hold a rough sketch map of Van Diemen's Land (4.2) sent home in January 1644 by the English resident at Bantam, annotated with the legend, 'A Draught of the South Land lately discovered 1643'. An accompanying letter noted that it had taken 'extraordinary friendschipp' to obtain the map, and went on to state that 'The Dutch have lately made a new discovery of the South Land'. Even though the writer was at pains to point out that 'the Dutch Generall intends to send thither again and fortifie, having mett with something worth the looking after', there is no likelihood that the English company considered spending any of its limited resources in vying with the Dutch in so remote a region.[2]

Among the first signs of recognition outside Holland of the significance of Tasman's explorations is an English world map of 1655 by Joseph Moxon (4.3). The section covering the area of (modern) Australia and New Zealand must have been based on a Dutch map, presumably one of Joan Blaeu's (4.1, 3.15).[3] There was no particular eagerness by the Dutch East India Company to publicize Tasman's explorations, nor should any be expected in this era of monopoly trade. His discoveries held out little prospect of immediate commercial gain, yet any foreign incursion into those waters would be seen as a threat to the Dutch position. As the directors noted in 1643 of another region, 'It were to be wished that the said land continued still unknown and never explored, so as not to tell foreigners the way to the Company's overthrow.'[4] On the other hand, there was little of the neurotic concern with secrecy which had marked earlier Spanish discoveries. If there had been, Tasman's explorations would hardly have been displayed on the great world map laid in about 1650 on the floor of the new city hall in Amsterdam for all the world to see. Nor would the superb Klencke Atlas have been presented to Charles II on the occasion of his restoration in 1660 with, among its maps, Joan Blaeu's 'Archipelagus Orientalis sive Asiaticus' (4.1) which showed New Holland and much else. Until the publication of Thévenot's map of 1663 (4.4), with its clear and comprehensive view of the Dutch explorations,

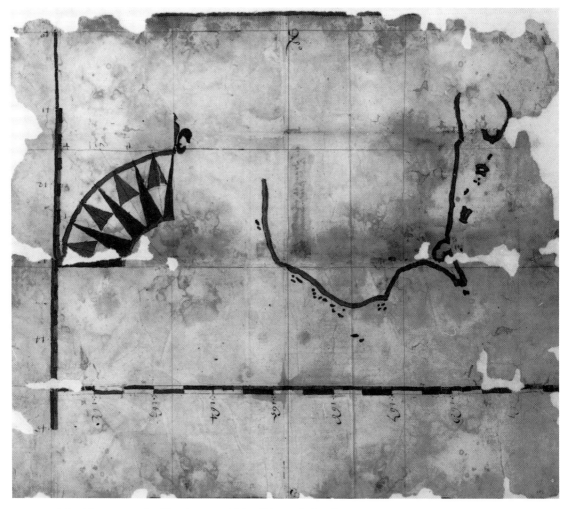

4.2 [Anonymous] Sketch map of Van Diemen's Land 1644

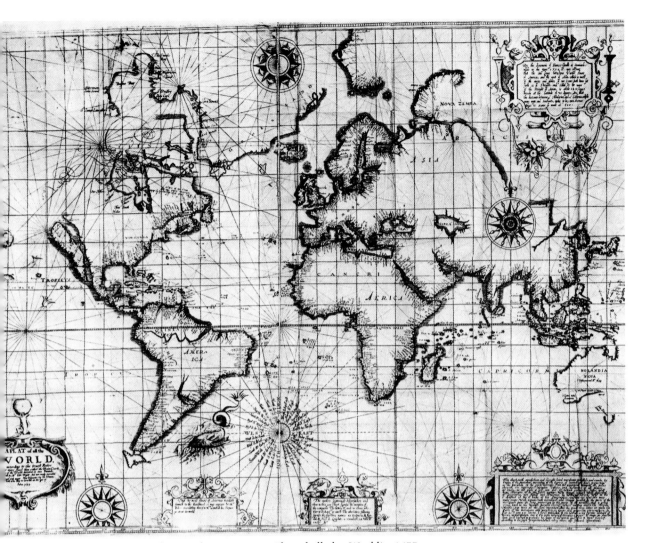

4.3   Edward Wright/Joseph Moxon   'A Plat of all the World'   1655

Moxon's was the best representation of Tasman's discoveries to be issued outside Holland; but located as it was in a technical treatise on navigation it made no impact on the English cartographers of the day.[5]

   Printed accounts of Tasman's voyages were even slower in appearing. A rather unsatisfactory narrative by the surgeon Hendrik Haelbos was published in Dutch in 1671, and in the same year an English translation found its way into John Ogilby's *America*. One of the interesting aspects of this version is that the English editor linked the Tasman voyage with the Quirós discoveries of 1606, pointing out that 'no Spaniard hath since that time set Foot on the unknown South-Land. But the [Dutch] East-India Company undertaking the Design with great eagerness, sent thither two Ships ... '.[6] It was this inclusion of the glowing Spanish predictions resulting from the approach to Australia from the east which helped to keep alive European interest despite the unenthusiastic reports which accompanied the approach from the west taken by Tasman and,

119

later, Dampier. The brief narrative was short on geographical detail, lacking any indication of the latitude or longitude of the 'South-Land', or an accompanying map. It had more to say on encounters with the 'Southlanders' in New Zealand, where the clash at Tasman's Murderers' Bay was described.

The second narrative of the Tasman voyage to appear in print was that of Dirck Rembrantsz van Nierop, based in part on Tasman's own journal. First published in Dutch in 1674, it was translated into English and printed in the *Philosophical Transactions* of the Royal Society in 1682. Twelve years later it was reprinted, with rather more elaborate introductory material, in a collection of voyages published in London. There was more precision and detail about the van Nierop account, though without a map the narrative must have been difficult to follow. In his introduction the unknown editor spelt out for the first time to English readers the significance of the Dutch discoveries, as well as hinting that there were others 'which they have not yet divulg'd'. Once more, a possible connection was indicated between the Dutch voyages and the earlier expedition of Quirós, which

sailed at several times above 800 Leagues together on the Coast of a Southern Continent, until they came to the height of 15 degrees of South Latitude, where they found a very fruitful, pleasant and populous Country ... This vast Tract of Land perhaps may be one side of, or may belong to, Jansen Tasman's Land, Van Diemen's Land, Zelandia Nova, Carpentaria, and New Guiney; which the Dutch afterwards coasted, detected, and gave Names to many Bays, Rivers and Capes.

After this overview of the Dutch voyages, Tasman's expedition of 1642 was put into perspective. It was, readers were told, 'the more considerable, in that 'tis the Discovery of a New World, not yet known to the English'. More precisely, ' 'tis probable by Abel Jansen Tasman's Navigation, that New Guinea, New Carpentaria, and New Holland, are a vast prodigious Island, which he seems to have encompassed in his Voyage'.[7]

The lucidity of these remarks stands in sharp contrast to the general air of muddle and uncertainty which overtook geographers when they contemplated this region. Older cartographic forms retained a tenacious grip long after the publication of maps by Blaeu (3.15, 4.1), Thévenot (4.4) and others, and to some editors Marco Polo remained more relevant than Tasman. Successive editions of the *Cosmography and Geography* of Varenius illustrate the point. In the first English edition of 1683, a mixture was concocted from Marco Polo's geography and the Dutch voyages before Tasman:

The Gulph Lantchidololinum floweth from the Indian Ocean, between the Provinces of the South Country Beach and New Guiney: it stretcheth from the North to the South, and terminateth at the unknown parts of the South Continent.

Another Gulph is near unto it towards the West, between Beach and the other procurrent land of the South, where is the Land called Anthonij à Diemen, which is the Name of a Dutch Master of a Ship by whom it was discovered.[8]

The 1703 edition of another standard geography, Peter Heylyn's *Cosmography*,

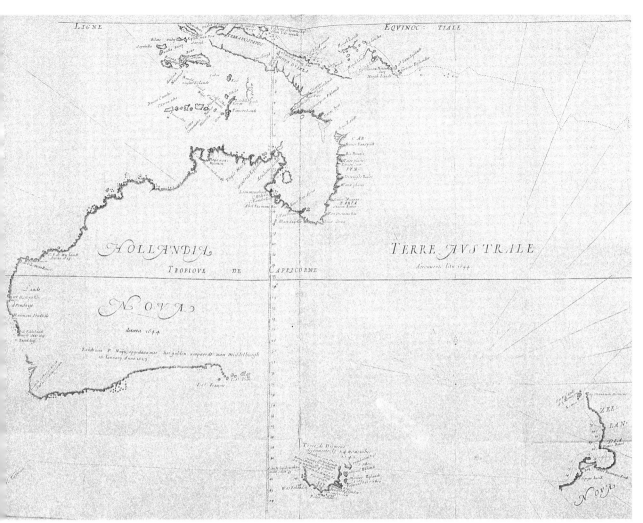

4.4 Melchisédec Thévenot New Holland and the Southern Continent ('Hollandia Nova/
Terre Avstrale') 1663

was even more laggard since it showed no knowledge either of Tasman or his
Dutch predecessors![9]

In one sense, this ignorance was a sign of the lack of European interest in so
remote a region. It is not altogether a chance matter that editors found difficulty
in deciding just where sections on 'Terra Australis Incognita' should be placed:
sometimes as an extension of South America, sometimes as an awkward append-
age to the East Indies. The hemispheric division of world maps had a similar
disjointing effect: New Guinea and New Zealand would be in one hemisphere,
New Holland in another. In a further category of maps, these areas had to be
studied in the difficult circular framework of a polar projection. Only Thévenot's
map (4.4) took as its centre point the Australian continent. It was to this scene of
geographical confusion and indifference that Dampier's voyages to New Holland
made their contribution—one whose effects were out of all proportion to their
geographical significance.

121

DAMPIER AND NEW HOLLAND, 1688 AND 1699

William Dampier's first visit to New Holland formed part of the global wanderings described in his *New Voyage round the World* published in 1697, and was a matter of accident rather than design. In the buccaneer vessel *Cygnet*, commanded by Captain Read, Dampier (4.5) journeyed through the East Indies to Timor on the southern fringe of the Dutch sphere of influence. In late December 1687, 'being now clear of all the Islands, we stood off South, intending to touch at New-Holland, a part of Terra Australis Incognita, to see what that Country would afford us. Indeed as the Winds were, we could not now keep our intended Course (which was first westerly, and then northerly) without going to New-Holland, unless we had gone back again among the Islands'.[10] The reference to New Holland as 'part of Terra Australis Incognita' (4.6) shows Dampier's confusion on this point, since Tasman had proved that the two were separated— if indeed both existed. A later passage shows the same confusion: 'New-Holland is a very large Tract of Land. It is not yet determined whether it is an Island or a main Continent.'[11] There was no knowledge of Tasman's voyage here, nor should any be expected. Dampier had left England on the start of his journeyings in 1679, at a time when nothing had been published in English on Tasman except the cryptic Haelbos account. Although Dampier had the opportunity to modify his journal before its belated publication in 1697, six years after his return home, the signs are that this section was written before, or at least without knowledge of, the fuller account of Tasman's voyage published in 1694. There is a ring of truth about the laconic admission in Dampier's preface to the *New Voyage*: 'Nor have I given my self any great Trouble since my Return, to compare my Discoveries with those of others.'

The *Cygnet* sighted the Australian coast on 4 January 1688, and the next day anchored in a bay in latitude 16°50′S later named after the vessel—'a pretty deep Bay, with abundance of Islands in it, and a very good place to anchor in, or to hale ashoar'.[12] According to Dampier's book, the vessel remained there until 12 March. However, a shorter manuscript account of the voyage in the British Library gives 12 February as the departure date, and if this is correct then the visit was much briefer than is generally thought.[13] Even so, it represents the longest known stay yet by Europeans on the Australian mainland. Tasman's visit to Van Diemen's Land, by contrast, had lasted only three days, and he himself had not gone ashore.

Dampier's description of the area around Cygnet Bay was curt and unenthusiastic—dry, sandy soil; no surface water; some thin grass and stunted trees; little animal or bird life. If the place was unattractive its human inhabitants were still less alluring, and Dampier's published description of the Aborigines was to live long in the European memory. Naked, black, without covering or habitations,

4.5 Thomas Murray William Dampier 1698

The Inhabitants of this Country are the miserablest People in the World ... setting aside their Humane Shape, they differ but little from Brutes. They are tall, strait-bodied, and thin, with small long Limbs. They have great Heads, round Foreheads, and great Brows. Their Eyelids are always half closed, to keep the Flies out of their Eyes ... They have great Bottle-Noses, pretty full Lips, and wide Mouths ... They are long-visaged, and of a very unpleasing Aspect, having no one graceful Feature in their Faces. Their Hair is black, short and curl'd, like that of the Negroes; and not long and lank like the Common Indians. The Colour of their Skins, both of their Faces and the rest of their Body, is Coal-black, like that of the Negroes of Guinea.[14]

They had no metal or implements; their only weapons were wooden swords and spears. They grew no crops, trapped nothing, and seemed to exist on the small fish left stranded at low tide. Their speech was guttural and unintelligible. Their first reaction to the intruders was a distant shaking of their wooden weapons, but the beating of a drum was enough to frighten them off, and subsequent contacts were peaceful enough. A few Aborigines were taken on board the ship, though they showed no curiosity about their new surroundings. Others were pressed into service carrying water casks—'But all the signs we could make were to no purpose, for they stood like Statues, without motion, but grinn'd like so many Monkeys, staring one upon another'.[15] As the *Cygnet* sailed away Dampier took with him an impression (summarized in a note among Hans Sloane's papers) of 'a Sad Country and miserable Inhabitants'.[16] It was an impression which was to be transmitted to generations of readers, for by the standards of the time Dampier's *New Voyage* became a best-seller. For this reason, if no other, it is of more than academic interest that Dampier's description of the Aborigines in his manuscript account, if shorter, was also more dispassionate, and with a significant difference on a point which has puzzled later investigators: the nature of their hair. 'They are people of good stature but very thin and leane I judge for want of food[;] they are black yett I belive their haires would be long, if it was comed out but for want of Combs it is matted up like a negroes haire.' He went on to describe how they moved from place to place, 'for they are not troubled with household goods nor cloaths ... '.[17]

It was the longer version which was to be printed, and become standard, for by 1699 the *New Voyage* was in its fourth edition, by 1717 in its sixth. The year 1729 saw a collective reprint of all Dampier's travel volumes, and individual reprints and abridgements were included in most of the numerous collections of voyages and travels during the century. Herman Moll's accompanying maps made the outline of New Holland familiar in England for the first time, and they also—consciously or otherwise—reflect Dampier's geographical notions at this time. Both on the 'A New Map of the Whole World' (4.9) and on the larger-scale 'Map of the East Indies' (4.6) there is a hint of continental rather than insular dimensions about the representation of New Holland, and indeed on the latter map the identification is made—'New Holland or Terra Australis Incognita'. The further question of whether New Holland and New Guinea were joined was left unanswered: a gap in the region of Torres Strait is shown on one

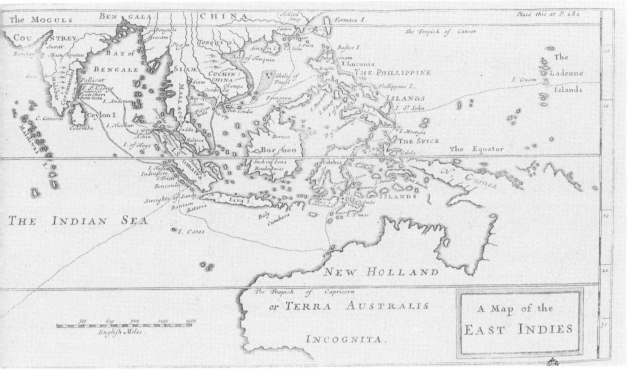

4.6   Herman Moll   'A Map of the East Indies'   1697

map, a continuous coast on the other. And although 'Dimens Land' appears faintly on the world map, the full message of Tasman's discoveries was blurred.

All this has a bearing on Dampier's second voyage to the region in 1699. The *New Voyage* appeared in 1697, and seems to have drawn the attention of ministers to Dampier's knowledge of regions now attracting official interest. In 1697 and 1698 Dampier made several appearances before the Council of Trade and Plantations to provide information on various parts of the world, and at about this time he was also in touch with the First Lord of the Admiralty,[18] the Earl of Orford. A series of letters from Dampier to Orford shows the genesis of the naval discovery expedition (a rarity in itself) which left England in 1699, and whose fortunes were recounted by Dampier in his *Voyage to New Holland*, published in two volumes in 1703 and 1709. Although both government and merchants were taking an increasing interest in the South Sea, attention was directed towards settled coasts and known trade rather than to trackless oceans and undiscovered lands. It was restricted, not to put too fine a point on it, to the waters which lapped the shores of Chile, Peru and Mexico.[19] There is no hint that Dampier's voyage represented any serious thrust of national policy, and one of his letters to Orford makes it clear that the choice of area to be explored was Dampier's rather than the Admiralty's:

Your Ldship has been pleased to order me to make a proposal of some voyage wherein I might be serviceable to my Nation. I know there are several places which might probably be visited with good Advantage: but as there is no larger Tract of Land hitherto undiscovered yn ye *Terra Australia* (if that vast space surrounding ye South Pole, and extend so far into ye warmer Climate be a continued Land, as a great deal of it is known to be) so 'tis reasonable to conceive yt so great a part of the World is not without very valuable commodities to incourage ye Discovery ...[20]

Circumstantial evidence suggests that at this time Dampier was in contact with Thomas Bowrey, a merchant with many years experience in the East Indies, who after his return to England in 1688 became an indefatigable promoter of schemes for South Seas enterprises.[21] Dampier first met Bowrey in 1688 in Achin a few months after his visit to New Holland. Bowrey was 'extraordinary kind' to Dampier, who was just recovering from illness, and at one stage hoped to take him to Persia. Even after Dampier declined the offer Bowrey gave him money, and 'treated me always with Wine and good Cheer'.[22] When Bowrey returned to England he took with him a collection of manuscript maps (now in the British Library), one of which (4.7) is a copy of a Dutch map showing Tasman's voyages of 1642–3 and 1644.[23] Apart from its obvious importance as a representation of Dutch explorations, it has a clear link with the English explorations of this period, for a copy of the map seems to have been taken by Dampier on his second voyage to New Holland—'Mr. Tasman's Draught', as he termed it. The correlation of place-names (many inaccurately translated or transcribed from the Dutch) as given on the map and in Dampier's published account, and the knowledge Dampier showed of Tasman's soundings on the north-west coast of Australia (also marked on the map) point firmly to this conclusion. How influential Bowrey might have been in the formulation of Dampier's plans is a matter for speculation, but the possibility is an intriguing one.

Although Dampier's letter to Orford laid heavy stress on Terra Australis, further letters as the preparations for the voyage slowly proceeded shifted the emphasis. In a note about possible routes, Dampier thought that he should sail straight from Madagascar

to the northernmost part of *New Holland* where I would water if I had occasion, and from thence I would range towards *New Guinnia*. There are many Islands in that sea between *New Holland* and *New Guinnia* which are not frequented by any Europeans, and it is probable that we may light upon some or other that are not without *Spice*; should I meet with nothing on any of these Islands I would range along the Main of New Guinia to see what that aforded; and from thence I would cross over to the East side of the *Island Gilolo* ... [then] range away to the Eastward of New Guinia and so direct my course southerly coasting by the land, and where I found a harbour or river I would land ...[24]

The stress here is on islands, preferably unexploited spice islands, rather than on the continent. Only after touching at these would Dampier bend his course around New Guinea and head south for unknown coasts. This westerly approach was for Dampier second-best, for another letter in the series reveals that originally

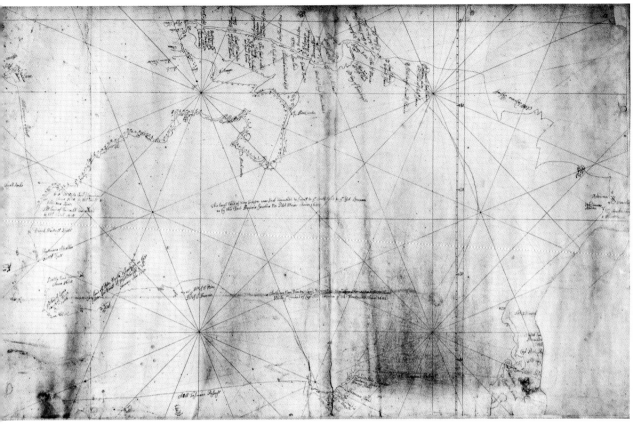

4.7   Thomas Bowrey   Copy of a chart of Tasman's discoveries and those of other Dutch
navigators   *c.* 1688

he had hoped to leave England in the early autumn (of 1698) so that he could
enter the Pacific by way of a summer rounding of Cape Horn, and then sail
between latitudes 35°S and 40°S to the east coast of Terra Australis before
turning north to New Guinea. This was in line with the suggestion he had made
in his *New Voyage* that the Cape Horn route was the 'easie way' to that 'vast
Tract of Terra Australis which bounds the South-Sea', and of which he thought
the 'long Tract of pretty high Land' allegedly sighted by his old captain, Davis,
five hundred leagues off the coast of Chile, might be part.[25] As it was, the loss of
the season forced his instructions, self-composed, to specify the Cape of Good
Hope route, 'and from thence to stretch away towards New Holland, and then to
New Guinea and Terra Australis'. He was to make careful observations, collect
specimens, and bring back 'some of the Natives, provided they shall be willing to
come along'.[26]

    To construct any systematic geography from these musings is not easy—
and indeed it is doubtful whether Dampier if allowed to explain himself in full

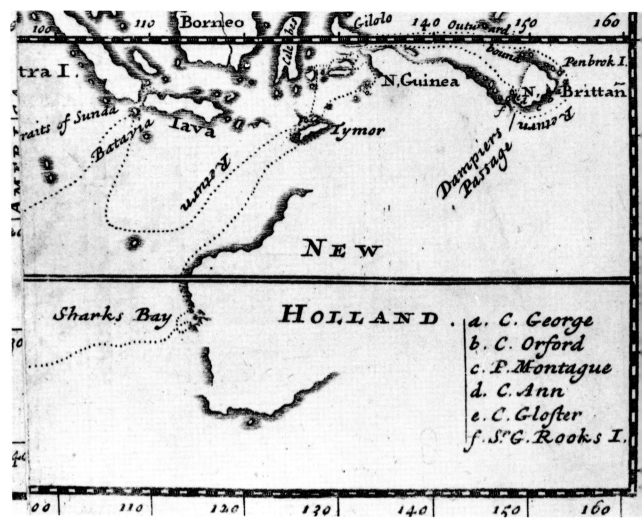

4.8   Herman Moll   section from his 'Capt. Dampier's New Voyage to New Holland &c in 1699'
1729

would have been totally consistent in his thinking. The reference in his first
letter to the possibility of 'a continued land' from the South Pole into warmer
latitudes seems to envisage a land mass separate from New Holland, though
perhaps approaching New Guinea fairly closely from the east, as New Holland
did from the west (4.8). It is possible to reconcile such speculation with Tasman's
discoveries on the assumption—which became a favoured one in the eighteenth
century—that the stretch of the New Zealand coast reached by Tasman was the
edge of the great southern continent, Terra Australis, and that he had sailed
north from there to New Guinea with the unknown east coast of New Holland
lying somewhere to port, and the equally unknown shoreline of the southern
continent to starboard. Whatever interpretation is favoured, one thing is clear:
Dampier saw New Holland as an obstacle, a barrier concealing more promising
lands to the east—hence the original plan for an approach from Cape Horn.

To look for precision of thought and expression from Dampier on this

128

matter is unrealistic: he had neither the evidence nor the methodology of the modern scholar at his disposal. His letters to Orford may have concealed as much as they revealed—a trading venture to islands just outside the Dutch sphere was possibly more appealing than a risky voyage to totally unknown shores, especially since despite his request for two vessels he had been given only one, the 290-ton *Roebuck,* and that with a crew of only 50 instead of the 70 he had wanted. The order in which he mentioned his objectives in an undated letter to Orford is perhaps significant: 'ye remoter part of the *East India Islands* and the neighbouring Coast of *Terra Australis'.*[27] Certainly Dampier, despite the modest fame which had come his way since the publication of the *New Voyage,* would have hoped for some financial gain from the undertaking over and above the £100 advanced him by the Admiralty 'upon my mencioning the Lowness of my present circumstances'.[28]

In the event, the voyage was a troubled and contentious one, and Dampier faced court-martial on his return. Not surprisingly, he threw little fresh light on the main geographical problems of the south Pacific. The *Roebuck* reached Australian waters in August 1699 and anchored in the bay visited by Dirk Hartog in 1616 and by Willem de Vlamingh only two years before. Situated in latitude 25°20'S, longitude 113°30'E, it is still known by Dampier's name of Shark's (now Shark) Bay (4.10). A week's search failed to find water, so Dampier sailed north as far as North West Cape, and then followed the coast around. In latitude 20°21'S he was running along a chain of islands (since named Dampier Archipelago) which he suspected might extend right back to Shark Bay. Like many seamen, he was predisposed to sense straits and passages through almost any coastline: 'by the great Tides I met with a while afterwards, more to the N.East, I had a strong Suspicion that here might be a kind of Archipelago of Islands, and Passage possible to the S.of N.Holland and N.Guinea into the great S.Sea Eastward; which I had thoughts also of attempting in my Return from N.Guinea ...'.[29] Tasman's chart on board showed, on the contrary, 'a firm, continued Land', but Dampier suspected from his soundings that Tasman had not approached the coast as closely in 1644 as his marked track indicated.[30] A few years later, the Dutch expedition of Marten van Delft in 1705 to Van Diemen's Gulf reached similar conclusions to Dampier's in that it noted of one opening that 'it was supposed by our people, that this inlet runs right through to the south side of New Holland, and not only this, but also others both east and west . From this it seems to follow, that the South Land in a great measure consists of islands'.[31]

Still looking for water, Dampier continued in a generally north-east direction, standing on and off from the shore. At the end of August he landed again, near latitude 18°S at Roebuck Bay, where digging produced some water, but so brackish that it was fit only for boiling oatmeal. Inland, all that could be seen were sand hills and some coarse grass. In a running skirmish with a dozen

Aborigines one was shot and wounded according to Dampier's account, while a seaman was struck in the face by a wooden spear which at first was thought to be poisoned. In Dampier's version there is little doubt but that the Aborigines were the aggressors—'menacing and threatning of us', 'coming on afresh with a great Noise'—and that he was forced, reluctantly, to open fire.[32] The journal of the *Roebuck*'s master, Jacob Hughes, gives an account—presumably at second-hand since normally he seems to have remained on the vessel during the shore excursions—which differs enough in emphasis for it to be worth giving here:

our Capt. endeavoured to speake with them but could not they being so very shy. Att last coming pritty nigh them one of our men Alexander Beale ran att them and came up with one who flung at him a stone, and having in his hand a wooden Lance he pusht heartily at hime so that he ran it through his Chin, when the saide Beale saw that he struck at him with his Cutlace cleaving one part of his head. The Blacks running to the others assistance our Capt. being by shott att one of them so that he fell down ...[33]

The encounter was too brief for Dampier to add anything to his earlier description. He thought that they were the same sort of people as he had met in 1688, with 'the most unplesant Looks and the worst Features of any people that ever I saw ... much the same blinking Creatures (here being also abundance of the same kind of Flesh-flies teizing them) and with the same black Skins, and Hair frizled, tall and thin, &c. as those were'. At this point, with scurvy affecting some of his crew, and with little hope of finding water or food, Dampier bore away for Timor after one final attempt to make his 1688 landfall had been thwarted by shoals.[34]

As he resumed his narrative in the *Continuation* published in 1709, Dampier retraced in some detail his thinking at this time. His coasting the shores of New Holland had been simply in search of refreshment—an optimistic plan given the barrenness of the region noted both by the Dutch and by himself on his earlier voyage:

for the further Discoveries I purposed to attempt on the *Terra Australis*. This large and hitherto almost unknown Tract of Land is situated so very advantageously in the richest Climates of the World, the *Torrid* and *Temperate* Zones; having in it especially all the Advantages of the Torrid Zone, as being known to reach from the *Equator* it self (within a Degree) to the *Tropick* of *Capricorn*, and beyond it; that in coasting round it, which I design'd by this Voyage, if possible: I could not but hope to meet with some fruitful Lands, Continent or Islands, or both ...[35]

Dampier made it clear that once on the west coast of New Holland he preferred a north-about approach to the alternative, which was to 'coast it to the Southward, and that way try to get round to the East of New Holland and New Guinea'. The likelihood of severe weather and intense cold, lack of enthusiasm among the crew—'heartless enough to the voyage at best'—and suspicion that far southerly latitudes would contain little of value, were produced as reasons for the northern track. All this seems an over-elaborate explanation (perhaps in response to some criticism, now lost to sight, of his lack of continental discoveries) of a course which was predicted by Dampier before the voyage began. His observations on

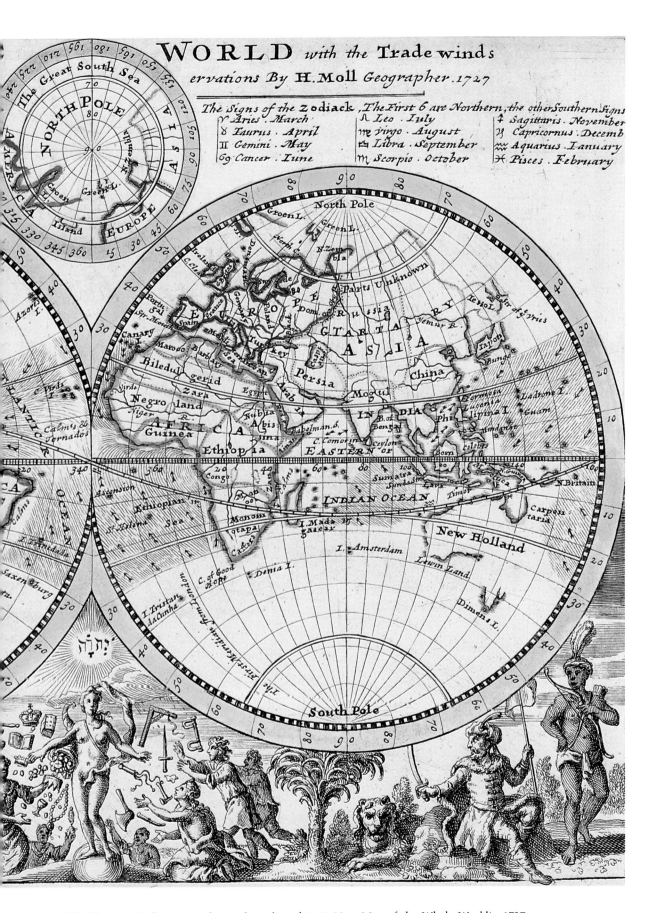

4.9 Herman Moll eastern hemisphere from his 'A New Map of the Whole World' 1727

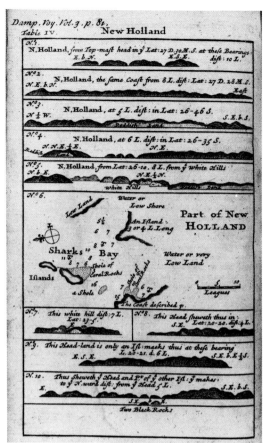

4.10 [Anonymous] Map of Shark Bay 1699

4.11 [Anonymous] Birds 1729

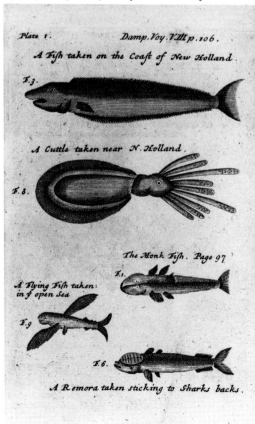

4.12 [Anonymous] Fish 1729

4.13 [Anonymous] Flora 1729

what he thought was the broken nature of the north-west coast had given him another reason for a clockwise course, for he pinned hopes on discovering a strait which would provide a short passage back from the seas to the east once he had rounded New Guinea. In the event, the onset of easterly winds, and damage to his pinnace, prompted Dampier to turn for home once he had discovered New Britain—a decision fully justified when the rotting *Roebuck* sank at Ascension Island. In the shipwreck many of Dampier's papers were lost, but among those which survived were illustrations of flora and fauna (4.11, 4.12, 4.13), from New Holland and elsewhere, and some coastal profiles, all done by 'a Person skill'd in Drawing' (as Dampier rather kindly described the unknown and untalented artist). Dampier also managed to save some plant specimens, which he presented to the geologist and physician Dr John Woodward, and a few of which still survive.[36]

For the English reading public, from the geographer or merchant to the casual browser, Dampier's main contribution on his two voyages was to make the western shoreline of New Holland a real, if unattractive, place rather than a wavering line on the map. He added little to the Dutch discoveries, but his published descriptions of the scrubby coastal area and its inhabitants, the drawings of its flora and fauna, and Moll's maps (4.8, 4.9), gave solidity to what had been a phantom presence. So vivid were Dampier's word-pictures of the Aborigines of the west and north-west coasts, 'the miserablest People in the World', and what the West Countryman saw as their arid, fly-blown habitat, that seventy years later and a continent's span away Cook and Banks looked at the Aborigines of Botany Bay through his eyes.

On the major geographical issues little progress had been made.[37] Seen through Dampier's eyes New Holland and Terra Australis resemble a case of intermittent double vision. Sometimes they blur into one, at other times they are separate and distinct. By the time of the second voyage, and with Bowrey's map of Tasman's discoveries on board, Dampier had accepted the fact of the insularity of New Holland; and indeed his inclination was to press further in that direction and to regard New Holland as at least two large islands. That Dampier had been reading accounts of earlier voyages to the area can be seen in a brief and cryptic statement made as he turned between Timor and Java on the homeward voyage in an attempt to find the Trial Rocks, 'which Discovery (when ever made) will be of great use to Merchants trading to these Parts'.[38] The reference is to the disaster of 1622, when the *Trial* was wrecked on reefs off the Monte Bello Islands on the north-west coast of Australia. What value such a discovery might be—apart from identifying a danger spot—is unclear, but the detour says something for Dampier's continuing interest in the region. His most important discovery on the second voyage was New Britain, and it was towards that island that he pointed his mercantile readers, 'since it is very probable that this Island may afford as many rich Commodities as any in the World'.[39]

PROJECTS AND FANTASIES

Dampier made further voyages before his death in 1715, but none in the employ of the Admiralty, and none in the direction of New Holland. There was, however, to be a curious if fruitless sequel to Dampier's association with Australia in the shape of proposals put forward for the discovery of 'Terra Australis Incognita' by his former crew-member, John Welbe. The story is a tangled one, which has to be teased out of scattered documents from the period, and much of it remains obscure. Welbe sailed in the *St George* with Dampier on his disastrous privateering venture of 1703–6. The vessel entered the Pacific by way of Cape Horn, and then followed a zig-zag route to Juan Fernandez, the coasts of Chile and Peru, the Galapagos Islands, the Panama Isthmus, and Mexico. Here a mutiny led by the mate William Funnell, Welbe, and the owner's representative Edward Morgan split the expedition into two separate parties. Of Morgan, one of Dampier's biographers has written: '[he] is a mysterious person ... he [gave] up buccaneering to become a thief, a Roman Catholic, and some sort of police spy. At one point in his murky career he was accused of smuggling French prisoners of war out of the country. There is reason to suppose that he was Dampier's evil genius on the unlucky voyage ...'.[40] The mutineers, as Dampier termed them, sailed off on a small barque, reached Amboina, and a Dutch prison, and made their way back to England in 1706. Dampier returned home more than a year later, and participated in the war of words which had broken out between the two sides. Welbe contributed to this in the form of a pamphlet entitled *Answer to Capt. Dampier's Vindication*, published in 1707.

That same year Welbe left England for Denmark, where he urged on the Danish court a discovery of the spice islands. Because of the outbreak of war this scheme came to nothing, and in 1713 Welbe returned home, bearing testimonials from Danish officials that they found his proposals 'plausible'.[41] Welbe now sought to interest the British government in a fully-fledged 'Scheme of a Voyage Round the Globe for the Discovery of Terra Australis Incognita'. He asked for the command of two naval vessels, a fourth-rate and a brig, with which he planned to sail into the Pacific by way of the familiar buccaneer's route of Cape Horn, Chile, Juan Fernandez and Peru.

Thence take my departure and Stear west to the Solomons Islands, which are reported by the Spanyards to abound in Gold ... From the Solomons Islands I propose to sail west to the Coast of Nova Guinea, which is the East Side of Nova Hollandia in the East Indies and make a true discovery of that coast, and search what the Country abounds in, it lying North and South as Peru does, and in the same lattd, I belive it abounds in Gold and Silver Mines (the Spanyards having found some there above 150 years ago) which if discovered and setled may be of vast advantage to great Britain.[42]

Welbe spent fourteen months being sent from pillar to post with his scheme, trying without success to interest the new monarch, George I, the South Sea Company, Secretaries of State Stanhope and Townshend, and the First Lord of the Treasury Robert Walpole. In a letter to the latter Welbe evidently hoped to strike a sympathetic chord by claiming to 'have studied Chymistry, and the Natur of Gold and Silver Mines, the want of which Qualifications, rendred the Discoverys of Capt Dampire of little or no efect, and retarded a farther Search of those Countrys'.[43] By 1716, having failed to enlist direct government support for his project, Welbe turned to other means, and outlined the prospectus for a new company, the London Adventurers, with a proposed joint stock of £2 500 000. The mines, he thought, would 'enrich the British Nation upwards of £50 000 000 sterling'.[44] Welbe's own circumstances went ill with so grandiose a prospectus, for at some time during 1716 he was committed to prison for a debt of £6. From gaol he sent pleading letters for support and money to Sir Hans Sloane, President of the Royal Society, accompanied by a recipe for 'an Anti-venerial Water', 'having expended', as he put it, 'my whole Substance to serve my Native Country'.[45]

Whether with help from Sloane or not, Welbe was discharged from prison, and next appears in 1719 as 'Master of a small ship in the River of Thames'.[46] He was still attempting to promote his discovery scheme, one of many being pushed in the feverish atmosphere of the South Sea Bubble months. Once more he found himself in prison—this time, according to his own account, for attempting to expose a marine insurance fraud organized by Edward Morgan. It was the 'Mr Edward Morgan a Roman Catholick liveing in Bloomsbury Square who was Round the Globe with Capt Dampire the same voyage that your Petitioner was . . . the said Morgan was afterwards the Ruin of the said Expedition and now endeavours to Ruin your Petitioner and thereby overthrow his Intended discovery'.[47] Once more, in or out of prison, Welbe bombarded ministers with details of his scheme—Townshend and Walpole again, the King, the Lords Commissioners of Trade and Plantations—all in the hope of being granted a charter. In May 1720 he went so far as to issue shares in his proposed company, and in December petitioned the Crown 'on behalf of himself and several Persons of distinction Merchants and others of the City of London touching the Establishing a Company by way of Charter for carrying on a Trade to Terra Australis'.[48] The easy optimism of his 1714–15 proposals had now veered perilously near total delusion as Welbe claimed (in his 1716 petition) that 'from the coast of Peru West to the East Indies is upwards of 2,500 Leagues, which to the south of the Line is undiscovered to any European, Captain Welbe excepted'.[49] His 1720 petition pursued the same assumptions of first-hand knowledge as he referred to his

proposed discoverys (viz) the Snt Georges Islands (so named by your Petitioner) which abound in Gold formerly Called the Solomons Islands being within and between the Equinoctial Line and the one and twentieth degree of South Latd about twelve hundred Leagues West from the Coast of Peru . . . and likewise New Wales so named by your Petitioner abounding with Gold and Silver Mines and several other adjacent Islands being farther west.[50]

A further petition to the King asserted 'that Columbus had nothing nigh the grounds to go upon as the said Captain hath who can plainly demonstrate the Situation of his intended discoveries which is an undoubted sign of his knowing the same'.[51]

At the end of 1720 Welbe's petition was referred to the Lords Commissioners of Trade and Plantations. Permission was sought to issue stock to the amount of £3 000 000, a sum dismissed by Welbe as insignificant compared with the riches which his discoveries would produce, and of which the Crown would retain one-fifth. With this wealth the government could maintain the balance of power in Europe, even pay off the National Debt.[52] When he wrenched himself away from this fantasy world Welbe was writing anxiously to the Lords Commissioners of Trade and Plantations about the efforts of his rivals 'to delude the people and extract their money by giving out shares, and all under a pretence of going on those discoverys',[53] and finally in July 1721 he gained an interview at the Board of Trade. After 'some discourse' with him the Lords Commissioners told Welbe that they could give him 'no encouragement as to the Charter desired'.[54] This final blow seems to have scattered what wits and fortune Welbe had left, and by 1722 he was once more writing from a debtors' prison, the King's Bench. His file in the Treasury Papers comes to an end with letters containing mingled appeals and threats of an increasingly distraught character. A letter to a legal adversary concluded with the archaic offer, 'What does you think of a fiery Tryall'.[55] His last known letter, of August 1722, appealed to Townshend for help, and offered him 'a Treatise of Philosophy proving the possibility of Regeneration and Transmutation called the Philosophers Stone which I wrott since my confinement in the Kings Bench to show what pains I have taken to qualify my self to serve my native country'.[56]

The frustrated and increasingly manic Welbe is more striking as a psychiatric case than as a potential explorer. His scheme itself, possibly like Dampier's of 1698–9, had more to do with gold, spices and shares than with geographical discovery. The quest for the islands of gold which had drawn the Spaniards was more evident than the definition of mainland coasts, known or unknown.[57] Since, despite his claims, he had never been near the regions of his projected discovery, Welbe clearly owed something to Dampier's writings, and perhaps something to his conversations on the *St George*. Certainly the insistence on sailing west across the Pacific from the South American coast towards the unknown southern lands reflected Dampier's strong preference. It is not without significance that during the closing stages of this particular saga Dampier's other old shipmate, Edward Morgan, was also pushing his own, rival scheme for a chartered company. These dimly-glimpsed manoeuvres and intrigues probably owed more to stock manipulation than to genuine commitment to overseas discovery, and in this they resembled the much greater schemes swirling around the South Sea Company in the same period.

The debacle of the South Sea Bubble had a chastening effect on government, promoters and investors alike. Defoe, in one of his last works, noted the change in attitude:

As for new Colonies and Conquests, how do we seem entirely to give over, even the Thoughts of them ... as if we had done our utmost, were fully satisfied with what we have, that the enterprising Genius was buried with the old Discoverers, and there was neither Room in the World nor Inclination in our People to look any farther.[58]

The South Pacific dropped out of reckoning as a sphere of activity for the English for more than a generation, and meanwhile it was safe for novelists, fantasists and satirists to continue pitching their stories in its unknown vastnesses. The geographical setting of Henry Neville's *The Isle of Pines: Or a late discovery of a fourth Island, in Terra Australis Incognita*, first published in 1688 and reprinted exactly one hundred years later as Cook set sail on his first voyage, was in the southern ocean somewhere between the Cape of Good Hope and the East Indies. The island's name was not a reference to trees but to the fictitious narrator, George Pine, shipwrecked there, and more specifically to his progeny; for the result of his stranding on the island with four women was that he fathered forty-seven children, and by his death boasted 1789 descendants! The island was a Utopia with heavy sexual overtones, but however benign its climate and lush its vegetation the handiwork of man was needed to control and improve nature. In a prefiguration of Cook and Phillip the author noted that the country would be a paradise, 'had it the culture that skilful people might bestow on it'.[59] Another work from the same period, Gabriel de Foigny's *La Terre Australe Connue*, appeared in English translation in 1693. It was fantasy based on fantasy, in so far as it was an extension and elaboration of the claims of Quirós: 'We found a Country much more Fertile and Populous than any in Europe; that the inhabitants were much Bigger and Taller than the Europeans; and that they lived much longer than they.' Logically and prophetically these splendid physical specimens, so superior to their European counterparts, were called, for the first time in English, 'Australians'.[60]

Both Defoe and Swift sent travellers to this region. Defoe took the title of his 1725 book, *A New Voyage Round the World*, straight from Dampier, although the anonymous narrator came across more exciting discoveries in southern waters than Dampier ever did—pearls, gold, fertile lands—certainly sufficient to justify Defoe's plea that Britain should colonize the area.[61] Closer to Dampier's disillusioning encounters with the Aborigines were Gulliver's experiences on the coast of New Holland. Of identifiable persons named in *Gulliver's Travels* 'My cousin Dampier' was the first, 'my worthy friend Mr Herman Moll' the last. Houyhnhnms Land was situated near the coast of New Holland (4.14), and when Gulliver escaped from it in 1715 he reached the mainland in two days in his crude canoe. 'The maps and charts placed this country at least three degrees more to the east than it really is', his account ran—a gloss on Dampier's note that the west coast of New Holland 'is less by 195 Leagues [from the Cape

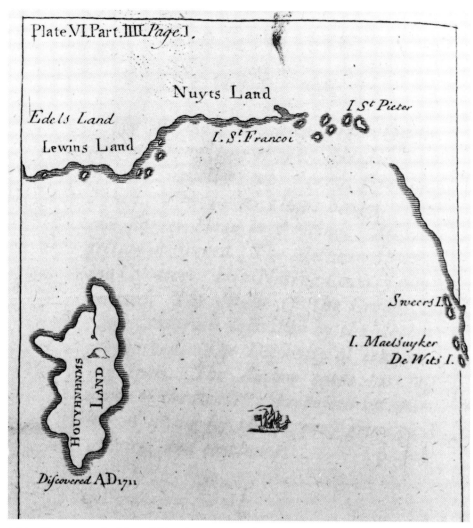

Plate VI. Part. IIII. *Page.*]

Nuyts Land

Edels Land

Lewins Land

I. St Francoi

I St Pieter

HOUYHNHNMS LAND

Sweers I.

I. Maelsuyker
De Wits I.

Discovered AD 1711

4.14   [Anonymous]   Map of Houyhnmns' Land   1726

of Good Hope] than is usually laid down in our common Draughts'. Gulliver's only meeting with the inhabitants was brief and hostile, and in Swift's account there is more than an echo of Dampier's brush with the Aborigines in 1699:

They were stark naked, men, women, and children, round a fire, as I could discover from the smoke. One of them spied me, and gave notice to the rest; five of them advanced towards me, leaving the women and children at the fire. I made what haste I could to the shore, and getting into my canoe, shoved off: the savages observing me retreat, ran after me; and before I could get far enough into the sea, discharged an arrow, which wounded me deeply on the inside of my left knee (I shall carry the mark to my grave). I apprehended the arrow might be poisoned, and paddling out of the reach of their darts (being a calm day) I made a shift to suck the wound, and dress it as well as I could.[62]

Except for the Dutch expedition to Carpentaria in 1756, there was no further European exploration of New Holland until Cook's landfall in 1770. What there was in this period, as chapter 1 explains, was a steady diffusion of existing knowledge, and an increase in speculation through maps and the printed

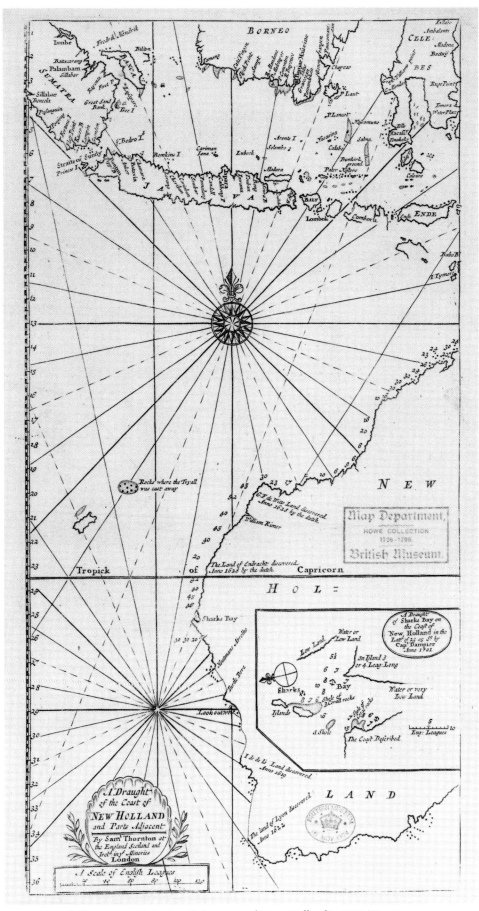

4.15   Samuel Thornton   'Draught of the coast of New Holland'   1703/40

word. In 1740, for example, Samuel Thornton's 1703 map of New Holland was re-issued (4.15). It is worth setting out what seemed the possibilities of discovery at the time Cook sailed. The framework of geographical knowledge remained the same as a century earlier, and was provided by the Dutch explorations, and particularly by the tracks of Tasman's two voyages. Within that framework something more than half of Australia's coastline had been sketched, though in places with a shaky hand. The outline of the Gulf of Carpentaria, and the coast to the west swinging first south and then back east to the Land of Pieter Nuyts, were marked. There was, though, no certainty as to whether this was a continuous shoreline or, as Dampier and some of the Dutch had suspected, one broken by straits. Away to the south-east was Van Diemen's Land, perhaps the southern extremity of New Holland, perhaps an island. Similarly, to the north, the question of whether New Guinea was part of New Holland had not found definite resolution. To the north-east the issue was whether the fashionable identification of Quirós's Espiritu Santo with the Australian mainland had any foundation save that of wishful thinking, for there had been no known European sighting of the east coast. In brief, the Australian problem was contained within a known compass; but inside the area bounded by Tasman's great sweep was more doubt than certainty.

COOK, BANKS AND NEW SOUTH WALES

In the new era of Pacific exploration which began in the 1760s, the definition of Australia had a low priority. The depressing image of New Holland cast a long shadow eastward, and the more exciting possibilities of an unknown southern continent, of which New Zealand perhaps formed the western tip, rather caught the attention. The arid reality of New Holland could not compete with excited speculation about lands unknown. As Dalrymple enthused: 'The number of inhabitants in the Southern Continent is probably more than 50 millions, considering the extent ... which in the latitude of 40 deg. amounts to 4596 geographic, or 5323 statute miles. This is a greater extent than the whole civilized part of ASIA, from TURKEY to the eastern extremity of CHINA.'[63] One will search in vain in the instructions of Byron, Wallis and Cook for any encouragement to venture within the sweep of Tasman's track, for the Lords of the Admiralty were rather exercised by the looming if shadowy presence of the southern continent. In Byron's orders of 1764 it is set in the Atlantic: 'Whereas there is reason to believe that Lands and Islands of great extent hitherto unvisited by any European Power may be found in the Atlantick Ocean between the Cape of Good Hope and the Magellanick Streight within Latitudes convenient for Navigation.'[64] Two years later Wallis was ordered to look for it in the Pacific: 'Whereas there is reason to believe that Lands or Islands of Great Extent, hitherto unvisited by any European Power may be found in the Southern Hemisphere between Cape Horn and New Zeeland.'[65] Neither voyage threw much light on the continent,

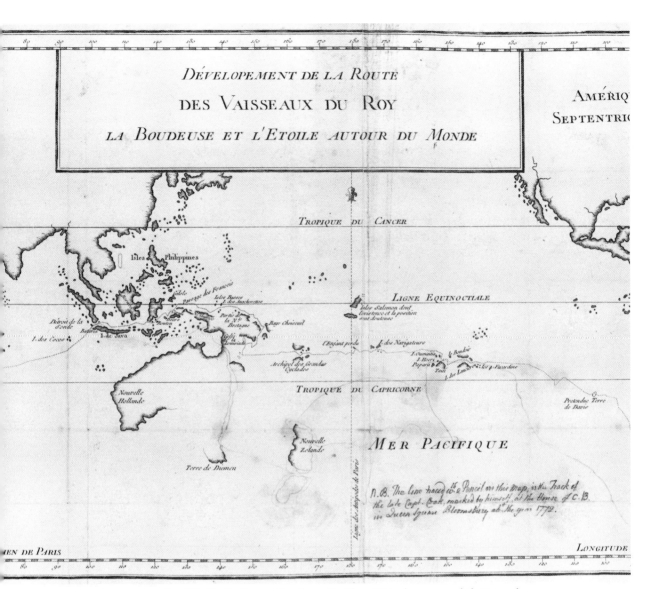

4.16 [Anonymous]   The Pacific Ocean after Bougainville   ('Développement de la Route des Vaisseaux du Roy')   1771

and Wallis's expedition rather introduced another element of error in the supposed sighting just south of Tahiti of 'the tops of several mountains the Extreems bearing from South to S.W. upwards of twenty Leag.^s'.[66] The instructions given to Lieutenant James Cook (4.18) in 1768, then, had a familiar ring with their information that 'there is reason to imagine that a Continent or Land of great extent, may be found to the Southward of the Tract lately made by Captn Wallis ... You are to proceed to the southward in order to make discovery of the Continent above-mentioned until you arrive in the Latitude of 40° ...'.[67] Of the explorers of this decade, only Bougainville was directed to investigate New Holland, and indeed his track took him to Espiritu Santo, islands not mainland, and from the New Hebrides (as Cook named them on his visit of 1774) he sailed west, only to be pushed away from the Queensland coast by warning signs of the Barrier Reef (4.16).[68]

By the time Bougainville had returned to France, Cook had already sailed. After Tahiti, if he found the southern continent, he was to survey and investigate it and 'with the Consent of the Natives to take possession of Convenient Situations in the Country in the Name of the King of Great Britain; or, if you find the Country uninhabited take Possession for His Majesty by setting up Proper Marks and Inscriptions, as first discoverers and possessors'. If he failed to find the continent, then his instructions were to explore New Zealand before sailing home 'either round the Cape of Good Hope, or Cape Horn, as from Circumstances you may judge the most eligible'. There was no reference to New Holland.[69]

By March 1770 Cook had completed his work at Tahiti, criss-crossed a large expanse of ocean as far as latitude 40°S in a vain search for the continent (4.17), and charted the New Zealand coastline. On the last day of the month, echoing the words of his instructions, Cook rehearsed in his journal the arguments concerning 'the most eligible way' home. The entry is worth quoting at length.

4.17   Sydney Parkinson   The *Endeavour* at Sea   1768–70

Capt. James Cook
of the Endeavour.

4.18   William Hodges   Captain James Cook   *? c.* 1775

143

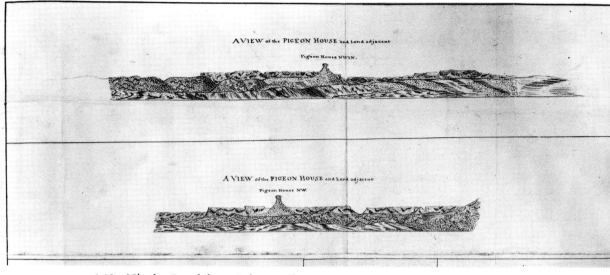

4.19 [Charles Praval from Sydney Parkinson or Herman Spöring], 'A View of the Pigeon House and land adjacent' 1770

To return by way of Cape Horn was what I most wish'd because by this rout we should have been able to prove the existence or non existence of a Southern Continent which yet remains doubtfull; but in order to ascertain this we must have kept in a high latitude in the very depth of winter but the condition of the ship in every respect was not thought sufficient for such an undertaking. For the same reason the thoughts of proceeding directly to the Cape of Good Hope was laid a side especialy as no discovery of any moment could be hoped for in that rout. It was therefore resolved to return by way of the East Indies by the following rout: upon leaving this coast to steer to the westward until we fall in with the East Coast of New Holland and than to follow the deriction of that Coast to the northward or what other direction it may take untill we arrive at its northern extremity, and if this should be found impractical than to endeavour to fall in with the lands or Islands discover'd by Quiros.[70]

Banks added in his journal, 'In doing this, although we hoped to make discoveries more interesting to trade at least than any we had yet made, we were obligd intirely to give up our first grand object, the Southern Continent; this for my own part I confess I could not do without much regret.'[71]

Without overwhelming enthusiasm, then, and moved by considerations of navigation rather than geography, the expedition headed westward for Van Diemen's Land, but narrowly missed sighting it. The first Australian landfall was of the mainland near Point Hicks (now Cape Everard), and the question of the insularity or otherwise of Van Diemen's Land was not to be settled for almost another thirty years. First glimpses of the mainland were reassuring: 'the face of the Country green and woody', as Cook noted; 'gentle sloping hills which had the appearance of the highest fertility', Banks wrote (cf. 5.4, 5.5).[72] It was Banks a few days later who came up with some imaginative phrases to describe this part of the New South Wales coast: 'The country tho in general well enough clothd appeard in some places bare; it resembled in my imagination the back of a lean Cow, coverd in general with long hair, but nevertheless where her scraggy hip bones have stuck out farther than they might accidental rubbs and knocks have intirely bard them of their share of covering.' (4.19)[73] As intriguing

144

4.20   [Joseph Banks ?]   Aborigines in canoes   1770

as the appearance of the landscape, clearly and hopefully different from the western shoreline of New Holland, were the distant sightings of the region's inhabitants. The preconceptions which came from reading Dampier were strong, especially for Banks, who wrote: 'we stood in with the land near enough to discern 5 people who appeard through our glasses to be enormously black: so far did the prejudices which we had built on Dampiers account influence us that we fancied we could see their Colour when we could scarce distinguish whether or not they were men'.[74] On 29 April the boats put ashore, at the spot soon to become celebrated as Botany Bay, where the first contact was made with the Aborigines, two of whom armed with spears and throwing-sticks seemed determined to resist the landing. It took the firing of several muskets loaded with small shot before they made off, and the Englishmen were able to investigate the half-dozen or so bark shelters, a huddle of frightened children, and a few canoes (4.20), 'the worst I think I ever saw', wrote Cook. Their 'lances' or 'darts' proved not to be smeared with poison, as Banks had suspected, and Cook thought they were 'more for strikeing fish than offensive weapons'.[75]

The following days brought further sightings of the Aborigines, and on occasion approaches to within twenty yards or so. Some half-hearted spear

4.21   George Stubbs   Kangaroo   *c.* 1771−2

throwing accompanied these encounters, but no serious violence (4.22). Banks's verdict was that the Aborigines were 'rank cowards'; Cook put a different interpretation on their distant gestures of defiance—'all they seem'd to want was for us to be gone'.[76] As Banks and Cook summed up their first impressions, both still had Dampier's comments in mind. Banks was careful to distinguish the Aborigines from Negroes: 'blacker than any we have seen in the Voyage tho by no means negroes . . . the hair of their heads was bushy and thick but by no means woolly like that of a Negro'.[77] Cook wrote that they 'were about as tall as Europeans, of a very dark brown colour but not black nor had they wooly frizzled hair, but black and lank like ours. No sort of clothing or ornaments were ever seen by any of us upon any one of them' (4.27).[78] Of the other logs kept on board only Pickersgill's struck an individual—though hardly original—note when he observed, 'The people have nothing to cover themselves, but go quite naked, men and women, and, in short, are the most wretched set I ever beheld or heard of.'[79]

The landing at Botany Bay (4.23, 5.6, 5.7) was significant in more than one respect. On 2 May a party including Cook and Banks made an inland 'excursion'. The country, Cook wrote, was 'deversified with woods, Lawns and Marshes; the woods are free from under wood of every kind and the trees are at such a distance from one a nother that the whole Country or at least great part of it might be cultivated without being oblig'd to cut down a single tree; we found the soil every where except on the Marshes to be a light, white sand and produceth a quant[it]y of good grass'.[80] Banks's reaction was less favourable: 'The Soil wherever we saw it consisted of either swamps or light sandy soil on which grew very few species of trees . . . but every place was coverd with vast quantities of grass.'[81] It was Cook's entry, rendered even more enthusiastically by Hawkesworth's pen, which appeared in print three years later.[82] The next descriptions of the two observers differed more significantly. Cook, accompanied by Solander and Monkhouse, went to the head of the bay where, he wrote, 'We found the face of the Country much the same as I have before described but the land much richer, for instead of sand I found in many places a deep black Soil which we thought was capable of produceing any kind of grain, at present it produceth besides timber as fine meadow as ever was seen.'[83] Banks, busy collecting plants, was not with Cook on this occasion, and when he went ashore the next day on the north-west side of the bay he gained rather a different impression: 'we went a good way into the countrey which in this place is very sandy and resembles something our Moors in England, as no trees grow upon it but everything is coverd with a thin brush of plants about as high as the knees'.[84] This entry found no place in Hawkesworth, where the map of the bay showed a tree-dotted, parklike landscape (4.23). Even the name added to the attraction, and it was perhaps not without significance to the future history of this spot that the first, rather unalluring name in Cook's journal of 'Sting ray's

Plate XXV.

S. Parkinson del. T. Chambers S.

Two of the Natives of New Holland, Advancing to Combat.

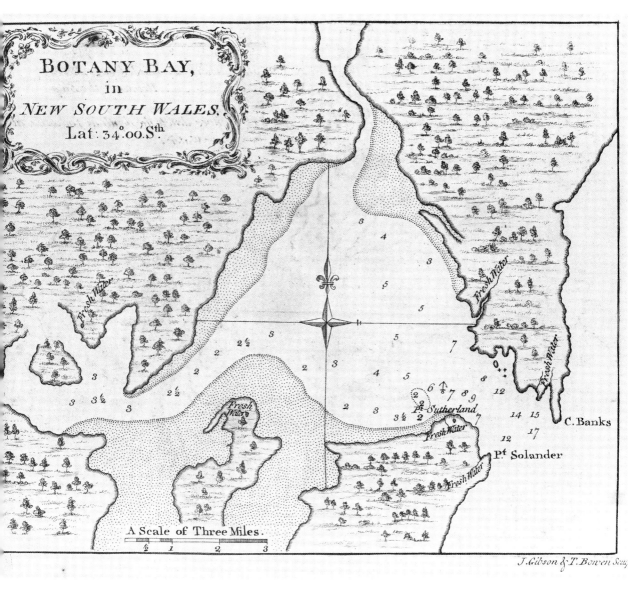

4.23   Engraved after James Cook/Isaac Smith, Map of Botany Bay   1770/3

4.22   Engraved by Thomas Chambers after Sydney Parkinson, 'Two of the Natives of
New Holland, Advancing to Combat' 1770/3

harbour' underwent successive modifications through 'Botanist Harbour', 'Botanist Bay', to the final, definitive 'Botany Bay'.[85]

From Botany Bay Cook took the *Endeavour* north, passing without investigation Port Jackson, and missing altogether Newcastle harbour. Both Cook and Banks continued to be impressed by the nature of the country they could see from the ship: 'it is diversified with an agreable variety of hils ridges Vallies and large planes all cloathed with wood' (Cook); 'well wooded and looked beautiful as well as fertile' (Banks).[86] However, as the ship kept north the coast became rugged and barren, and at Bustard Bay Cook reported that 'The Country is vissibly worse than at the last place we were at, the Soil is dry and sandy'.[87] At Thirsty Sound the expedition failed, for the first time, to find water, and Cook noted, 'No signs of fertility to be seen upon the land'.[88] Throughout the latter part of May and into June the ship kept north along the Queensland coast (5.1), without incident until the night of 11 June when in latitude 16°S low-lying islands or rocks were sighted ahead, and the *Endeavour* hauled away from shore in a northeasterly direction. 'My intention', explained Cook, 'was to stretch off all night as well to avoid the dangers we saw ahead as to see if any Islands lay in the offing, especialy as we now begin to draw near the Latitude of those discover'd by Quiros which some Geographers, for what reason I know not have found proper to tack to this land.'[89] Quirós and his discoveries were soon forgotten, for just before 11 p.m. the *Endeavour* struck on the reef now named after her. The story of the striking, the floating off of the vessel, and the desperate attempts to stop the leak will not be retold here. It was a chilling illustration of the danger of carrying out exploration in a single vessel. As Banks pointed out, if the *Endeavour* had gone down, any survivors would have been 'debarred from a hope of ever again seeing their native countrey or conversing with any but the most uncivilized savages perhaps in the world'.[90] Once off the reef, and with the leak temporarily muffled, the damaged vessel made for the nearby mainland, and found harbour on the south shore of the Endeavour River (4.24), the site of today's Cooktown. Here the expedition stayed for six weeks, while the *Endeavour* was repaired (4.25).

On shore glimpses were caught of strange, leaping animals, and finally one was shot (and eaten). Banks wrote that, 'To compare it with any European animal would be impossible as it has not the least resemblance of any one I have seen. Its forelegs are extreemly short and of no use to it in walking, its hind again as disproportionately long; with these it hops 7 or 8 feet at each hop.'[91] It was given what seemed to be the natives' name for it, 'Kanguru' (4.21, 4.26). The Aborigines themselves were at first as elusive as at Botany Bay, and Banks grumbled at their 'unaccountable timidity'. Then came the first real contacts, with the 'Indians' introducing themselves by name, and visiting the ship. Banks now wrote that they 'became our very good friends'; Cook noted more cautiously that they 'came to us without shewing the least signs of fear'.[92] But the women

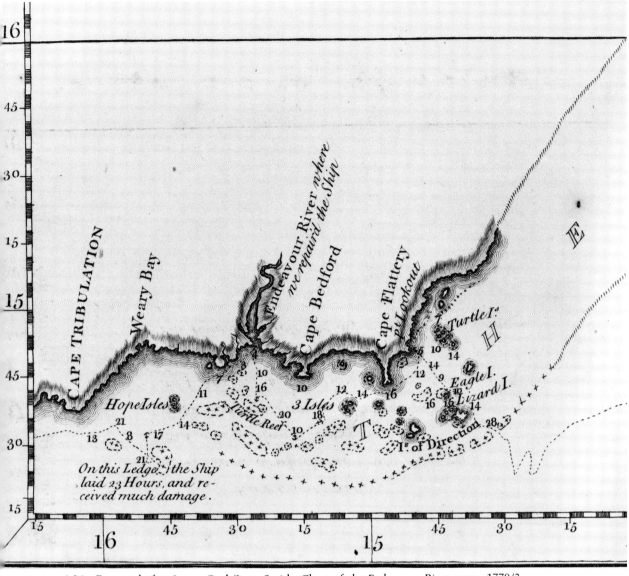

On this Ledge the Ship laid 23 Hours, and received much damage.

4.24 Engraved after James Cook/Isaac Smith, Chart of the Endeavour River area 1770/3

4.25 Engraved probably after Sydney Parkinson, 'The *Endeavour* being careened' 1770/3

4.26 Sydney Parkinson Kangaroo 1770

kept well away, and in mid-July an incident occurred which showed the fragility of the relationship. A refusal to allow the Aborigines to take away turtles which were lying on the deck of the *Endeavour* led to a fine display of temper by the visitors and some pushing and shoving. When the Aborigines paddled ashore they lit grass fires which threatened to engulf fishing nets, washing and a tent, and retreated only when Cook fired small shot at them. One man was hit, but after a while the rest returned, 'making signs as they came along that they would not set fire to the grass again and. we distributing musket balls among them and by our signs explaining their effect'.[93]

Although relations seemed to have been repaired after all the excitement, this was apparently the last occasion on which the Aborigines ventured near the ship. Occasional encounters away from the beach, fires in the hills at night, and empty huts or canoes, became the only entries in the journals about the Aborigines. Characteristic was the note of disillusionment in a journal entry by Banks: 'In Botanizing today on the other side of the river we accidentaly found

4.27   Sydney Parkinson   Aborigines, canoes, huts   1770

the greatest part of the clothes which had been given to the Indians left all in a heap together, doubtless as lumber not worth carriage'.[94] This lack of interest in their gifts was a matter of continuing bafflement. In a way it was welcome relief from the never-ending demands elsewhere for iron, clothes, firearms, trinkets; on the other hand, to find their accoutrements treated with disdain clearly produced feelings of unease and bewilderment among the crew.

On 3 August the *Endeavour* was warped from her mooring to face once more the offshore reefs and islands, until Cook reluctantly decided 'to quit this coast unexplored to its No[r]thern extremity which I think we were not far off, for I firmly believe it doth not join to *New Guinea*'.[95] Mention of this point of geography evidently jogged Cook's memory on another matter in dispute, for later in the same entry he reverted to Quirós:

I had forgot to mention in its proper place that not only on these Islands but in sever¹ places on the Sea beach in and about Endeavour River we found Bamboos, Cocoa-nutts, the Seeds of Plants, and Pummick Stones which were not the produce of this Country from all the discoveries we have been able to make in it. It is reasonable to suppose that they are the produce of some Country lying to the Eastward and brought here by the Easterly Trade winds. The Islands discover'd by *Quiros* call'd by him Astralia del Espiritu Santo lays in this parallel but how far to the East is hard to say, most charts place them as far to the west as this Country, but we are morally certain that he never was upon any part of this coast.[96]

Another fearsome encounter with the Great Barrier Reef led to a change of mind by Cook and a change of course for the *Endeavour*; for he now decided ('let the concequence be what it will') to keep close to the mainland in order to determine whether it was joined to New Guinea.[97]

On the morning of 21 August (nautical time) Cook reached, and named, Cape York, and before sunset went ashore to take possession in the name of George III of the east coast of Australia from his landfall of latitude 38°S to this spot (5.1). He made no attempt, more than one critic has pointed out, to follow his orders to gain 'the Consent of the Natives' for this act of possession.[98] It must be said that Cook had long since discarded this part of his instructions, even in regions where finding, and communicating with, the native inhabitants were easier than at Cape York. Earlier in the year he had taken possession of Queen Charlotte Sound in New Zealand without reference to its inhabitants— unless the handing to an old man present at the ceremony of an empty wine bottle once the toasts had been drunk can be taken as evidence of negotiation.[99] As he sailed north-west from Cape York into the Endeavour Strait, Cook became convinced that there was 'an open Sea to the westward, which gave me no small satisfaction not only because the dangers and fatigues of the Voyage was drawing near to an end, but by being able to prove that New-Holland and New-Guinea are two Seperate Lands or Islands, which until this day hath been a doubtfull point with Geographers'.[100] With Torres Strait opening before him, the way was clear for a run to Batavia before the north-west monsoon set in. The alternative would have been a semi-circular detour 'backwards' around New Guinea, an unwelcome prospect as the expedition moved into the third year of the voyage. The mystery of Quirós's Espiritu Santo (1.7), already half-solved by Bougainville (4.16), would have to wait. When, four years later, Cook on his second voyage reached the New Hebrides, he paid tribute to his Spanish predecessor: 'The Northern islands of this Archipelago were first discovered by that great Navigator Quiros in 1606, and not without reason supposed to be a part of the Southern Continent.'[101] His second lieutenant, Charles Clerke, was less complimentary, referring to Quirós's 'most pompous description of this Country ... Mr Quiros's zeal and warmth for his own favourite projects has carried him too far in the qualities he has attributed to this Country'.[102]

As the *Endeavour* finally left the Australian coast Cook and Banks composed their customary descriptions of the land, its products and its inhabitants. Cook made some perceptive comments on the Aborigines, and showed more ability than most to relate their lifestyle to their environment. He concluded his observations with a passage which stood as a direct challenge to the earlier remarks of Dampier and the Dutch navigators.

From what I have said of the Natives of New-Holland they may appear to some to be the most wretched people upon Earth, but in reality they are far more happier than we Europeans: being wholy unacquainted not only with the superfluous but the necessary Conveniences so much sought after in Europe, they are happy in not knowing the use of them. They live in a Tranquillity which is not disturb'd by the Inequality of Condition: The Earth and sea of their own accord furnishes them with all things necessary for life.[103]

These comments were not to see the light of day until the publication of Cook's manuscript journal in 1893, for when the mangled amalgam of the accounts of Cook and Banks was published in 1773 Hawkesworth omitted altogether Cook's reflective observations on the Aborigines, while those of Banks were transferred by editorial sleight of hand to the inhabitants of Tierra del Fuego.[104]

As far as the resources of the newly-discovered land were concerned, neither man was smitten by great enthusiasm, though Cook finished on a cheerful note. He pointed out that New South Wales—to give the country the name he was eventually to settle on—bore little resemblance to the 'barren and miserable' coastline of Dampier's experience, that there were good harbours, and potential for agriculture. 'In this extensive Country it can never be doubted but what most sorts of Grain, Fruit, Roots &c of every kind would flourish here were they once brought hither, planted and cultivated by the hand of Industry'.[105] Banks was harsher in his evaluation of the region. 'Barren it may justly be called and in a very high degree, that at least that we saw. The Soil in general is sandy and very light ... the fertile soil Bears no kind of Proportion to that which seems by nature doomd to everlasting Barrenness.' The most he would concede was that there was probably enough in the way of indigenous resources to support a shipwrecked crew. In making this gloomy assessment of a country which the expedition had only skirted, Banks was influenced by the backwardness of the inhabitants, and their thinness on the ground—a state of affairs he suspected also held good for the interior. When he looked for an explanation of this lack of population his general conclusion was far from reassuring: 'perhaps the Barreness of the Soil and scarcity of fresh water; but why mankind should not increase here as fast as in other places unless their small tribes have frequent wars in which many are destroyed'.[106]

Even though the east coast had been shown to be more fertile and accessible than the west, to both Cook and Banks it compared poorly with New Zealand as far as possible European settlement was concerned. Despite Cook's mention of the 'deep black Soil' of Botany Bay which later arrivals were to seek in vain, there was no equivalent in his account of those enthusiastic remarks on the

North Island of New Zealand with its 'rich and fertile' soil, where 'an Industrious people ... would very soon be supply'd not only with the necessarys but many of the luxuries of life'.[107] Banks, visualizing a future settlement along the banks of the Thames (Waihou), added that its 'noble timber' could be used for building houses and ships, while 'the River would furnish plenty of Fish, and the Soil make ample returns of any European Vegetables sown in it'.[108] And the pages of Hawkesworth reflect this preference for New Zealand over New South Wales. Despite his inclusion of Cook's favourable comments on Botany Bay the overall impression was not one to catch the eye—'the soil in some parts seemed to be capable of improvement, but the far greater part is such as can admit of no cultivation'.[109]

It would be going too far to say that the long-awaited European discovery of the east coast of Australia was an anti-climax; but certainly to contemporaries, who viewed it after all in the context of the complete voyage, and through the eyes of Hawkesworth, it seems to have made little immediate impact. In the same way that Banks rather than Cook dominated attention once the *Endeavour* returned, so Tahiti took the imagination of readers. New Zealand ran second in interest, and New South Wales a poor third. So, in a geographical and mercantile encyclopedia published shortly after Hawkesworth's *Voyages*, whereas the revelation of New Zealand—'the finest climate in the world, possesses a most fruitful soil, and numerous valuable productions'—was judged to be 'of the highest consequence', Cook's exploration of the east coast of Australia was not even mentioned.[110] To the casual reader at least, the main impression of New South Wales given in Hawkesworth might well have been of an uninspiring two thousand miles of coastline with dangerous reefs, a backward naked people, and an eccentric hopping animal. It provided neither the exotic customs and dazzling landscape of Polynesia, nor the imposing warrior inhabitants and magnificent scenery of New Zealand. What might in other circumstances have been seen as a major step forward in Europe's knowledge of the Pacific remained, for almost another twenty years, a marginal matter.

Notes

1 See *Australia's Oldest Wreck: the historical background and archaeological analysis of the wreck of the English East India Company's ship 'Trial'* ed. J. N. Green (British Archaeological Reports, Supplementary Series 27, Oxford, 1977).

2 For the map and letter see Günter Schilder, *Australia Unveiled: the share of the Dutch navigators in the discovery of Australia* (Amsterdam, 1976), pp. 145, 189.

3 See ibid., map 76, and *supra*, chapter 3.

4 *Abel Janszoon Tasman's Journal of his discovery of Van Diemen's Land and New Zealand in 1642 ...* ed. J. E. Heeres (Amsterdam, 1898), p. 74. (Amsterdam, 1898, reprinted Los Angeles, 1965 [1898]), p. 74.

5 The map's title is 'A Plat of all the World ... first set forth by MʳEdw. Wright And now newly Corrected and inlarged with many New Discoveries by Jos. Moxon ... 1655'. It is placed at the end of *Certain Errors in Navigation Detected and Corrected by Edw. Wright ... With many Additions ... Printed by Joseph Moxon* (London, 1657). For a discussion of the map see Schilder, *Australia Unveiled*, pp. 394–5.

6 John Ogilby, *America ...* (London, 1671), p. 654.

7 *An Account of several late Voyages & Discoveries to the South and North* (London, 1694), pp. x, xxvii–xxviii, 131.

8 *Cosmography and Geography in Two Parts ...* (London, 1683), Pt 1, p. 61.

9 See Peter Heylyn, *Cosmography ... 7th Edition corrected & inlarged by Edmund Bohun* (London, 1703), p. 1127, appendix on 'Endeavouring a Discovery of the Unknown Parts of the World: especially of Terra Australis Incognita, or the Southern Continent'.

10 William Dampier, *A New Voyage round the World* [1697], ed. A. Gray (London, 1937), p. 310.

11 Ibid., p. 312.

12 Ibid., p. 311.

13 See BL Sloane MS 3236, ff. 222d.–223. It is difficult to be certain on the question of the length of the stay, but the dates given in the manuscript account seem more likely than those in the book. The two accounts retain their difference of a month in dates from Dampier's departure from the coast of New Holland to his arrival in Achin in early May 1688 (manuscript version) or early June 1688 *(New Voyage)*. The latter seems unlikely, since according to this version Dampier reached Achin sometime in the first week of June, remained seriously ill for at least a week after his arrival, then after a partial recovery met Thomas Bowrey, agreed to accompany him on a voyage, and still set off 'about the Beginning of June'. The manuscript version, which allows a month for these events to take place, is clearly more convincing.

14 Dampier, *New Voyage*, pp. 312–13.

15 Ibid., p. 315.

16 BL Sloane MS 3986, f. 44.

17 BL Sloane MS 3236, ff. 222–222d.

18 See *Calendar of State Papers Colonial, America and West Indies, 1696–7*, 1120; *1697–8*, 830, 850, 851.

19 See G. Williams, ' "The Inexhaustible Fountains of Gold": English Projects and Ventures in the South Seas, 1670–1750', in *Perspectives of Empire: Essays presented to Gerald S. Graham*, ed. J. E. Flint and G. Williams (London, 1973), pp. 27–53.

20 Dampier's correspondence with the Admiralty for this period is in PRO ADM 2/1692 (no folio numbers); the main documents are printed in John Masefield, ed., *Dampier's Voyages* (London, 1906), II, 325–30.

21 Details of some of them are in BL Add MS 28, 140, ff. 31–33d; Guildhall MS 3041/2.

22 Dampier, *New Voyage*, pp. 337–8.

23 The map is in BL Sloane MS 5222 (12). For brief analyses of it see Heeres, *Tasman's Journal*, pp. 73n, 119n; and Schilder, *Australia Unveiled*, p. 358.

24 Masefield, *Dampier's Voyages*, II, 326.

25 Dampier, *New Voyage*, p. 240.

26 Masefield, *Dampier's Voyages*, II, 331.

27 First letter in Dampier file, n.d., PRO ADM 1/1692.

28 Letter of 27 September 1698, ibid.

29 William Dampier, *A Voyage to New Holland*, ed. J. A. Williamson (London, 1939), p. 94.

30 In a letter to this author dated 10 January 1986, Professor Leslie R. Marchant of the University of Western Australia writes: 'Dampier was justified in criticizing Tasman's latitudes. On his map, Tasman sketches the coast lying between North West Cape and just near Roebuck Bay as lying south of the 19 degree south parallel. This is not so. All of that coast up to the De Grey River lies below the 20 degree parallel of latitude indicating that Dampier was correct and therefore justified in criticizing Tasman's assessment. Dampier is also right when he criticizes Tasman

in drawing in rivers where in fact there are none. This indicates that Dampier made a more precise, closer in-shore survey than Tasman who no doubt used the technique of "masthead" surveys which can be very misleading.'

31 Quoted in *Early Voyages to Terra Australis, now called Australia*, ed. R. H. Major (London, 1859), p. 169.
32 Williamson, *Voyage to New Holland*, pp. 111–12.
33 1 September 1699, PRO ADM 52/94.
34 Williamson, *Voyage to New Holland*, pp. 102–3.
35 Ibid., p. 121.
36 See Christopher Lloyd, *William Dampier* (London, 1966), p. 78.
37 The same holds true for some of the minor ones. There is considerable doubt about the precise identification of Dampier's landing-places of Cygnet Bay on his first voyage and Roebuck Bay on his second. The Mitchell Library holds a large file of correspondence (97 9338) between J. W. Forsyth and Trevor Tuckfield in the 1950s discussing—in spirited but eventually inconclusive fashion—these and other problems relating to Dampier. Professor Marchant is currently engaged on the task of identifying Dampier's landfalls and landing-places in Australia, and when his work is complete we can expect fuller answers to a whole range of navigational queries arising from Dampier's two Australian coastings.
38 Williamson, *Voyage to New Holland*, p. 236. The rocks are marked incorrectly on the Tasman map in BL Sloane MS 5222 (12).
39 Ibid., p. 217.
40 Lloyd, *Dampier*, p. 98.
41 See BL Sloane MS 4044, f. 214.
42 Ibid., f. 214d.
43 Ibid., f. 217.
44 The 1716 proposal is printed in G. B. Barton, *History of New South Wales from the records* (London, 1889), II, 567–8.
45 BL Sloane MS 4044, ff. 212–13.
46 See BL Add MS 33, 054, f. 75.
47 PRO T 1/240, No. 38, f. 182.
48 Ibid., f. 192.
49 George Collingridge, *The Discovery of Australia* (Sydney, 1895), p. 301.
50 PRO T 1/240, No. 38, f. 191.
51 Ibid., ff. 195–6
52 Ibid.
53 Ibid., ff. 192d–193.
54 *Journal of Commissioners of Trade and Plantations* (London, 1925), p. 301.
55 PRO T 1/240, No. 38, f. 198.
56 Ibid.
57 See Celsus Kelly, 'Geographical Knowledge and Speculation in regard to Spanish Pacific Voyages', *Historical Studies*, 9 (1959–61), 12–18.
58 [Daniel Defoe], *A Plan of the English Commerce* (2nd edn, London, 1730), pp. xiii–xiv.
59 See W. T. James, 'Nostalgia for Paradise: Terra Australis in the Seventeenth Century', in *Australia and the European Imagination* (Canberra, 1982), p. 79.
60 *A New Discovery of Terra Incognita Australis, or the Southern World. By James Sadeur ...* (London, 1693), preface.
61 [Daniel Defoe], *A New Voyage round the World ...* (London, 1725), pp. 176–8. See also Ross Gibson, *The Diminishing Paradise: Changing Literary Perceptions of Australia* (Sydney, 1984), pp. 11–14.
62 Jonathan Swift, *Gulliver's Travels* [1726] (Harmondsworth, 1967), p. 333.
63 Alexander Dalrymple, *An Historical Collection of the several Voyages and Discoveries in the South Pacific Ocean* (London, 1770–1), I, xxviii–ix.
64 *Byron's Journal of his Circumnavigation 1764–1766*, ed. R. E. Gallagher (London, 1964), p. 3.
65 *The Discovery of Tahiti*, ed. Hugh Carrington (London, 1948), p. xxii.
66 Ibid., p. 135.
67 *The Journals of Captain James Cook*, ed. J. C. Beaglehole (Cambridge, 1955–68), I, cclxxxii.
68 Jean-Etienne Martin-Allanic, *Bougainville Navigateur et les Découvertes de son Temps* (Paris, 1964), I, 475.
69 Cook, *Journals*, I, cclxxxiii.
70 Ibid., pp. 272–3.
71 *The Endeavour Journal of Joseph Banks 1768–1771*, ed. J. C. Beaglehole (Sydney, 1962), (hereafter Banks, *Journal*), 38.
72 Cook, *Journals*, I, 299; Banks, *Journal*, II, 49.
73 Banks, *Journal*, II, 51.
74 Ibid., 51.
75 Cook, *Journals*, I, 306.
76 Banks, *Journal*, II, 59; Cook, *Journals*, I, 306.
77 Banks, *Journal*, II, 55.
78 Cook, *Journals*, I, 312.
79 HRNSW, I, ii, 215.
80 Cook, *Journals*, 307.
81 Banks, *Journal*, II, 57.
82 John Hawkesworth, comp., *An Account of the Voyages undertaken ... for making Discoveries in the Southern Hemisphere* (London, 1773), III, 498.
83 Cook, *Journals*, I, 308–9.
84 Banks, *Journal*, II, 60.
85 See Cook, *Journals*, I, ccix, 310.
86 Cook, *Journals*, I, 316; Banks, *Journal*, II, 63.
87 Cook, *Journals*, I, 325.
88 Ibid., p. 322.
89 Ibid., p. 343.
90 Banks, *Journal*, II, 79.
91 Banks, *Journal*, II, 93–4. For a recent discussion of a complex subject see Denis J. Carr, 'The identity of Captain Cook's kangaroo' in *Sydney Parkinson: Artist of Cook's Endeavour Voyage*,

ed. D. J. Carr (London and Canberra, 1983), pp. 242−9.

[92] Banks, *Journal*, II, 95; Cook, *Journals*, I, 360.

[93] Cook, *Journals*, I, 361−2.

[94] Banks, *Journal*, I, 98−9.

[95] Cook, *Journals*, I, 376.

[96] Ibid.

[97] Ibid., p. 380.

[98] Ibid., p. 385; see e.g. Keith Willey, *When the sky fell down: the destruction of the tribes of the Sydney region 1788−1850s* (Sydney, 1979), p. 30.

[99] Cook, *Journals*, I, 243.

[100] Ibid., p. 390.

[101] Cook, *Journals*, II, 520−1.

[102] Ibid., pp. 516n−517n.

[103] Cook, *Journals*, I, 399.

[104] See Glyndwr Williams, '"Far more happier than we Europeans": Reactions to the Australian Aborigines on Cook's Voyage', *Historical Studies*, 19 (1981), 499−512.

[105] Cook, *Journals*, I, 397.

[106] Banks, *Journal*, II, 122−3.

[107] Cook, *Journals*, I, 276.

[108] Banks, *Journal*, II, 4.

[109] Hawkesworth, *Voyages*, III, 622.

[110] *The Politician's Dictionary* ... (London, 1775), II, 259.

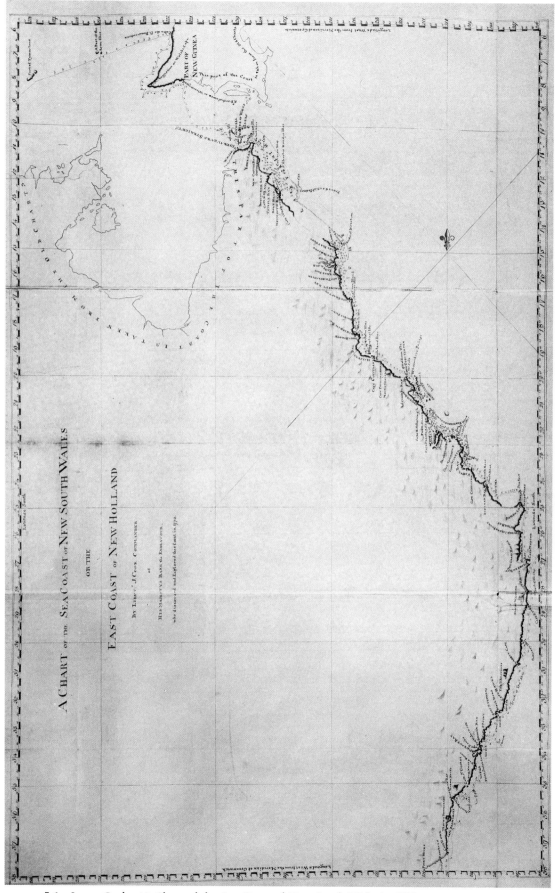

5.1   James Cook   'A Chart of the Sea Coast of New South Wales'   1770

Chapter 5

New South Wales: Expectations and Reality

Glyndwr Williams and Alan Frost

EXPECTATIONS

By the mid-1780s, Cook's and Banks's descriptions had given rise to a prevailing image of New South Wales, which reached the British public mainly through the pages of Hawkesworth, but also in a variety of other ways. As described in the eighth (1783) edition of William Guthrie's *Geography*, the region was 'rather barren than fertile', yet with 'in many places the rising grounds ... chequered by woods and lawns, and the plains and vallies covered with herbage'.[1] Three years later, with the plan for colonization announced, Thomas Bankes and his colleagues elaborated. New Holland was an island of 'vast extent, reaching from 10 to 44 degrees south, between 110 and 154 degrees east of London'. New South Wales, the eastern part of it, was an 'immense track'. It was 'in general low and level, and, upon the whole, rather barren than fruitful, yet the rising ground is chequered with woods and lawns, the vallies and plains are, in many places, covered with herbage'. Though there were no 'great' rivers, the 'whole eastern coast [was] well watered by small brooks and springs'. There was a variety of 'gum' and palm trees, and some fruit trees. Among the few animals were the native dog (5.12); a 'kind of opossum' (5.2), with a 'membraneous bag near the stomach, in which it conceals and carries its young'; and the 'remarkable' kangaroo (4.21, 4.26), 'which, when fully grown, is as large as a sheep ... It goes in an erect posture, and its motion is by successive leaps or hops of a great length'. The coastal waters contained an 'abundance' of fish, together with shellfish of various kinds.[2]

Despite this image of a moderately-endowed environment, there were some who entertained additional expectations. Sir George Young, for example, observed in 1784−5 of New South Wales:

The variety of Climates included between the forty-fourth, and tenth Degrees of Latitude, gives us an Opportunity of uniting in one Territory, almost all the Productions of the known World; to explain this more fully, I will point out some of the Countries which are situated within the same extent of Latitude, on either side of the Equator; they are *China, Japan, Siam, India, Persia, Arabia-felix, Egypt, Greece, all Turkey, the Mediterranean Sea, Italy, Spain, South of France and Portugal, with Mexico, Lima,*

5.2 [Anonymous] Opossum 1786

Baldavia, and the greatest part of the *Pacific Ocean;* to which may be added the *Cape of Good Hope,* &c, &c.[3]

From more limited—and more realistic perspectives—Banks in 1785 advised that 'the Soil of many Parts of the Eastern Coast of New South wales between the Latitudes of 30 & 40 [degrees] is sufficiently fertile to support a Considerable Number of Europeans who would cultivate it in the Ordinary Modes used in England'.[4] Even more to the point was his opinion the next year that the climate of New South Wales was likely to prove 'similar to that of the South of France',[5] a perception which determined the kinds of grain and vegetable seeds and fruit trees (5.3) that he gathered for the colonizing party.[6]

Such expectations derived both from the long-held sense of Terra Australis and from knowledge of the world at large; and the experience of the Pacific explorers gave a number of them particular point. From the 1760s until the end of the 1770s, Cook and his colleagues had made the lush islands of the central Pacific an essential part of their operations. At Tahiti, at Fiji and Samoa and the Cook Islands, and then at the Hawaiian Islands, the captains had taken respite from the ocean, and obtained water and fresh foods to succour their crews; and the crews themselves had enjoyed the compliant women. The prospect of importing Polynesian women to redress the sexual imbalance among the proposed colonists appeared early in the discussion of the New South Wales scheme. 'Do you think

162

in a Climate similar to that of the South of France which Botany Bay Probably is the following Vegetables that are propagated by Engrafting because they cannot be Otherwise raised will be highly usefull

Peaches	Apples	Cherries	Lemons
Nectarines	Pears	Pomgranates	Limes
Apricots	Plumbs	Oranges	Shaddocks

The following also should be Carried there because being uncertain & Tedious, when raised from seed they are usualy Cultivated by Layers.

Mulberry	Gooseberry	+Strawberry	+Walnut
Fig	Raspberry	Filbert	
Vine	Currant	+Almond	

Artichokes	Baum	Garlick	Chamomile
Horse Raddish	Sage	Sives	
Sorrell	mint	Tarragon	

• These marked thus may be raised but seed but young Plants are the Preferd

5.3 Joseph Banks List of fruit trees, etc., to be taken to New South Wales 1786

Women co.[d] be induced to go from thence for the Use of the European Men at the New Settlement', the members of the Beauchamp Committee asked James Matra in May 1785, who replied: 'Yes—in any Number—they are more partial to Europeans than to their own Countrymen.'[7]

Yet there was a good deal more to this suggestion than the simple redressing of sexual imbalance. As developed by officials in 1786, the idea involved bringing Polynesian women to become wives for the marines who wished to settle in the new land, rather than to meet the sexual needs of the male convicts. It was Governor Arthur Phillip's intention that these women should first be kept apart in 'a proper place', and supported from the government store. He would 'punish with severity . . . any Insult offer'd to them', and they would be 'free to choose Husbands, or to live in private'. On marriage to 'the Soldiers of the Garrison', they would receive grants of land.[8] That is, from the union of marines and island women would arise a body of sturdy yeomen farmers able to spring to the colony's defence as needed, but, more importantly, able also to supply that range of garden products necessary for the colonists' general health. To British eyes in the mid-1780s, New South Wales was likely to prove as abundant as a tropic isle.[9]

The British also expected that this agricultural progress, so desirable and so necessary, was to be easily achieved. Cook and Banks had noticed how the New South Wales trees grew apart from each other, and the absence of underwood. These features gave rise to the hope that 'a plantation might easily be established, without much trouble in clearing',[10] and the size of the trees pointed to intrinsic fertility. A similar perception attached to the raising of animals. Banks told the Beauchamp Committee that the 'vast Quantities of Grass' at Botany Bay suggested that European cattle would 'thrive'. Matra pointed out that animals might be easily obtained from the East Indies.[11] And then there was the fecundity of the coastal waters, so apparent during the *Endeavour's* stay.[12]

A particular set of expectations of the Botany Bay region's fertility therefore prevailed in the mid-1780s. As Evan Nepean, undersecretary at the Home Office, and the official most concerned with the colonization, put it in October 1786, Botany Bay 'on the coast of New South Wales, situated in the Latitude of 33° 30′ S°., or some other place contiguous thereto, . . . appears to be a Country peculiarly adapted for a Settlement, the Lands about it being plentifully supplied with Wood and Water, the Soil rich and fertile, and the Shores well stocked with Shell and other Fish'.[13] The *St James Chronicle's* leader-writer went further, when he wrote that

by the number of Cattle now sending over of various sorts, and all the different Seeds for Vegetation, a capital Improvement will be made in the Southern part of the New World; and our Ships, which may hereafter sail in that Quarter of the Globe, must receive Refreshment in greater Plenty, than from the Exhausted Soil of Europe, considering that all [New] South Wales is formed of a Virgin Mould undisturbed since the Creation.[14]

Just as the colonists should reap a rich agricultural, pastoral, and coastal harvest, so too should they reap a rewarding one of natural history. During their seven days at Botany Bay, Banks and Solander had found themselves in a naturalist's wonderland, and gathered an extensive collection. The six weeks' sojourn at the Endeavour River provided further opportunities for collecting, and they added that surprising marsupial the kangaroo as well as tropical plants. These specimens were significant in making the pair's collection 'the greatest treasure of Natural History that ever was brought into any country at one time by two persons'.[15] Banks's and Solander's correspondence, Banks's and Cook's descriptions of the kangaroo in Hawkesworth,[16] and George Stubbs's elaboration of Parkinson's drawing of it (4.21, 4.26), whetted the interest of the specialist and general public alike. Furneaux's and Cook's brief visits to Van Diemen's Land subsequently added more items of interest. New South Wales was potentially a scientific treasure trove.

And the region's bounty might be gathered under a benign climate. Cook and his companions on the *Endeavour* had experienced the Botany Bay region in May. Fifty years' colonization showed this end-of-autumn month to be habitually the 'finest [one] in the year, and the most congenial to the European constitution; weather clear, cool, and bracing; the sun sets and rises in a cloudless sky for weeks together, and the scenery of the heavens at night is sublime beyond description'.[17] The *Endeavour* also ran up the tropical coast at a propitious time. Though the days in North Queensland in June, July and August are warm, with the monsoon and cyclone season over, the weather is generally most pleasant. It is small wonder, then, that these explorers should have concluded that the climate of New South Wales was likely to prove a nurturing one. Matra reported to the Beauchamp Committee that they 'found the Climate perfectly agreeable to European Constitution'.[18] Writing to the *Gentleman's Magazine* to refute suggestions of government callousness towards the convicts, 'T. W.' emphasized this feature. 'Consider first', he urged, the 'lot' of the American Loyalists now relocated in Canada; 'See them encounter the difficulties of an inhospitable shore;—see them in latitudes to which their constitutions were strangers, struggling to begin the world afresh. Revolve, immediately, in your mind the mild latitude of 34°—the very name of the spot the convicts are going to—the characters of the [explorers], who declare it favourable to vegetation and agriculture—and say if the delinquents are not bountifully provided for?'[19]

As the explorers' reconnaissances also indicated that there were no predatory animals in New South Wales, there seemed nothing from the points of view of geography and natural history that might stand in the way of rapid progress at colonization.[20] Nor was it likely that the indigenous inhabitants would constitute any impediment. From the pages of Hawkesworth, an image emerged of the Aborigines as a naked, wandering people with no fixed habitations, no agriculture, no possessions of any consequence. They lived in families, but of larger social groupings there was no sign, let alone of political institutions or recognized authority.[21] These latter features were particularly stressed by Banks in his evidence to the Beauchamp Committee in 1785; and his remarks were taken as showing that New South Wales was *terra nullius*, belonging to no-one, ready for occupation and exploitation.[22] There were 'very few' Aborigines at Botany Bay, he said, and 'though they seemed inclined to Hostilities they did not appear at all to be feared. We never saw more than 30 or 40 together'. During their stay there had been no prospect of 'obtaining any thing either by Cession or purchase as there was nothing we could offer that they would take except provisions and those we wanted ourselves'. He could give the Committee no idea 'whatsoever' of their form of government or of their language. He was convinced that those at Botany Bay 'wo.^d speedily abandon the Country to the New Comers'.[23] Altogether, his evidence confirmed Cook's earlier perception: 'We are to Consider that we see this Country in the pure state of Nature, the Industry of Man has had nothing to do with any part of it.'[24]

The next year, Thomas Bankes's description conveyed this image to the public in all its essentials. The coastal regions of New South Wales were 'very thinly inhabited', and the interior was probably deserted. Both sexes went 'stark-naked, not having any conscious sense of indecency, in discovering the whole body', though they did wear some bone and shell ornaments and scarify and paint themselves. They made no attempt to cultivate the land, subsisting instead almost entirely on the products of the sea. Neither was there to be seen 'town or village in the whole country, nor did either art or industry appear in the construction of their houses'. Their utensils were 'a vessel made of bark to hold the water they fetch from springs and a bag about the size of a moderate cabbage-net, which the men carry upon their backs with a string which passes over their heads. It contains paint, fish-hooks, darts, and bracelets, which compose the whole property of the richest men amongst them' (5.16). Their canoes were 'made of one piece of bark, tied together at the ends and kept open in the middle by small bows of wood' (4.20, 4.27). Their weapons consisted of 'spears or lances of different sorts' (4.22). Their 'principal means of annoying their European visitors, was by setting fire to the high grass in the neighbourhood of the place where the tents were fixed'. They had 'no idea of traffic'. 'The cause of the small number of the human species which are to be met with throughout this country cannot be ascertained', Bankes summed up, 'but from their total ignorance of agriculture, commerce, and the means of procuring the comforts and conveniences of life, it is plain that they are amongst the most miserable of beings, that can be stiled human.'[25]

From the point of view of the character and social organization of the indigenous inhabitants, then, Botany Bay seemed an ideal location for the new settlement. There was no necessity for negotiations with indigenous states, for none existed. There were no formidable warriors, as in New Zealand; no distrustful chieftains, as in Africa. Precisely what was to be the status of the Aborigines in the new dispensation is not clear. As subjects of the king, they were certainly to enjoy the protection of British law, but there is extant no discussion of how this protection was to be extended. The point seems to have rested in the general humanitarianism that, by and large, governed the British penetration of the Pacific from the 1760s. Phillip was instructed 'to endeavour by every possible means to open an intercourse with the natives, and to conciliate their affections, enjoining all our subjects to live in amity and kindness with them. And if any of our subjects still wantonly destroy them, or give them any unnecessary interruption in the exercise of their several occupations, it is our will and pleasure that you do cause such offenders to be brought to punishment'.[26] Time was to show how unrealistic were these instructions.

Based on Hawkesworth's renderings of Cook's and Banks's journals, bolstered by discussion with some who had sailed to the Pacific, and disseminated in lively conversation, all these various expectations constituted a rich freight for Phillip and the First Fleet officers to sail from Portsmouth with. These officers' sense of other European colonial ventures—in North America and the West Indies, in South America, at the Cape of Good Hope and in India and the East Indies—added to their cargo, especially as the welcome respites offered by Teneriffe, Rio de Janeiro and Cape Town during the course of a long and tedious voyage brought home to them how much they were merely the latest players of an eternal European drama.[27]

At the same time, though, sailing with convicts to establish a colony in a scarcely-visited region 12 000 miles distant from their homeland, Phillip and his colleagues knew they were also first colonists, with a new world all before them. The abundance of the records of the venture—a number, indeed, from the first kept with a view to publication—indicates their sense of its historicity. Major books on the early settlement were put together from the first reports of the governor, Arthur Phillip, and some of his officers (in 1789); by marine captain Watkin Tench (two books, one in 1789, and a fuller sequel in 1793); and by David Collins, judge-advocate of the colony (1798, with a supplementary volume in 1802). In addition to these published accounts, many manuscript journals, letters and narratives have survived, including those of Arthur Bowes Smyth, surgeon; John Easty, marine private; Henry Waterhouse, midshipman; John Harris, surgeon; George Worgan, surgeon; Philip Gidley King, naval lieutenant and later governor of the settlement; Ralph Clark, marine lieutenant; James Campbell, marine captain; David Blackburn, ship's master; William Bradley, naval lieutenant; Robert Ross, commandant of marines, and as lieutenant-governor Phillip's deputy; James Scott, marine sergeant; Jacob Nagle, seaman; Daniel Southwell, ship's mate; Richard Johnson, first chaplain to the colony. There are also extant many hundreds of charts and plans, drawings and water-colours of New South Wales scenes, by Bradley, Raper, the mysterious 'Port Jackson

Painter',[28] and others. The roll-call is impressive but far from representative. The majority of those who landed from the First Fleet—the convicts—are not represented here. Nor are the other unwilling participants in the enterprise, the Aboriginal inhabitants of the Sydney and Botany Bay areas. With one or two exceptions, it is a record from the top, with all the problems that presents. Even so, these records constitute an unparalleled account of the first years of a European colonization, and are a rich source of information about how the colonists responded to the environment and its inhabitants. A central feature is the often sharp conflict between expectation and reality.

REALITY: THE LAND

One expectation at least was never in doubt of realization. Sharing his time's perceptions of disease-laden miasmas, Phillip chose Sydney Cove as the site of first settlement partly because the rising ground behind would permit him to lay out a township through which air might circulate freely.[29] And from the first, even given the summer heats and fierce thunderstorms and heavy autumn rains, the colonists found the New South Wales climate a life-enhancing one. 'The climate is a very fine one, and the country will ... when the woods are cleared away, be as healthy as any in the world', Phillip wrote in July 1788. 'The climate is equal to the finest in Europe', he remarked in September. Early in 1790 he pronounced authoritatively: 'I believe a finer or more healthy climate is not to be found in any [other] part of the world.'[30]

This opinion was shared by all those who commented on the point,[31] and was amply justified by the health record. At the beginning of 1790 Phillip reported:

Of 1030 people who landed, many of whom were worn out by old age, the scurvy, and various disorders, only seventy-two have died in one-and-twenty months, and by the surgeon's returns it appears that twenty-six of these died from disorders of long standing ... which it is more than probable would have carried them off much sooner in England.[32]

While there was heavy mortality among the convicts who arrived on the Second and Third Fleets (1790, 1791), many of these were old or decrepit and in any case not well treated on the voyage out, and had no realistic prospects of survival.

At the same time, the fertility of European women in New South Wales was striking. Tench commented in some amazement on the 'great number of births which happened, considering the age, and other circumstances, of many of the mothers. Women, who certainly would never have bred in any other climate, here produced as fine children as ever were born'.[33] Though there were a number of factors involved in the remarkable burgeoning, the more significant one is likely to have been that, despite the long periods of rationing, the basic food intake was sufficient to increase the women's general health to a level

5.4 [Anonymous] 'A View of the Land to the Southward of Botany Bay with the entrance of the Harbour...' 1788

where many became fertile again after years of barrenness. And because the children were at least adequately fed, and not ravaged by such banes as typhoid, measles, scarlet fever, whooping cough and smallpox, they did not die at the rates usual in Britain. Quickly, New South Wales became known as a place where children thrived.

If the expectation concerning climate was vindicated, though, others were immediately disappointed. Cook and Banks had reported on Botany Bay (4.23, 5.6, 5.7) from the point of view of the needs of a small exploring party, rather than of those of a large colonizing group; and seeing it in May, after autumn rains had filled the creeks and nurtured a lush cover of grasses on the grounds the Aborigines had cleared with fire, they had been favourably impressed. The First Fleet officers saw it in late January, at the height of summer, before the seasonal rains had offered their succouring. In the summer of 1788 the area was scarcely recognizable as that described by the explorers. The grass cover was strikingly absent: 'The fine meadows talked of in Captain Cook's voyage I could never see, though I took some pains to find them out, nor have I ever heard of a person that has seen any parts resembling them', John White wrote bitterly.[34] There was only a small volume of running water, there were some ominous swamps, and there was no obviously fertile soil—as White again recorded, the ground was 'sandy, poor, and swampy, and but very indifferently supplied with water'.[35] While some 'good situations offered for a small number of people', Phillip found none 'that appeared calculated for our numbers'.[36] In addition,

169

5.5   [Anonymous]   'A View of the Land from Botany Bay to Port Jackson'   1788

there was the discouraging fact of a bay 'so shoal that ships of even a moderate draught of water are obliged to anchor [and] with the entrance ... open, are exposed to a heavy sea that rolls in when it blows hard from the eastward'.[37]

It was small wonder that the governor decided to look for another site. In Port Jackson (6.1) he found an incomparable harbour, one where 'a thousand sail of the line may ride in the most perfect security',[38] and at Sydney Cove (5.8, 5.11) he found an acceptable site—one where 'ships can anchor so close to the shore that at a very small expence quays may be made at which the largest ships may unload' (5.9); where there was a good 'spring of water'; where there was reasonably clear land that might be cultivated; and where, to the south and south-east, there was land over which the intended town might spread.[39]

Unfortunately, like Botany Bay, this new site also promised but deceived. Immediately Phillip set the colonists to clearing, building, and planting, difficulties appeared. The soft steel of the English axes broke against the ironbarks and redgums; the trunks of the trees were often so large as to be scarcely manageable, and the roots spread widely—it was 'hardly possible' to give 'a just idea' of the labour involved in clearing the site, the governor reported.[40] The vegetables and grains which were first planted sprang up only to wither in the late summer heat: 'whether from any unfriendly, deleterious Quality of the Soil or the Season', Worgan observed, 'nothing seems to flourish vigorously long, but they shoot up suddenly after being put in the Ground, look green & luxuriant for a little Time, blossom early, fructify slowly & weakly, before they come to their

170

5.6   William Bradley   'Botany Bay. *Sirius* & Convoy going in: *Supply* & Agent's division in the Bay. 21 Jan[ry] 1788'

5.7   Charles Gore   'Botany Bay 1788'   before 1790

171

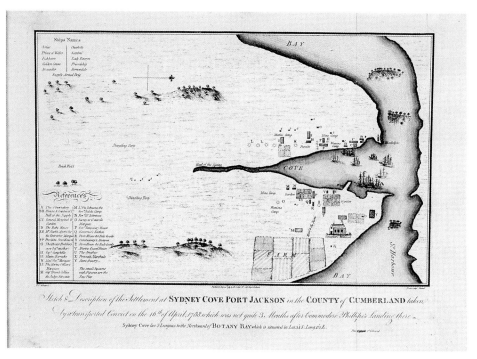

5.8 Francis Fowkes 'Sketch & Description of the Settlement at Sydney Cove Port Jackson in the County of Cumberland...16.th of April, 1788'

5.9 [George Raper] 'His Majesty's Brig *Supply* of Lord Howe's Island 1790' and 'His Majesty's Ship *Sirius* in Sidney Cove 1789'

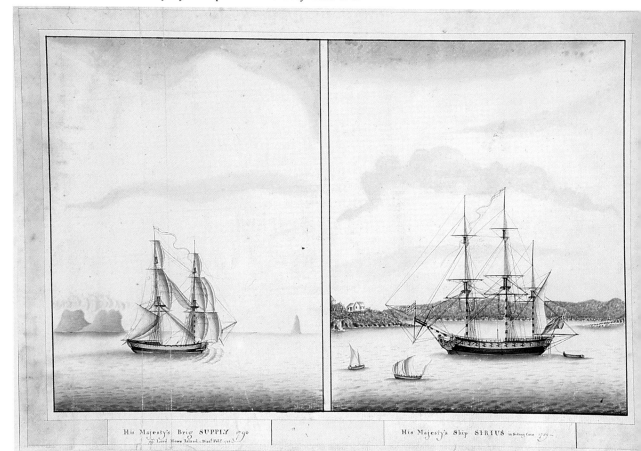

proper Size. Indeed, many of the Plants wither long ere they arrive at these Periods of Growth'.[41] The colonists did find an area of reasonable soil bordering the next cove to the east, where Phillip established the government farm (5.8), but this also offered only a limited promise; and probes in the immediate vicinity did not reveal better ones.

Geology and geography were against the colonists. Bordered by the ocean on one side and by an encompassing plateau of (Hawkesbury) sandstone on others, Port Jackson, Botany Bay and the Nepean River define a geologically discrete section. This small, bulbous area consists principally of Triassic shales and sandstones, with some tertiary sand, silt, clay, and basalt and with some more recent deposits of alluvium, gravel, sand and clay. There are a few patches of better soils, but by 1788 aeons of rains and floods had largely leached them of their nutrients (a result perhaps aided by the Aborigines' habit of burning off), so that they required fertilizing to be really suitable for the cultivation of vegetables and grains—and the colonists lacked the herds and flocks to provide the necessary manure.[42] In this area of limited fertility, the indigenous sclerophyll vegetation also deceived. So well had it adapted to its environment that trees grew large; the dull-leaved shrubs proliferated most in the poorest sections; and, uncropped by voracious cattle and sheep, and growing in ground not yet compacted by these animals' hooves, native grasses flourished after rain.

Across the first year, the colonists planted repeatedly, only to learn the area's limitations. Maize grew better than wheat, but the results were none the less only moderate. Vegetables did not grow particularly well—as Tench recorded, 'the soil would produce neither [grain nor vegetables] without manure; and as this was not to be procured, our vigour soon slackened'.[43] 'Thus situated', he added,

the scurvy began its usual ravages, and extended its baneful influence, more or less, through all descriptions of persons. Unfortunately the esculent vegetable productions of the country are neither plentiful, nor tend very effectually to remove this disease. And the ground we had turned up and planted with garden seeds, either from the nature of the soil, or, which is more probable, the lateness of the season, yielded but a scanty and insufficient supply of what we stood so greatly in need of.[44]

In these circumstances Phillip gave up any pursuit of the scheme to fetch Polynesian women, telling Sydney, 'I am certain your Lordship will think that to send for women from the Islands, in our present situation, would answer no other purpose than that of bringing them to pine away in misery'.[45]

It was quickly apparent that the colonists needed better land to cultivate if they were to succeed; and this Phillip finally found at Parramatta at the head of the harbour. Here, relatively clear of trees and shrubs, were deposits of clay, which also required manuring to produce abundantly but which were none the less intrinsically more fertile than the Sydney sands; and, at Prospect Hill, a little to the west, there was an irregular vein of rich volcanic soil. Phillip began

173

to place settlers in this area in November 1788. By the beginning of 1791 there were over 70 acres under maize, and government and private barns, granaries, and cottages had been erected (5.10). By the end of 1792 there were 1000 acres of grain under government cultivation, and 400 acres worked privately (5.28).[46] Simultaneously, the colonists had found that European fruit trees and vines thrived in the Sydney sands and light loams. Phillip reported in July 1790 that he had more than a thousand cuttings of grape vines in the ground, and that his fruit trees were bearing (5.11).[47] Later, Tench observed that

vines of every sort seem to flourish: melons, cucumbers, and pumpkins, run with unbounded luxuriancy; and I am convinced that the grapes of New South Wales will, in a few years, equal those of any other country ... Other fruits are yet in their infancy; but oranges, lemons, and figs ... will, I dared believe, in a few years become plentiful. Apples, and the fruits of colder climes, also promise to gratify expectation.[48]

In March 1793 the officers of Malaspina's expedition inspected the colony (5.27, 5.28). Going to Parramatta, they found

along both shores ... farms with residences of some of the colonists. Corn, wheat, and barley, though not too abundant, were giving signs of an attractive harvest. More flourishing certainly was the potato, which promised a less doubtful future. The fruit trees, vegetable patches, and especially the lemon and the grapevine, gave new stimulus to the common activity and aspirations. Finally, the first young livestock, though very few in number, of cattle, sheep, and horses, gave good hopes for combining, in this new centre of national wealth, English energy and policy with a climate and soil not unlike that of our own Andalucia.[49]

The comparison was an appropriate one, and the observations acute. When Phillip left the colony in December 1792, he did so knowing that he had won the battle to establish it, even if it still lacked herds and flocks.

As the colonists consolidated their initial settlement, and as Phillip and his colleagues explored the environs, inevitably they acquainted themselves with its natural history. In May, the governor observed that the 'large gum-tree ... splits and warps in such a manner when used green ... that a store-house boarded up with this wood is rendered useless. The timber which in its growth resembles the fir-tree warps less, but we are already obliged to fetch it from some distance, and it will not float'. There was a 'variety' of palm trees; and 'the heaths that are free from timber are covered with a variety of the most beautiful flowering shrubs, wild celery, spinages, samphose, a small wild fig, and several berries, which have proved very wholesome, particularly the leaves of a small shrub which is found in such plenty that it has not yet failed us as most of the others have done'.[50] John White noted how on one occasion he collected 'in the distance of about half a mile, twenty-five flowers of plants and shrubs of different genera and species' (5.15).[51]

Nor was the officers' interest confined to plants. Birds and animals also caught their attention. The kangaroo was naturally of immediate concern. In July 1788, Phillip told Banks that the animal grew 'to a great size. One has been killed that weigh'd very near Two hundred weight, & one was found dead in the

174

5.10 [Port Jackson Painter] 'A View of Government Farm at Rose Hill N.S. wales 1791'

5.11 [Port Jackson Painter] 'A View of Sydney Cove Port Jackson March 7ᵗʰ 1792'

A View of Sydney Cove - Port Jackson   March 7ᵗʰ 1792

5.12 [Anonymous] Dingo *c.* 1788−92

5.13 [Port Jackson Painter] Black Swan *c.*1788−92   5.14 [Anonymous] Emu *c.* 1788−92

Woods, the Tail of which I have, that measures Eighteen inches in circumference'.
About this time, the opportunity to tame a young one arose. 'It uses the fore
feet to clean the face as a Cat does & by no means seems to avoid the fire',
Phillip observed, to continue:

I rather think that the Kanguroo is fond of fire, as I once saw two very near a Tree that
was on fire, & this young one jumped into the fire & singed it self. It is handsome the
Eye very sharp, attentive to the least Noise & lays the Ears back, or points them
different ways to listen, with the fore feet if they can be call'd so, it takes hold of you, or
anything it is going to eat, like a Monkey; it weights about twenty five pounds.[52]

Such acquaintance led the officers into observing the animal's anatomical curio-
sities. Tench opined that it was 'a new species of opossum, the female being
furnished with a bag, in which the young is contained; and in which the teats
are found'; and he pointed out that 'the testicles of the male are placed contrary
to the usual order of nature'.[53] Phillip was more explicit on this latter point:
'The situation of the Penis ... appears ... uncommon, between the Anus & the
Testicles, & very close to the former.'[54] At the same time Phillip also reported
that there was 'a variety of small Animals, several of which leap like the
Kangurroo & never put the fore feet to the ground'.[55]

Then there were the unusual birds—the 'noble' black swan (5.13), of which
the colonists saw many, but managed to kill only one by mid-1788; and the
unexpected 'cassowary' or 'emu' (5.14), one of which Phillip's gamekeeper shot.
Its weight, Tench recorded, was

seventy pounds, and its length from the end of the toe to the tip of the beak, seven feet
two inches ... On dissection many anatomical singularities were observed: the gall-
bladder was remarkably large, the liver not bigger than that of a barn-door fowl, and
after the strictest search no gizzard could be found; the legs, which were of a vast length,
were covered with thick, strong scales, plainly indicating the animal to be formed for
living amidst deserts; and the foot differed from an ostrich's by forming a triangle,
instead of being cloven ... The wings are so small as hardly to deserve the name, and
are unfurnished with those beautiful ornaments which adorn the wings of the ostrich: all
the feathers are extremely coarse, but the construction of them deserves notice—they
grow in pairs from a single shaft ... Though incapable of flying, they run with such
swiftness, that our fleetest greyhounds are left far behind in every attempt to catch
them.[56]

There were also those birds 'of the most exquisite beauty of plumage'[57]—the
parrots, paroquets, and cockatoos. And, of course, the dingo or native dog, which
the Aborigines had domesticated.

It was Phillip's and his colleagues' clear perception that there was 'such
variety of plants ... that it merits the attention of the naturalist and the
botanist'.[58] Through a misunderstanding, there was no botanist in the group,[59]
so the officers did the next best thing, and gathered specimens and seeds to send
home. At the same time, they obtained specimens of the fauna. In mid-1788
Phillip sent Banks one stuffed kangaroo and a young one preserved in spirits,
and several skins. He sent Lord Sydney the skin of the emu, and as well one of a
'Tingo'. Later in the year, he sent Banks a kegful of 'Young Kangurroo rats,

177

Nat. size.
Flowers in October.

Warratta.
Grows to the height of 8 or 10 feet.

5.15   [Thomas Watling]   'Warratta'   ? c. 1792–3

Birds, Young Kangurroos &c', and two 'Tubs of Plants', the one containing 'twenty plants of pepper in very fine Order, the other several flowering shrubs of this place'.[60] John White despatched specimens of birds to his patrons.

From 1790 this commerce became extensive. In April 1790 Phillip sent Banks six tubs of plants by the *Justinian*,[61] and the following March several 'cases of seeds', a keg containing 'a young kanguroo, a Porcupine, a Rat kanguroo ... & various other animals, & a skin of the *ma-ra-ong* (the Emu)'.[62] Subsequently, he sent three cases of seeds and four tubs of plants, and late in the year no fewer than sixty tubs of plants.[63] Simultaneously, Considen sent the famous naturalist kangaroo skins and stuffed birds, live opossums and parrots, dried flowers and seeds.[64] Inevitably, given his position as President of the Royal Society and his acquaintance with and abiding interest in New South Wales, Banks was the scientist to be first supplied, but he was not the only one. Phillip and White both sent specimens to J. E. Smith, the founder of the Linnean Society.[65] Phillip sent seaweeds to Thomas Velley.[66] White sent mammals, reptiles, birds, plants, shells, and fishes to his patron Thomas Wilson.[67] Considen supplied his friend Charles Hamilton.[68] Presumably, there were also numerous unrecorded parcels to reach London.[69] And in any case, Banks shared generously the contents of those that he received.

REALITY: THE INHABITANTS

Just as from the first they recorded their impressions of the country and its fauna and flora, so too did the First Fleet writers note details of the indigenous inhabitants from the moment of arrival at Botany Bay.[70] They were not, of course, inscribing their remarks on blank slates. Some of them would have read the comments made by Dampier on his visits to New Holland in 1688 and 1699, most would have had some knowledge of the more recent contact of 1770, but be unaware that the observations of Cook and Banks had been censored and mangled in the amalgam of their journals which appeared in Hawkesworth.[71] In the eighteenth-century discussions on the origins and nature of man, the Aborigines, together with the Hottentots and Fuegans, were invariably slotted into the first and most rudimentary stage of human development as a nomadic, non-agricultural people, either backward or degenerate. The influential Buffon in his *Variétés dans l'espèce humaine*, published in 1749, took his description of the Aborigines straight from Dampier—'perhaps the most miserable people in the world, those who most nearly approach animals'.[72] (5.16)

Predictably, the nakedness of the Aborigines was one of the first points described by the journal keepers, as were the initial hostile if distant demonstrations of shouting and spear-shaking (4.22). Only King seemed to have sensed any surprise or shock among the Aborigines, and he had his own interpretation of this. An Aborigine he saw on shore 'seemed quite astonished at ye figure we cut in being cloathed & I think it is very easy to conceive ye ridiculous figure we

179

must appear to those poor creatures who were perfectly naked'.[73] Although these first contacts were as peaceable as could be expected, an underlying tension was sensed by some of the newcomers. Even the sentence in William Bradley's journal, which provides the firmest evidence of some mingling between the seamen and the Aborigines as the ships came into Botany Bay, seems to end with a reservation: 'our People & the Natives were mixed together, the Boats Crews amused themselves with dressing the Natives w^h paper & other whimsical things to entertain them, with which they were pleas'd for the moment'.[74] The next day he made a more serious point when he described how a party was sent 'to clear away to a run of water on the S.° side of the Bay: The Natives were well pleas'd with our People until they began clearing the Ground at which they were displeased & wanted them to be gone'.[75] At the same time George Worgan noted that 'Some of the Natives ... expressed a little Anger at seeing us cut down the Trees, but it was only by jabbering very fast & loud'.[76] Others thought all was well. David Collins insisted that at Botany Bay 'the natives had hitherto conducted themselves sociably and peaceably towards all the parties of our officers and people with whom they had hitherto met, and by no means seemed to regard them as enemies or invaders of their country and tranquillity'.[77] Tench put it more starkly when he wrote, 'Our first object was to win their affections, and our next to convince them of the superiority we possessed.'[78] A demonstration of the use of firearms was sufficient to make the latter point, to the extent that White noted that 'from the first, they carefully avoided a soldier, or any person wearing a red coat'.[79]

The pattern of reasonable relations seemed to be maintained when within a week the whole expedition moved a few miles north along the coast to Port Jackson, and re-established itself at Sydney Cove. Phillip's first encounter with the Aborigines there 'gave me', he wrote, 'a much higher opinion of them than I had formed from the behaviour of those seen in Captain Cook's voyage, and their confidence and manly behaviour made me give the name of Manly Cove to this place'. He went on to describe how, 'As their curiosity made them very troublesome when we were preparing our dinner, I made a circle round us. There was little difficulty in making them understand that they were not to come within it, and they then sat down very quiet'.[80] When this was incorporated into the published account of Phillip's *Voyage* in 1789 the unknown editor added that this was 'another proof how tractable these people are when no insult or injury is offered, and when proper means are employed to influence the simplicity of their minds'.[81] A comment by Tench suggests that the circumstances of the meeting were given a greater significance by Phillip and his officers than they perhaps merited. 'It seems, that on that occasion, they not only received our people with great cordiality, but so far acknowledged their authority as to submit, that a boundary, during their first interview, might be drawn on the sand, which they attempted, not to infringe, and appeared to be satisfied with.'

The Aborigines helped with the hauling of the seine, pointed out the best landing places, and often left their weapons behind when coming down to the beach to greet the incoming boats. 'But in a few days', wrote Tench, 'they were observed to be more shy of our company. From what cause their distaste arose we never could trace, as we had made it our study, on these occasions, to treat them with kindness, and load them with presents. No quarrel had happened ....'.[82]

Some indication of the timing and nature of the change is given by Bradley, whose daily journal records his survey at this time of parts of the great harbour. Contact with Aborigines, helpful but alert, on 28 January, 'increased my favourable opinion of them very much', he wrote, and he gave the first full description of their canoes, spears, and fishing methods. On 30 January he met Aboriginal women, usually a sign of relaxed relations, though (as Bradley's painting (5.18) shows), armed men remained, 'silent & attentive', in the background, spears 'poised ready for throwing'. Despite these grim attendants, who were no doubt matched by watchful marines in the boats, 'Our people and these mixed together and were quite sociable, dancing and otherwise amusing them'. Within days there was a sudden and, to Bradley, inexplicable, change. On 2 February Aboriginal canoes turned and fled at his approach. Then, the next day, as a group of Aborigines spotted his surveying boat, 'the moment they perceiv'd us, they ran off in great confusion & hurry not taking time to make the canoes fast or haul them ashore ... their fright was so great that they went off without taking their fishing lines, spears or any thing with them'. On 4 February he was confronted by 'an astonishing number of the Natives all armed', and turned back.[83]

Several factors are probably involved. It may be, as some writers have speculated, that the Aborigines at first regarded the white arrivals as spirits, and that realization that this was not so led to an abrupt change of attitude.[84] After a few days, as more and more convicts disembarked, it must have been clear to the watching Aborigines that the white men were neither spirits, nor were transient visitors—as the *Endeavour's* crew had been—for the surveying and building operations indicated an intention of remaining in their country. Tench was writing quite openly about the problem of establishing good relations 'between the old, and new, lords of the soil'[85]—a change marked in formal fashion in a ceremony on 7 February during which Phillip had read the royal commission proclaiming his authority over New South Wales, there defined as extending from South Cape to Cape York, and inland as far as 135°E.[86] To Cook's original act of taking possession of most of the east coast of Australia in August 1770 was added the new fact of occupation and settlement, and neither in London nor at Sydney Cove was there any mention of native rights.

To the Aborigines the growing huddle of tents and shacks which formed the first settlement at Sydney Cove must have been a fearful place, to be shunned by most. There were the hospital tents with their sick and dying, the floggings

181

5.16 [Philip Gidley King] An Aboriginal Family ? 1788

5.17   William Bradley   'View in Broken Bay New South Wales. March 1788'

5.18   William Bradley   'First interview with the Native Women at Port Jackson   New South Wales'   1788

and less frequent but well-publicized hangings, the drunken brawls, the armed marines. To a people whose livelihood depended on their thin spacing across the land, the crowding of a thousand humans onto one site must have been at once incomprehensible and threatening. It appeared as 'a horrendous avalanche'[87] which threatened to sweep them and their customs away as the newcomers spilled out from the cramped shoreline of Sydney Cove. The violation, accidental or otherwise, of sacred sites almost certainly accounts for some of the resentments and outbursts of hostility which the new arrivals found difficult to understand. A reference by Bradley on 22 April to digging up an Aboriginal grave clearly represents a widespread practice, for before the end of the year he was writing that 'we have every reason to suppose that they burn the dead, from the number of graves we have open'd & . . . found the ashes with many pieces of bone not quite consumed'.[88] Later, Phillip promised Banks to send some Aboriginal skulls home, though he pointed out that their cremation customs might make this difficult.[89] Looming over such specific violations was the more general problem of incompatibility between the settlers' way of life and that of the Aborigines. At no point did the two touch and, as W. E. H. Stanner has put it, the English 'had no idea, it seems, that they were crowding at every place on to a confined estate whose every feature and object entailed proprietary rights and religious significances'.[90]

Another unsettling development was the violence which occurred back at Botany Bay between the Aborigines and the Frenchmen of the Lapérouse expedition which arrived there on 26 January within a few days of the English. The ships remained for six weeks, and as early as 1 February King reported that the French had thrown up a stockade around their tents and work-site. On 9 February a French officer visiting Port Jackson reported that 'they had been obliged to fire on the Natives at Botany Bay to keep them quiet'.[91] As Collins put it, 'This circumstance materially affected us, as those who had rendered this violence necessary could not discriminate between us and them.'[92] He thought that only 'the greatest necessity' would have led the Frenchmen to this pitch, but it is clear that their recent experiences at Samoa where a dozen crew-members had been killed in an attack by the islanders had produced an attitude at once more wary and embittered than that of Phillip's officers.[93]

Even so, it is unlikely that the violence had broken out so soon after the French arrival as to explain the mood, first of fear and then defiance, which Bradley noted some miles away at Port Jackson in the first days of February. A more probable explanation is that Phillip's instructions to conciliate and protect the native inhabitants—a difficult aim at the best of times given the massed nature of the intrusion—were being ignored by some of the ships' crews and convicts almost from the beginning. Although he put no precise date to it, Collins wrote of this period that 'the convicts were every where straggling about, collecting animals and gum to sell to the people of the transports, who at the same time were procuring spears, shields, swords, fishing-lines, and other articles from the natives, to carry to Europe; the loss of which must have been attended with many inconveniences to the owners'.[94] The lack of control over the movements of the convicts was shown by the muster of 23 February, at which ten were reported missing, and by the number who during the same month slipped across country to Botany Bay in hopes of finding a passage back to Europe in the French ships. The Aborigines reacted by stealing implements and tools, so that by mid-February Lieutenant Ralph Clark of the marines was writing, 'they are the Greatest thefs that ever lived—I think that we are in a fine stat we brought nothing but thefs out with us to find nothing but thefs'.[95]

The journals for the next few months show occasional signs of friendly contact. On 15 February Phillip met some Aborigines, one of whom was persuaded to try his hand at rowing. On 2 March boats' crews were given a friendly reception 'by a great number of the Natives' at Broken Bay, as shown in another of Bradley's paintings (5.17). On 25 April Bradley described how some officers returned overland from Botany Bay and 'met several of the Natives, all very friendly; One party which they met at close of the evening shewd them a Hut, making signs for them to sleep there, they also brought them Fire & Water & came to visit them in the morning'.[96] On 24 May Worgan wrote of an encounter with native women—'some shew no signs of Fear, but will laugh and Frisk about You like a Spaniel, and put on the Airs of a Tantalizing Coquet'.[97] But such entries were accompanied by others showing evidence of increased friction between the Aborigines and the settlers—an indication of the difficulty, indeed unreality, of attempting to confine the different experiences of scattered observers into a single interpretative framework. On 19 February Aborigines stole shovels and a pickaxe, and had 'their skin well pepper'd with small shot'. On 10 March Bradley, whose surveying duties took him farther afield than most of the journal keepers, met a native with 'marks on his body where he had been beat & also on the Shoulder by the people who landed here from two Boats'.[98] And in his first letter home on 15 May Phillip admitted that because of the clashes with the Lapérouse expedition and 'the bad behaviour of some of the transports' boats and some convicts, the natives have lately avoided us'.[99]

'Proper measures', Phillip wrote, were to be taken to regain the confidence of the natives, but instead events took a more serious turn in the last week of May. On 23 May an Aborigine was killed in a scuffle with convicts, knowledge of which seemed slow to come to official attention. A week later two convicts out cutting rushes were speared to death by Aborigines (5.19). The details of these, the first known deaths on either side, repay examination. Most of the journal keepers were agreed in linking the two incidents, and in apportioning blame. Phillip was convinced that in both cases the convicts had been the aggressors.[100] Collins, who reporting an earlier incident had remarked that there was 'too much reason to believe that our people had been the aggressors', noted that the dead convicts had earlier stolen a canoe, 'for which act of violence and injustice they paid with their lives'.[101] Hunter wrote, 'It has been strongly suspected that these people had engaged in some dispute or quarrel with them, and as they had hatchets and bill-hooks with them, it is believed they might have been rash enough to use violence with some of the natives, who had, no doubt, been numerous there.'[102] Seaman Richard Williams thought that 'It was supposed to have been done thro' revenge for taking away one of their canoes'.[103] Bradley had perhaps the most interesting entry, a day after the discovery of the bodies of the two slain convicts. He heard that 'a Convict had killed one of the Natives some days before by cutting him across the belly with his knife. I have no doubt but this Native having been murder'd occasioned their seeking revenge & which proved fatal to those who were not concern'd. They have attack'd our people when they have met them unarmed, but that did not happen until they had been very ill treated by us in the lower part of the Harbour & fired upon at Botany Bay by the French'.[104]

For the Englishmen, a surprising development followed hard on these killings. Taking a dozen armed men with him to recover the implements of the dead convicts and to attempt a reconciliation, Phillip had to turn back after encountering more than two hundred armed Aborigines—by far the largest force seen by white men in Australia, and quite unexpected. A similar, sobering encounter took place a few days later, as related by Blackburn. 'A Party of Gentlemen with their servants & 4 soldiers were walking to Botany Bay—Met with a Body of 300 & upwards all arm'd with spears & Targets. They did not seem to feel their superiority of Numbers but walk'd out of the Track our People were in & let them pass without showing any Mischievous Intention.'[105] Of the impressions passed on to the First Fleet from Cook's visit one of the first to be modified was that there were very few Aborigines even in the coastal area, and none in the interior. Even before the ships sailed David Collins had wondered about this, and had worried whether the settlement would be able to defend itself against possible native attacks.[106] Phillip himself had suggested while still in England that 'on landing in Botany Bay it will be necessary to throw up a slight work as a defence against the natives—who, tho' only seen in small numbers by Captn. Cook, may be very numerous on other parts of the coast'.[107] By mid-1788 Phillip considered that there were probably about 1500 Aborigines in the Botany Bay—Port Jackson—Broken Bay area, and that they were 'far more numerous than I expected'. He had come across traces of them 30 miles into the interior, and had seen smoke 50 miles inland, so 'there cannot be the least doubt but that there are Inhabitants in the interior parts of the Country'.[108] To the anxieties and tensions inevitable in a mixed group of convicts and their guards as they struggled to come to terms with an alien environment was added the fear that unknown numbers of probably hostile natives might be gathering in the bush. The reassuring comments of Cook and Banks about the land and its

186

5.19   [Port Jackson Painter]   An Attack by Aborigines   *?c.* 1788

5.20   [Port Jackson Painter]   'Mr White, Harris & Laing with a party of Soldiers visiting
       Botany Bay Colebee...'   *?* 1788–92

inhabitants seemed to be losing relevance by the day.

The second half of 1788 saw little change in the pattern of mistrust and occasional violence. While Phillip in his letters of July 1788 to be taken on the homeward-bound ships wrote of his hopes 'to persuade some of them to live near us ... to reconcile them to us, & to render their situation more comfortable',[109] Major Ross, the edgy commandant of the marines, was arguing the necessity for some sort of defences against possible native attacks, for 'I am by no means of opinion that they are that harmless, inoffensive race they have in general been represented to be'. As evidence of this he pointed to the fearsome injuries suffered by the two convict rush-cutters, 'most barbarously mangled and murther'd by the natives. One of the bodys had no less than seven spears in it, some of which went through and through, and the skulls of both were fractured'.[110] A letter from Tench in the same month blamed the convict deaths on the 'brutal and undistinguishing ferocity' of the natives.[111] There were still amicable encounters, but little trust on either side. White wrote of a meeting with Aborigines in July, friendly and relaxed, when 'all on a sudden they paddled away from us. On looking about to discover the cause, we perceived the gunner of the *Supply* at some little distance, with a gun in his hand'.[112] Daniel Southwell, mate of the *Sirius*, described another meeting in August with seventy or eighty Aborigines at Manly Cove. 'They affected a deal of good humour and unconcern; but 'tis believed they do not much like our coming amongst them. The watchful eye they keep upon our people's musquets is very likely the effect of fear; but it also seems expressive of disappointment, and leads to a doubt of their sincerity if not thus overawed.'[113]

Two days later, after cautiously remaining in the boats on glimpsing 200 Aborigines on shore, the crews heard what appeared to be fierce fighting just out of sight. Phillip, following his policy of trying to calm settler alarm and to reassure the Aborigines, commented that the affray was probably 'no more than an exercise'[114]—an interpretation Southwell refused to accept. He wrote that 'At first the noise was simply that of men's voices wrangling with the most barbarous dissonance and savage agitation; but now the clashing of spears and the strokes of lances against the target was very distinctly heard'. Three possible explanations of this tumult came to mind, none of them particularly reassuring to the boat crews as they lay offshore. It might represent 'the first dictates of passionate resentment'; possibly it was an attempt 'to impress us with formidable sentiments of their native savage bravery'; or it could be 'a stratagem to draw us on shore'. As dusk fell the boats pulled away to avoid possible involvement, but spears were thrown, 'for so depraved are their sentiments', Southwell concluded, 'that forbearance, instead of having the use intended, only led them to despise our seeming imbecility'.[115]

In September Phillip wrote to Lord Sydney in somewhat despondent tones. 'They certainly are not pleased with our remaining amongst them, as they see we deprive them of fish, which is almost their only support; but if they set fire to the corn, necessity will oblige me to drive them to a greater distance.'[116] Perhaps in conformity with this, the garrison now opened fire as soon as the Aborigines threatened, 'it having now come absolutely necessary to compel them to keep at a greater distance from the settlement', Collins wrote.[117] By the beginning of October Bradley was convinced that the natives were well disposed only 'when they suppose we have them in our power or are well prepared by being armed. Latterly, they have attack'd almost every person who has met with them that has not had a musquet & have sometimes endeavoured to surprise some who had'.[118] The situation was, in Tench's words, one of 'unabated animosity', 'petty warfare', and 'endless uncertainty',[119]—although these remarks should be seen in the light of the convict casualty figures as recorded by Collins. By the end of the year fifty-six had died of natural causes, fourteen were missing, five had been hanged, and only four killed by the Aborigines.[120]

By the end of the first year a flickering picture of Aboriginal life was emerging in the journals, particularly those of Tench, Hunter and Bradley. The remarks of Tench and Hunter, written with publication in mind, followed the conventional classification of eighteenth-century travel accounts: the physical appearance, means of subsistence, government, war and religion of the native inhabitants.[121] Neither man showed complete confidence in his observations. As Tench pointed out, his chapter was 'made up of detached observations, taken at different times, and not from a regular series of knowledge of the customs and manners of a people, with whom opportunities of communication are so scarce, as to have been seldom obtained'.

On the appearance of the Aborigines, Tench noted that they were 'nimble sprightly, and vigorous', Hunter that they were 'a straight, thin, but well made people, rather small in their limbs, but very active'. Both men were repelled by further features of the Aborigines' appearance—Tench by their custom of scarifying themselves ('It is hardly possible to see anything in human shape more ugly, than one of those savages thus scarified, and further ornamented with a fish bone struck through the gristle of the nose'), Hunter by the fact that 'They are abominably filthy'. The reader is left in no doubt that even by eighteenth-century European standards of hygiene the Aborigines were 'dirty'; but two points should be kept in mind. The neglect of any form of sanitation was that of a people living in the open, and on the move; and some of the layering of grease which Europeans found so nauseating was a deliberate precaution to keep out the cold and to fend off biting insects.[122] Like all the observers, Tench and Hunter stressed the total nudity of the Aborigines (5.21), though without the moral censure shown, for example, by Robert Brown when he encountered some Aboriginal women: 'stark naked, and did not show the least signs of shame'.[123] What intrigued Tench and Hunter was how exposed the lack of clothes left the Aborigines to the elements—'shivering, and huddling them-

5.21   Engraved by J. Stothard after John Hunter   Terrified Aboriginal mother and child 1793

selves up in heaps', as Tench put it. All the observers had descriptions of their bark shelters, often simply windbreaks, their fishing nets and bone fish-hooks, spears and stone hatchets. Even though White on one occasion saw a hut 'with more comfort and convenience' than usual, his experience on the West Indian station led him to declare that 'in improvements of every kind, the Indians of this country are many centuries behind' those he had seen on the Mosquito Shore (5.20).[124]

Tench provided as good a description as could be expected of the means of subsistence of the Port Jackson Aborigines:

To cultivation of the ground they are utter strangers, and wholly depend for food on the few fruits they gather; the roots they dig up in the swamps; and the fish they pick up along shore, or contrive to strike from their canoes with spears. Fishing, indeed, seems to engross nearly the whole of their time, probably from its forming the chief part of a subsistence, which observation has convinced us, nothing short of the most painful labour, and unwearied assiduity, can procure.

Bradley's surveying expeditions had shown him that the means of subsistence of a particular tribe depended on its location, and that some of the natives further inland hunted kangaroo, set traps for catching ducks, and had snares for taking smaller animals. After the first assumption that the Aborigines lived almost entirely on fish (5.22), some understanding began to emerge of the complexity of an economy based on the varied but exiguous resources of a natural environment. Failure to 'improve' this environment, in particular the refusal or inability to

190

5.22   [Port Jackson Painter]   'A New South Wales native stricking fish while his wife is
        employed fishing with hooks & lines in her canoe'   1788—92

cultivate, remained a perplexing matter. As Bradley stressed, 'we never met with
the smallest appearance of any kind of Cultivated ground'.[125] That the indigenous
seeds were not suitable for arable farming, nor kangaroos and emus controllable
in a pastoral economy, seemed not to have occurred to the critical observers of
the First Fleet.[126] The economy of effort and the simplicity of implements which
characterized the Aborigines' way of life were seen by the newcomers as
evidence only of indolence and poverty.

As far as their government was concerned, Tench could see—to use his
rather stilted language—no sign of 'civil regulations, or ordinances . . . excepting
a little tributary respect which the younger part appear to pay those more
advanced in years, I never could observe any degree of subordination among
them'. Hunter differed to the extent that he thought that 'In all their quarrels
with one another, they put themselves under the direction of a chief: how those
chiefs are chosen we have not learnt, but have reason to believe it is from an
opinion of their dexterity in war'. Neither observer could discern any religious
rites or beliefs. This conclusion was not surprising, for the complex spiritual life
of the Aborigines was impenetrable to observers intent on finding evidence
among the natives of belief in 'a Deity'. Hunter and Tench had not progressed
further than Dampier a hundred years earlier: 'I did not perceive that they did
worship any thing.'[127] Finally, the two men differed on the more limited but
crucial question of the future relationship between the settlers and the natives.
Hunter thought 'it will be no very difficult matter, in due time, to conciliate

191

their friendship and confidence'; Tench suspected that 'the fickle, jealous, wavering disposition' of the natives would block all such attempts. Away from the formal observations of journal keepers writing for publication, David Blackburn, master of the *Supply*, summed up in more laconic fashion what may have been for most of the newcomers the immediate impression of the natives—'to all appearance the Lowest in Rank among the Human Race. They go Quite Naked & very Dirty. They do not seem to Live in Community, but by separate familys in Caves & Hollows of the Rocks & as far as we know live only on fish & the Root of the Fern which Grows here in Plenty'.[128]

Most of the accounts modified in some respects the descriptions given in Hawkesworth. The Aborigines were more numerous, and potentially more formidable, than Cook and Banks had thought, and they seemed livelier altogether than the incurious, apathetic groups encountered in 1770. But the baffling inability to make real contact with them, the difficulty of interpreting their attitudes and actions, exercised Phillip and his officers as it had done Cook and Banks eighteen years earlier. The most frustrating aspect of the situation as seen through the eyes of the officers of 1788 was the conviction that they intended the native inhabitants no harm, and that any misbehaviour on the part of the convicts or marines towards them would be punished. How to convey this to a people as elusive, fearful and sporadically violent as the Aborigines, particularly given the language barrier, was not easy. Phillip had explained the problem in a letter of July 1788: 'Of these people we know little; for though I go amongst them as often as the many circumstances which draw my attention permit, yet not being able to remain any time with them, and they never coming near us, but when we are near the coves in which they reside, or for a few minutes in their canoes alongside the *Sirius*, very few words of their language are attained.'[129] By the end of the year attempts were made to capture one or more of the Aborigines in the hope, as Tench put it, that this 'would induce an intercourse, by the report which our prisoners would make of the mildness and indulgence with which we used them'.[130] There seems to have been little awareness of the inherent paradox of this policy, with a tension between the means and the end which would not be easy to resolve. The editor of Phillip's *Voyage* built onto the decision a spiralling staircase of an argument: 'It will probably turn out to be the kindest piece of violence that could be used . . . They will then perhaps acquire sufficient confidence in their new countrymen to mix with them, to enrich themselves with some of their implements, and to learn and adopt some of the most useful and necessary of their arts.'[131]

On the last day of 1788 an Aborigine named Arabanoo was finally taken. The first actions of his captors were characteristic of the whole approach: they washed and shaved him, cut his hair, put clothes on him, then tethered him to a convict by handcuffs. Arabanoo's fellow Aborigines made strenuous efforts to save him at the time of his capture, but seemed to take no further interest in his

5.23   William Bradley   'Taking of Colbee & Benalon   25 Nov.ʳ 1789'

fate. The dreadful epidemic of smallpox at that time swept him away as it did many of the Aborigines of the Port Jackson region, where unburied corpses lay scattered at the water's edge. The onset of the disease was sudden and unexpected. James Scott seems to have come across the first victims while out cutting grass on 15 April, but soon Tench reported 'repeated accounts brought by our boats of finding bodies of the Indians in all the coves and inlets of the harbour'.[132] 'In the caves of the rocks', Hunter wrote, 'which used to shelter whole families in bad weather, were now to be seen men, women, and children, lying dead.'[133] A few of the sick were brought into the settlement, and a boy (Nanbaree) and a girl (Abaroo) recovered.

The origins of the outbreak puzzled the surgeons, who insisted that there was no smallpox on the First Fleet, and the matter has recently engaged the attention of scholars once more. A list of possible causes has been advanced at one time or another: that the disease was not smallpox at all; that smallpox was already endemic among the Aborigines; that it reached the Sydney area, coincidentally just after the European arrival, by overland transmission from the north coast where it had been introduced among the Aborigines by Macassan traders; that it came from the Lapérouse expedition; that the First Fleet carried, unnoticed, some latent form of smallpox which wrought havoc among the unprotected Aborigines; that the 'variolus matter' (probably dried smallpox scabs used in the

5.24 [Port Jackson Painter] 'The Governor making the best of his way to the Boat after being wounded with the spear sticking in his Shoulder'   1790

primitive inoculation process of the period) known to have been brought out by the fleet surgeons was still potent after two years, and somehow—by accident or design—had infected the Aborigines.[134] How many died in what was the first recorded instance of the vulnerability of the Aborigines to an unfamiliar disease is not known. Phillip thought that half the local population had been wiped out in a matter of weeks, and that the disease had spread along the coast and inland. It was little wonder, as Tench put it, that 'the same suspicious dread of our approach, and the same scenes of vengeance acted on unfortunate stragglers, continued to prevail'.[135]

After several further attempts, two more Aborigines were taken in November 1789 (5.23). Bradley was in charge of the operation, which he both drew and described in his journal—'The two poor devils were seiz'd & handed into the boat in an instant ... it was by far the most unpleasant service I ever was order'd to Execute.'[136] One of the prisoners, Colby, soon escaped, fetters and all; but the other, Bennelong, 'acquired knowledge, both of our manners and language, faster than his predecessors had done'.[137] Then, in May 1790, he too escaped. Both he and Colby were seen from time to time on the edge of the settlement, and in a chance meeting with them and a group of other Aborigines, Phillip received a serious, though not fatal, wound when a strange Aborigine suddenly threw a spear into his shoulder (5.24). It was generally accepted that 'the action proceeded from a momentary impulse of fear'[138]—understandable in

194

the light of the several kidnap attempts—but a more general sense of mistrust was revealed in the inquiries which followed the incident. Two Aborigines 'expressed great dissatisfaction at the number of white men who had settled in their former territories', while Bennelong complained that 'his countrymen had lately been plundered of fish-gigs, spears, a sword, and many other articles, by some of our people'.[139]

Before the end of 1790 relations were patched up, and to some extent put on a new footing. This came about partly through Bennelong and Colby, who began coming into the settlement after the former had been restored to favour following the help he gave a boat's crew in trouble, partly through the efforts of Abaroo, the Aboriginal girl recovered from smallpox who was in the care of the Reverend Johnson. After preliminary contacts on the north shore of the harbour, Bennelong, Colby and two other Aborigines visited the governor on 8 October, but only on condition that Johnson, Abaroo, and a convict were held among the Aborigines 'as a Pledge'.[140] Hunter noted that Bennelong and Colby 'were kindly received, went from house to house, and saw all their old acquaintances; they received many little presents, and returned to their friends when they thought proper'.[141] By 19 October James Scott was writing that 'the Natives Come in frequently', and that the governor was building a small house for them; and by the end of the month that 'Great Numbers' were daily at the settlement.[142] The other journals confirm this change, which was marked in spectacular fashion when twenty-six Aboriginal men and women performed a corroboree for the officers under the direction of Bennelong and Colby. As Tench put it, 'From this time our intercourse with the natives, though partially interrupted, was never broken off'.[143]

There is something baffling about this development. In March 1791 Captain Campbell of the marines was still puzzled. 'The accident has, somehow or other, tho' I cannot account for the reason, it being diametrically opposite to what might naturally have been expected, produced one advantage, for the natives have almost ever since, appeared perfectly reconciled to us.'[144] One writer has recently seen the willingness of the Aborigines to come into the settlement as a surrender—a recognition at one level that the spear was no match for the musket, and at another that with traditional sources of food obliterated by the arrival of the Europeans a new relation of dependence on the strangers was both possible and necessary.[145] There is some evidence for this in the journals. Hunter, for example, wrote that 'whenever they were pressed for hunger, they had immediate recourse to our quarters, where they generally got their bellies filled'.[146] Such a collapse of confidence and resistance is easier to understand after the catastrophic casualties of the smallpox epidemic the previous year.

The change of attitude had important implications, not least in the half-hidden area of sexual contact between the settlers and Aboriginal women. On this the journals are mostly reticent, but it must have been at about this time that the change began to take place from the situation described by Bradley in October 1788 when he wrote, 'To speak of the virtue of the Ladies of this Country, I believe no one in the Colony can boast of having received favours',[147] wording which points to female unavailability rather than female unattractiveness as the reason for settler abstinence. To Captain Campbell, contemptuous of the natives and all their ways, the native women, 'the filthiest of all God's creatures', were 'an antidote to all desire'; but this was not a universal opinion.[148] George Worgan, while also deploring the women's dirt and grease, wrote with some enthusiasm about the 'Proportion, . . . Softness, . . . roundness, and Plumpness in their Limbs & Bodies'. He pronounced that were it not 'for the nauseous, greasy, grimy appearance of these *naked* Damsels, one might be said to be in a state of *Tantalism*, whenever they vouchsafe to permit Us to come near them'.[149] With male convicts outnumbering female by three to one, and with, as Campbell put it with some irritation in March 1791, 'morning, noon & night, [Aboriginal] men, women and children, and all, without even madam Eve's covering, rambling about our Huts',[150] it was not likely that widespread sexual contacts would be further delayed. By the time Collins left Sydney in 1796 Aboriginal women were being kept both in the settlement and on board the ships in the harbour as virtual prostitutes.[151]

Despite the improvement in relations at the end of 1790 contact remained brittle and fragile. Bradley wrote in his journal that 'Notwithstanding this apparent friendly intercourse I cannot think they are to be trusted.'[152] Dr John Harris noted that 'the Governor Built a House for them to which they come and go at pleasure. I know of no good they have as yet been to us nor do I think they ever will . . . I am certain they will never be in friendship with us especially when their party is stronger than ours'.[153] Phillip wrote to Banks that although the natives 'are now as much at home at Sydney as they are in their woods . . . very little information has been obtained, & what I have sent to Mr. Nepean on the subject, I send merely because I suppose something would be expected'.[154] Great hopes were pinned on Bennelong, but in many ways he was a sad disappointment. His conversation, when it could be understood, seemed to dwell excessively on his disputes with other Aborigines over women. He had been given clothes, 'but he did not always condescend to wear them'. In brief, as Tench put it in some despair, 'inexplicable contradictions arose to bewilder our researches, which no ingenuity could unravel, and no credulity reconcile'.[155] Hunter's comment on Bennelong's progress revealed something of the super-ficiality of the whole exercise. 'Considering the state of nature which he has been brought up in, he may be called a polite man, as he performs every action of bowing, drinking healths, returning thanks, &c. with the most scrupulous attention.'[156] Similar problems hampered the attempt to convert and civilize Abaroo (5.35). Once her fellow Aborigines began coming into the settlement, 'she has not behaved so well or so complying', complained the Reverend Johnson.

'Once and again she has been off in the woods for sometime.'[157]

Two characteristics of the Aborigines, in particular, bothered the observers. The first was their disinclination to improve their lot by following the European example now displayed to them of cultivation and industry; the second was the level of apparently gratuitous violence in Aboriginal society, especially towards women. Soon after his arrival in the settlement in April 1792 Richard Atkins wrote: 'The people of this Country show not the least disposition to profit by our example. Industry even to procure those articles they seem so fond of, as Potatoes, Greens &c they have no idea of, their whole thoughts seem to be emply'd in fishing and hunting the Kangaroo, and as soon as their appetites are satisfied they lay down to sleep.'[158] An even more severe judgement was made by Daniel Paine, who arrived in 1795 as a boatbuilder:

The Native Inhabitants are the most irrational and ill formed Human beings on the Face of the Earth destitute in every Thought for future Comfort and deriving as yet no benefit from Civilization ... they have no Idea of profiting by the Example of our Settlers to sow Corn for a sure Provision ... nothing but the Inclemency of Weather or Hunger makes them Visitants for they will not attempt to assist you by working.[159]

As far as the lot of the Aboriginal women was concerned, the observers were united in pity and condemnation. Campbell wrote: 'The women seem to be under the greatest subjection to the men, and, if we may judge from the number of them that come in, with broken heads, which the men boast of having given them, they are most cruelly treated.'[160] Tench sounded the same refrain—'the women are in all respects treated with savage barbarity; condemned not only to carry the children, but all other burthens, they meet in return for submission only with blows, kicks, and every other mark of brutality'. It would be an over-simplification to insist that one reason for the increasingly critical attitude to the Aborigines was their failure to conform to the standards of a polite Englishman, but there is something of this in the reaction. It is there in the despairing cry of Tench:

A thousand times ... have I wished, that those European philosophers, whose closet speculations exalt a state of nature above a state of civilization, could survey the phantom, which their heated imaginations have raised: possibly they might then learn, that a state of nature is, of all others, least adapted to promote the happiness of a being ... that a savage roaming for prey amidst his native deserts, is a creature deformed by all those passions, which afflict and degrade our nature.[161]

All the difficulties of perception and understanding experienced by Europeans in their confrontations with the peoples of the Pacific in this period seemed to be summed up in their most acute form in the encounter with the Aborigines. The ethnocentric attempts of the observers of the previous decades to find evidence in the Pacific islands of familiar figures and structures—of kings and chiefs, priests, villages, cultivation—ran into a dead end of incomprehension at Sydney Cove.[162]

In general, the continuance of attacks, thefts and killings on both sides bears the depressingly familiar stamp of frontier violence. Attitudes were hardening.

In 1788 Blackburn thought the Aborigines 'a Quiet Inoffensive People'; in 1791 he wrote, 'they are very treacherous & however friendly they may Appear whilst amongst us, Experience has taught us, that they are not to be trusted in the Woods, without an Apparent Superiority on our side'.[163] Phillip, attempting at one and the same time to restrain and protect the convict settlers, and to conciliate and fend off the natives, was in danger of failing in all respects. Floggings seemed to have no effect on the convicts; while two punitive expeditions mounted against the Aborigines after the spearing of the governor's gamekeeper, John McEntire, returned without any sightings. The circumstances of McEntire's death afford a glimpse of the unrecorded history of the relations between the settlers and Aborigines at this time, away from the gaze of Phillip and his officers. Despite McEntire's death-bed denials of ever having attacked Aborigines, there seems no doubt that Bennelong regarded him with 'dread and hatred'. The witness to this, Tench, continued, 'From the aversion uniformly shewn by all the natives to this unhappy man, he had long been suspected by us of having in his excursions, shot and injured them'.[164] These suspicions were presumably not shared by Phillip, and if the original intentions of the retaliatory expeditions had been carried out—ten Aborigines to be killed, and their heads brought back, as punishment for the gamekeeper's death—the governor's reputation for humanity would have taken a hard knock. Fortunately for all concerned, the chances of the cumbersome, heavily-armed punitive expeditions coming within firing distance of Aborigines on their own terrain were slight, and meanwhile Phillip had time for second, and third, thoughts.

Reflecting upon the situation in February 1791, Collins moved nearer the core of the problem as far as the Aborigines were concerned: 'While they entertained the idea of our having dispossessed them of their residences, they must always consider us as enemies; and upon this principle they made a point of attacking the white people whenever opportunity and safety concurred.'[165] Here, and in Phillip's acknowledgement that the Aborigines had lost their fishing grounds in the harbour, there is some realization of the clash of material interests which followed the European arrival. But the matter went further than that. Two totally incompatible cultures had been thrust against each other. Aboriginal culture was one based on family bands which ranged over a given territory, and whose intimate knowledge of it—the location of plants, animals, water—allowed them to exist in an environment where strangers would have perished. It is therefore ironic that for all the much-vaunted technical superiority of the First Fleet, the failure of the follow-up expedition to arrive when expected brought the settlers near starvation and death. As White wrote in April 1790, rations were being reduced to such a level 'as will enable us to drag out a miserable existence for seven months. Should we have no arrivals in that time, the game will be up with us ... '.[166] There was, and could be, no understanding among the newcomers that the bond between an Aboriginal band or clan and its traditional territory was fundamentally a religious one. 'The Aborigines conceived it as a union of earth, sky and water on the one hand with spirit, body and personality on the other. A band did not "own" land in the European sense. It and territory were twain; the connection was inextinguishable; the territory inalienable.'[167] Equipment, material possessions, dwellings, were minimal, light, and above all portable or dispensable. No greater contrast could exist between this culture, tracing its activities with the lightest of touches upon the surface of the land, and the incessant digging, enclosing and improving activities of the newcomers, who were determined to stamp their imprint on their surroundings, using military discipline or concepts of individual ownership as the means to that end. The acquisitive, accumulative instincts of the European had nothing in common with a way of life where unnecessary possessions or a static location could mean death.

Despite his insistence on treating the indigenous inhabitants with courtesy and kindness, Phillip could have had no answer to the problem of co-existence. His formal statement before he left England of how he intended to deal with the Aborigines was both optimistic and inadequate: to 'proceed in this business without having any dispute with the natives, a few of which I shall endeavour to persuade to settle near us, and who I mean to furnish with everything that can tend to civilize them, and to give them a high opinion of their new guests'.[168] The gulf in comprehension was almost complete, and attempts to bridge it were hindered by the language barrier. Slowly, it became clear to the Europeans that it was not a question of mastering a single Aboriginal language. Even within the limited range of these first contacts, several different linguistic groupings had been dimly discerned which the settlers characterized as 'tribes'—the Camaraigal on the north shore of Port Jackson, the Cadigal along the south shore, the Wangal near Parramatta, and the Gayiumai north of Manly. As Phillip wrote to Banks in 1791, 'it was a matter of great surprize to me when I first arrived in this Country, to find that the words used by the natives when you was here, were not understood by the present inhabitants'.[169] Collins admitted that 'our knowledge of their language consisted at this time of only a few terms for such things as, being visible, could not well be mistaken'.[170] The limits of this knowledge were shown by Tench when he noted that they had been at Port Jackson for almost three years 'before we knew that the word Bée-al signified no, and not good'.[171]

The new familiarity of some Aborigines with the settlement compounded rather than eased the problem of relations. It was the beginning of the process which brought them into a state of mendicity, even parasitism. At the same time as one group of Aborigines, dressed in cast-off European clothes, were carrying wood and water for the settlers at Sydney Cove, another band might be attacking convicts as they were on the move between the outlying settlements. Either reaction, the dependent or the aggressive, would have put difficulties in the way of establishing a steady relationship between the European newcomers and the Aboriginal inhabitants. The apparently unpredictable fluctuations between the two made such a relationship impossible. As one scholar has put it, 'Permanent settlement left them dispossessed, with only two courses open—pauperism and clash',[172] and the origins of this bleak dilemma can be seen as early as 1790.

EPILOGUE

When Governor Arthur Phillip left New South Wales in December 1792 he took with him 'various specimens of the natural productions of the country, timber, plants, animals, and birds. Among the animals were four fine kangaroos, and several native dogs'.[173] Also with him went two Aborigines, Bennelong and Yemmerrawannie, 'who withstood at the moment of their departure the united distress of their wives, and the dismal lamentations of their friends, to accompany him to England, a place they well knew was a great distance from them';[174] and he took as well a portfolio of drawings, of Aborigines, fauna and flora.[175]

Reaction to Phillip's arrival back in England in May 1793 with these samples of the antipodean world was various. Phillip himself gave the major share of the content of his fifty tubs of plants to Banks, who established them with their predecessors at Kew, and much lesser portions to Lord Hawkesbury and others such as John Sibthrop, Sherardian Professor at Oxford, and J. E. Smith; and Banks and Smith in turn distributed their largesse.[176] In reporting Phillip's arrival, the *Dublin Chronicle* observed that he 'has brought home with him two of the natives of New Holland, a man and a boy, and brought them to town'. 'From the description given of the natives of Jackson's Bay', the report

5.25   Engraved by J. Neagle after [Anonymous]   Bennelong in European dress   1798

THE WONDERFUL

KANGUROO,

FROM

BOTANY BAY,

(The only One ever brought alive to Europe)

Removed from the HAY-MARKET, and now exhibited at the LYCEUM, in the STRAND, from 8 o'Clock in the Morning, till 8 in the Evening.

THIS amazing, beautiful, and tame Animal, is about five Feet in Height, of a Fawn Colour, and diftinguifhes itfelf in Shape, Make, and true Symmetry of Parts, *different from all other* QUADRUPEDS. Its Swiftnefs, when purfued, is fuperior to the Greyhound: to enumerate its extraordinary Qualities would far exceed the common Limits of a Public Notice. Let it fuffice to obferve, that the Public in general are pleafed, and beftow their Plaudits; the Ingenious are delighted; the Virtuofo, and Connoiffeur, are taught to admire! impreffing the Beholder with Wonder and Afto-nifhment, at the Sight of this unparalleled Animal from the Southern Hemifphere, that almoft furpaffes Belief; therefore Ocular Demonftration will exceed all that Words can defcribe, or Pencil delineate........Admittance, ONE SHILLING each.

5.26 [Anonymous] Kangaroo Broadside 1791

continued, 'they appear to be a race totally incapable of civilisation, every attempt to that end having proved ineffectual and yet they discover an astonishing art and cunning in their mode of fishing and entrapping the kangeroo and birds, the only animal food found there.'[177] None the less, His Majesty graciously received Bennelong at St James (5.25).[178] And the public wondered. 'Have you no kind friends among the *virtuosi*', a correspondent asked the editor of the *Gentleman's Magazine*,

that will give you some account, though but a hasty one, of the *gamgarou,* the new animal just brought to England from South Wales by Governor Philips. Certainly, Sir, it would give much satisfaction to many of your readers to be informed of the colour of the creature, his size and figure; whether he be wild or domestic; together with such of his qualities and properties as are known at present; so that one may be able to judge to what class or species of animals to refer him.[179]

British responses to the general experience of the First Fleet officers as reported in the years 1789–93 were similar.[180] Inevitably, some of the British public's interest was simply sensational. When a kangaroo sent by John White reached England alive in 1791, an entrepreneur quickly exhibited it to his profit and Phillip's distress (5.26). On being informed by Banks that the animal had been valued at £500, the governor scornfully denied that he had sent it, asking 'surely it is not supposed in England that I am in partnership with a Show man?'[181]

Perhaps ephemeral in itself, such charlatanism might act to spur a more serious interest. As the correspondent to the *Gentleman's Magazine* pointed out, the public stood in need of the virtuosi's assessment of New South Wales's many wonders. And the experts, both amateur and professional, high and low, were not backward in deploying their knowledge. From 1789 London nurserymen were cultivating antipodean plants to meet a lively demand from wealthy amateur collectors.[182] The leading ornithologist John Latham advised on the plates for *The Voyage of Governor Phillip to Botany Bay* (1789). The zoologist George Shaw, the botanist J. E. Smith, and the anatomist John Hunter all advised Thomas Wilson, the editor of John White's *Journal of a Voyage to New South Wales* (1790), in which appeared 'Sixty-five Plates of Non descript Animals, Birds, Lizards, Serpents, curious Cones of Trees and other Natural Productions'. The great German anatomist Johann Blumenbach asked Banks for specimens of Aboriginal skulls, so that he might further his studies of the origin and divergence of the human race.[183]

This concerted study quickly led to a recognition of the diversity and frequent uniqueness of things antipodean. J. E. Smith, for example, began his *Specimen of the Botany of New Holland* (1793−4) with the observation that

When a botanist first enters on the investigation of so remote a country as New Holland, he finds himself as it were in a new world. He can scarcely meet with any certain fixed points from which to draw his analogies; and even those that appear most promising are frequently in danger of misleading him. Whole tribes of plants, which at first sight seem familiar to his acquaintance, as occupying links in Nature's chain ... prove, on a nearer

5.27   Fernando Brambila   View of Sydney ('Vista de la Colonia Inglesa de Sydney en la Nueva Gales Meridional')   1793

examination, total strangers, with other configurations, other oeconomy, and other qualities; not only the species that present themselves are new, but most of the genera, and even natural orders.[184]

It was a perception that Erasmus Darwin, encouraged by some of Captain John Hunter's remarks, soon after applied to branches of the fauna; and it became an important strand in the development of an evolutionary world view.[185]

The First Fleet officers' experience of New South Wales constitutes the substantial beginning of the modern sense of the southern continent,[186] and from it arose a series of vivid images. There was the image of a reasonably fertile coastal area; and that of a benign climate in which Europeans might flourish. There was that of a land of odd animals, birds, and plants; and that of an indigenous people equally mysterious in their innate and continuing otherness. Inevitably, the picture was not a complete one. No European in the mid-1790s understood that the cycle of drought, fire, and flood was usual, rather than an aberration; nor did anyone fully comprehend either the nature of the continent's interior, or the extent of divergence from known norms of the fauna and flora, or the complexity, diversity and the uniqueness of Aboriginal culture. Before there could be complete understanding, there had to be much more charting of coastlines, the vast interior had to be explored and its aridity faced, myriad specimens had to be gathered, as also had volumes of ethnographic information. Still, no-one now viewing the images of the Sydney region presented in these years can fail to find them to embody, in however muted a way, the beginnings of the modern idea of Australia.

5.28   Fernando Brambila   View of Parramatta   ('Vista de la Colonia de Paramata')

Notes

1 William Guthrie, et al., *A New Geographical, Historical and Commercial Grammar*, 8th edn (London, 1783), p. 797.

2 Thomas Bankes, et al., *A New Royal Authentic and Complete System of Universal Geography* (London, [1786−7]), pp. [5]−11.

3 *Dreams of a Pacific Empire*, ed. Alan Frost (Sydney, 1980), p. 34.

4 Banks, Testimony to the Beauchamp Committee, 10 May 1785, PRO HO 7/1.

5 Banks, 'Scheme of Plant[s] for Botany Bay', undated but *c*. October/November 1786, SUTRO Banks Papers SS1/48.

6 See ibid.; and Banks, List of seeds supplied, undated but November 1786, PRO T 1/639.

7 Matra, Testimony to the Beauchamp Committee, 9 May 1785, PRO HO 7/1.

8 Phillip, Memorandum on the colonization, undated but *c*. September 1786, and Comments on his Instructions, *c*. 11 April 1787, PRO CO 201/2, ff. 92, 130.

9 The idea that spices might be easily cultivated in New South Wales also turned on a similar perception of fertility:

> Most of the Asiatic productions may also without doubt be cultivated in the new settlement, and in a few years may render our recourse to our European neighbours for those productions unnecessary. — 'Heads of a Plan', HRNSW, I, ii, 19.

10 *Gentleman's Magazine*, 44 (1774), 71.

11 Banks, Testimony, 10 May 1785, and Matra, Testimony, 23 May 1785, PRO HO 7/1.

12 In answer to the Beauchamp Committee's question, 'Does the Coast abound with Fish and is it easily to be taken?' Banks replied: 'Yes, particularly Sting Rays of a great Size which are very good Food and which were easily caught at high Water by being struck with a Boat Hook or Friz gig'—PRO HO 7/1.

13 Nepean to Sackville Hamilton, 24 October 1786 (draft), PRO HO 100/18, ff. 369−70.

14 *St James Chronicle*, 16−18 January 1787.

15 Ellis to Linnaeus, 16 July 1771, quoted in *The 'Endeavour' Journal of Joseph Banks*, ed. J. C. Beaglehole, 2nd edn (Sydney, 1963), I, 53.

16 John Hawkesworth, comp., *An Account of the Voyages undertaken by the Order of His Present Majesty for making Discoveries in the Southern Hemisphere* (London, 1773), III, 561.

17 'The Australian Year', *Sydney Herald*, 8 January 1835.

18 Matra, Testimony, 9 May 1785, PRO HO 7/1.

19 *Gentleman's Magazine*, 56 (1786), 1019.

20 Banks told the Beauchamp Committee that he had seen 'no wild Beasts'—Testimony, 10 May 1785, PRO HO 7/1. Cf. *The Journals of Captain James Cook*, ed. J. C. Beaglehole (Cambridge, 1955−68), I, 394.

21 See Hawkesworth, *An Account of the Voyages*, III, passim, but especially 631−46.

22 For a full discussion of this point, see Alan Frost, 'New South Wales as *terra nullius*: The British denial of Aboriginal land rights', *Historical Studies*, 19 (1981), 513−23.

23 Banks, Testimony, 10 May 1785, PRO HO 7/1.

24 Cook, *Journals*, I, 397.

25 Bankes, *System of Geography*, pp. 6−7.

26 George III, Instructions to Phillip, 25 April 1787, HRNSW, I, ii, 89.

27 See Alan Frost, 'Towards Australia: The Coming of the Europeans, 1400−1788', in *Australians to 1788*, ed. D. J. Mulvaney and J. Peter White (Sydney, 1987), pp. 368−411.

28 For a discussion of his possible identity and of his work, see *The Art of the First Fleet and other early Australian Drawings*, ed. Bernard Smith and Alwyne Wheeler (Melbourne, 1988), pp. 220−8.

29 Phillip to Sydney, 9 July 1788, HRNSW, I, ii, 147.

30 Ibid., p. 150; and Phillip to Sydney, 28 September 1788 and 12 February 1790, ibid., pp. 190, 298.

31 Cf., for example, Watkin Tench, *Sydney's First Four Years*, ed. L. F. Fitzhardinge (Sydney, 1979), p. 69.

32 Phillip to Sydney, 12 February 1790, HRNSW, I, ii, 298.

33 Tench, *Sydney's First Four Years*, p. 267.

34 John White, *Journal of a Voyage to New South Wales*, ed. A. H. Chisholm (Sydney, 1962), p. 110.

35 Ibid.

36 Phillip to Sydney, 15 May 1788, HRNSW, I, ii, 122.

37 Ibid., p. 121.

38 Ibid., p. 122.

39 Ibid., pp. 122, 124; and Phillip to Sydney, 9 July 1788, ibid., p. 147.

40 Phillip to Sydney, 15 May 1788, ibid., p. 123.

41 George B. Worgan, *Journal of a First Fleet Surgeon* (Sydney, 1978), p. 12.

42 This brief account is based on the fuller one in T. M. Perry, *Australia's First Frontier* (Melbourne, 1963), pp. 7−15, 17−20.

43 Tench, *Sydney's First Four Years*, p. 135.
44 Ibid., p. 59.
45 Phillip to Sydney, 15 May 1788, HRNSW, I, ii, 127.
46 Phillip to Sydney, 12 February 1790, HRNSW, I, ii, 296; Phillip to Dundas, 2 and 4 October 1792, HRNSW, I, ii, 645, 653−61; David Collins, *An Account of the English Colony in New South*, ed. B. H. Fletcher (Sydney, 1975), I, 209.
47 Phillip to Banks, 26 July 1790, Mitchell MS C213, pp. 55−60.
48 Tench, *Sydney's First Four Years*, p. 264.
49 Francisco Xavier de Viana, 'Diario', in *The Spanish at Port Jackson* (Sydney, 1967), p. 26.
50 Phillip to Sydney, 15 May 1788, HRNSW, I, ii, 128.
51 White, *Journal*, p. 158.
52 Phillip to Banks, 2 July 1788, Mitchell MS C213, pp. 8, 13.
53 Tench, *Sydney's First Four Years*, pp. 67−8.
54 Phillip to Banks, 2 July 1788, Mitchell MS C213, p. 8.
55 Phillip to Banks, 2 July 1788, ibid., pp. 15−16.
56 Tench, *Sydney's First Four Years*, pp. 66−7.
57 Ibid., p. 66.
58 Phillip to Sydney, 15 May 1788, HRNSW, I, ii, 128.
59 Banks had intended that Francis Masson, then collecting for the King's garden at the Cape of Good Hope, should go with the First Fleet. After the ships had left England in May, though, he learned that Masson declined to do so; and it was then impossible for him to send another botanist on them—see Alan Frost, *Arthur Phillip, 1738−1814: His Voyaging* (Melbourne, 1987), p. 159.
60 Phillip to Banks, 10 July 1788, Mitchell MS C213, p. 29; Phillip to Sydney, 6 July 1788, Dixson MS Q162, p. 11; Phillip to Banks, 16 November 1788, Mitchell MS C213, p. 42.
61 Phillip to Banks, 22 August 1790, Mitchell MS C213, p. 62.
62 Phillip to Banks, 24 March 1791, ibid., p. 70, and List, ibid., p. 93.
63 Phillip to Banks, 17 November 1791, ibid., p. 81.
64 Considen to Banks, 18 November 1788, HRNSW, I, ii, 220.
65 Information kindly supplied by Dr John Edmondson, of the Merseyside County Museum.
66 Information kindly supplied by Dr John Edmondson, of the Merseyside County Museum.
67 See 'Introduction', White, *Journal*, pp. 9−16.
68 See Considen to Banks, 18 November 1788, HRNSW, I, ii, 220.
69 It is known, for example, that Phillip from time to time sent plants and seeds to friends and acquaintances—see his letters to Sydney, 21 March 1791, Dixson MS Q162, p. 27; and to Banks, 24 March 1791, Mitchell MS C213, pp. 71−2.
70 Although 'aborigine' and 'aboriginal' were words in common literary usage in this period, they were not used specifically to refer to the original inhabitants of Australia until well into the nineteenth century—see the *Oxford English Dictionary* for examples from Trollope and others. The First Fleet observers used, more or less indiscriminately, 'natives', 'blacks', 'Indians', 'savages'.
71 See Glyndwr Williams, '"Far more happier than we Europeans": reactions to the Australian Aborigines on Cook's Voyage', *Historical Studies*, 19 (1981), 510.
72 For Buffon's views see M. Duchet, *Anthropologie et histoire au siècle des lumières* (Paris, 1971), pp. 255 ff.
73 *The Journal of Philip Gidley King . . . 1787−1790*, ed. P. G. Fidlon and R. J. Ryan (Sydney, 1980), pp. 32−3.
74 *The Voyage to New South Wales: The Journal of Lieutenant William Bradley RN of HMS Sirius 1786−1792* (Sydney, 1969), p. 59.
75 Ibid.
76 Worgan, *Journal*, p. 28.
77 Collins, *Account*, p. 2.
78 Tench, *Sydney's First Four Years*, p. 37.
79 White, *Journal*, p. 111.
80 Phillip to Sydney, 15 May 1788, HRNSW, I, ii, 129.
81 *The Voyage of Governor Phillip to Botany Bay*, ed. J. A. Auchmuty (Sydney, 1970), p. 26.
82 Both extracts from Tench, *Sydney's First Four Years*, p. 40.
83 For this paragraph see Bradley, *Voyage*, pp. 65−75.
84 See, for example, Ronald M. Berndt and Catherine H. Berndt, *The World of the First Australians* (Sydney, 1968), p. 422.
85 Tench, *Sydney's First Four Years*, p. 46.
86 See Bill Gammage, 'Early boundaries of New South Wales', *Historical Studies*, 19 (1981), 524−31.
87 The phrase is that of A. T. Yarwood and M. J. Knowling, *Race Relations in Australia: A History* (Melbourne, 1982), p. 10.
88 Bradley, *Voyage*, pp. 102, 142.
89 Phillip to Banks, 26 July 1790, 17 November 1791, Mitchell MS C213, pp. 59, 81.
90 W. E. H. Stanner, *White Man Got No Dreaming: Essays 1938−1973* (Canberra, 1979), p. 173.
91 Bradley, *Voyage*, p. 81.
92 Collins, *Account*, p. 13.
93 See *A Voyage Round the World . . . by J. F. G. de la Pérouse*, ed. M. L. A. Milet-Mureau (London, 1799), II, 134−40.
94 Collins, *Account*, p. 13.
95 *The Journal and Letters of Lt. Ralph Clark*, ed.

P. G. Fidlon and R. J. Ryan (Sydney, 1981), p. 100.

[96] Bradley, *Voyage*, pp. 89, 103.

[97] Worgan, *Journal*, p. 47.

[98] Bradley, *Voyage*, pp. 85, 94.

[99] Phillip to Sydney, 15 May 1788, HRNSW, I, ii, 128.

[100] Phillip to Sydney, 9 July 1788, ibid., pp. 146, 148.

[101] Collins, *Account*, pp. 18, 24.

[102] John Hunter, *An Historical Journal of Events at Sydney and at sea 1787–1792*, ed. John Bach (Sydney, 1968), p. 54.

[103] John Cobley, *Sydney Cove 1788* (London, 1962), p. 153.

[104] Bradley, *Voyage*, p. 112.

[105] Blackburn to [Knight], 12 July 1788, Mitchell MS Ab 163.

[106] David Collins to George Collins, 1 February 1787, Mitchell MS 700.

[107] Phillip, Memorandum of c. September 1787, HRNSW, I, ii, 52.

[108] Phillip to Banks, 2 July 1788, Mitchell MS C213, pp. 10, 18.

[109] Phillip to Sydney, 5 July 1788, Dixson MS Q162, p. 8.

[110] Ross to Stephens, 10 July 1788, HRNSW, I, ii, 171.

[111] Mitchell ML 990/80, p. 27.

[112] White, *Journal*, p. 153.

[113] Cobley, *Sydney Cove 1788*, p. 208.

[114] Phillip to Sydney, 28 September 1788, HRNSW, I, ii, 191.

[115] Southwell to Butler, 12 July 1788, HRNSW, II, 702–3.

[116] Phillip to Sydney, 28 September 1788, HRNSW, I, ii, 192.

[117] Collins, *Account*, p. 36.

[118] Bradley, *Voyage*, p. 126.

[119] Tench, *Sydney's First Four Years*, pp. 137–8.

[120] Collins, *Account*, p. 41.

[121] Unless otherwise indicated, the observations in this and the following three paragraphs are taken from Tench, *Sydney's First Four Years*, pp. 46–53 and Hunter, *Historical Journal*, pp. 41–5.

[122] See A. A. Abie, *The Original Australians* (London, 1969), p. 64.

[123] Quoted in Cobley, *Sydney Cove 1788*, p. 90.

[124] White, *Journal*, pp. 157, 160.

[125] Bradley, *Voyage*, p. 110, 133–4, 135, 166.

[126] See A. P. Elkin, *The Australian Aborigines*, 4th edn (Sydney, 1964), p. 51.

[127] William Dampier, *A New Voyage round the World*, ed. Albert Gray (London, 1937), p. 314.

[128] Blackburn to [Knight], 12 July 1788, Mitchell MS Ab 163.

[129] Phillip to Stephens, 10 July 1788, HRNSW, I, ii, 168.

[130] Tench, *Sydney's First Four Years*, p. 138.

[131] Phillip, *Voyage*, p. 79.

[132] James Scott, *Remarks on a Passage to Botany Bay 1787–1792* (Sydney, 1963), p. 47; Tench, *Sydney's First Four Years*, p. 146.

[133] Hunter, *Historical Journal*, p. 93.

[134] An intemperate scholarly controversy has flared around this last explanation. See Noel Butlin, *Our Original Aggression: Aboriginal Populations of Southeastern Australia 1788–1850* (Sydney, 1983); Charles Wilson, 'History, Hypothesis and Fiction: Smallpox and Aboriginal Genocide', *Quadrant* (March 1985), 26–32; Noel Butlin, 'Reply ...', ibid. (June 1985), 30–3; Charles Wilson, 'A Rejoinder ...', ibid., (July 1985), 17–19.

[135] Tench, *Sydney's First Four Years*, p. 151.

[136] Bradley, *Voyage*, pp. 182–3.

[137] Tench, *Sydney's First Four Years*, p. 160.

[138] Detailed accounts of the episode were given by Henry Waterhouse, writing some weeks later (Mitchell MS Aw 109/2, pp. 1–3) and by Dr John Harris, writing six months later (Mitchell MS A 1597, pp. 3–4).

[139] Tench, *Sydney's First Four Years*, p. 181.

[140] Scott, *Remarks*, p. 58.

[141] Hunter, *Historical Journal*, p. 139.

[142] Scott, *Remarks*, pp. 58, 59.

[143] Tench, *Sydney's First Four Years*, p. 190.

[144] James Campbell to Farr, 24 March 1791, Mitchell doc. 1174.

[145] Keith Willey, *When the Sky Fell Down: The Destruction of the Tribes of the Sydney Region 1788–1850s* (Sydney, 1979), pp. 118–20.

[146] Hunter, *Historical Journal*, p. 139. See also the unknown letter-writer of January 1791 quoted in John Cobley, *Sydney Cove 1791–1792* (Sydney, 1965), p. 40, who made the same point.

[147] Bradley, *Voyage*, p. 141.

[148] Campbell to Farr, 24 March 1791, Mitchell doc. 1174, p. 7.

[149] Worgan, *Journal*, pp. 47–8.

[150] Campbell to Farr, 24 March 1791, Mitchell doc. 1174, p. 5.

[151] Collins, *Account*, p. 464.

[152] Bradley, *Voyage*, p. 230.

[153] Harris to [?], 20 March 1791, Mitchell MS A1597, p. 7.

[154] Phillip to Banks, 24 March 1791, Mitchell MS C213, p. 77.

[155] Tench, *Sydney's First Four Years*, pp. 200, 203.

[156] Hunter, *Historical Journal*, p. 269.

[157] *Some Letters of Rev. Richard Johnson ... ed.* George Mackaness (Sydney, 1954), p. 38.

[158] Richard Atkins, Journal entry, 26 April 1792, Mitchell MS 737.

[159] *The Journal of Daniel Paine 1794–1797*, ed. R. J. B. Knight and Alan Frost (Sydney, 1983), p. 39.

160 Campbell to Farr, 24 March 1791, Mitchell doc. 1174, p. 9.

161 Tench, *Sydney's First Four Years*, pp. 290−1.

162 On this see P. J. Marshall and Glyndwr Williams, *The Great Map of Mankind: British Perceptions of the World in the Age of Enlightenment* (London, 1982), especially ch. 9.

163 Blackburn to [?], 12 July 1788, 19 March 1791, Mitchell MS Ab163.

164 Tench, *Sydney's First Four Years*, pp. 205−9.

165 Collins, *Account*, p. 122.

166 *Gentleman's Magazine*, 61 (1791), 79.

167 Stanner, *White Man Got No Dreaming*, p. 161.

168 Phillip, Memorandum of *c.* September 1787, HRNSW, I, ii, 52.

169 Phillip to Banks, 3 December 1791, in Cobley, *Sydney Cove 1791−1792*, p. 177.

170 Collins, *Account*, p. 122.

171 Tench, *Sydney's First Four Years*, p. 231.

172 Elkin, *Australian Aborigines*, p. 363.

173 Collins, *Account*, p. 211.

174 Ibid.

175 In a letter of 13 April 1790 (Mitchell MS C213, p. 54), Phillip told Banks: 'I am now getting drawings of all the Flowering Shrubs in the Country'. In one of 2 April 1792 (ibid., p. 89), he said: 'I continue to procure drawings of all the shrubs & plants, but the variety is so great that it will be a long time before drawings of the whole can be collected.' Presumably, on his return he gave many of these drawings to Banks, to copy or keep; but he must also have retained numbers of them, for he directed in his will (PRO PROB Bridport 579) that 'my drawings made in New South Wales' be sold immediately on his death. The identity of the artist is most uncertain, as is the subsequent fate of the works,

although a number of them must now be among those in the British Museum (Natural History), where there are some annotated in Phillip's hand.

176 See Bernard Smith, *European Vision and the South Pacific*, 2nd edn (Sydney, [1984]), pp. 163−9.

177 *Dublin Chronicle*, 4 June 1793.

178 John Kenny, *Bennelong: First Notable Aboriginal* (Sydney, 1973), p. 54.

179 *Gentleman's Magazine*, 63 (1793), 531.

180 As well as through the published First Fleet journals, the public received information from the periodicals of the day, which gave generous space to letters from the colony, and which reviewed the journals at length.

181 Phillip to Banks, 15 October 1792, NLA MS 9/134.

182 See Smith, *European Vision*, pp. 163−4.

183 *The Banks Letters*, ed. Warren R. Dawson (London, 1958), pp. 110−12. Phillip wrote to Banks on 17 November 1791: 'The natives burn their dead, but when Skulls can be got they shall be sent' (Mitchell MS C213, p. 81). Despite his reservations, he evidently did return with some, for Blumenbach wrote to Banks on 1 November 1793 to thank him for the New Holland skulls.

184 Quoted in Smith, *European Vision*, p. 168.

185 For the importance of Australian species in Charles Darwin's development of his theory of divergence by natural selection see, e.g., his *Notebooks on Transmutation of Species*, ed. Sir Gavin de Beer, et al. (London, 1960−7).

186 For another view of the establishment of the colony see Geoffrey Blainey, 'Sydney 1788', in *Australians to 1788*, ed. John Mulvaney and J. Peter White (Sydney, 1987), pp. 413−44.

6.1   [Anonymous]   'New South Wales. Port Jackson from the Entrance up to Sydney Cove taken in Oct[br]. 1788'

208

Chapter 6

Australia: The Emergence of a Continent

Alan Frost

Governor Arthur Phillip's settlement of his colonists at Port Jackson constituted the end of a long and noteworthy voyage. It also marked the beginning of detailed exploration of Australian seas and the painstaking charting of the coastline of the continent.

Phillip's instructions included the proviso that he obtain information about 'the several ports or harbours upon the coast, and the islands contiguous thereto';[1] and interested seaman and diligent officer that he was, he soon acted on this. On 15 February 1788 he despatched Philip Gidley King with a small party of marines and convicts to occupy Norfolk Island, some 1000 miles to the east of Port Jackson. Sailing in the *Supply* commanded by Lieutenant Henry Ball, King reached his destination two weeks later. Simultaneously, Phillip had Hunter and Bradley survey Port Jackson (6.1). For some weeks, working from small boats, they sounded and charted for the benefit of future shipping. Subsequently, they extended their work to include Broken Bay and Botany Bay. Later, the wreck of the *Sirius* on Norfolk Island gave them the enforced occasion likewise to chart its shores, outliers, and encircling reefs. By the time Phillip left New South Wales in December 1792, the main features of the coasts about the settlement had been identified and recorded.

The Europeans enlarged their knowledge of the surrounding seas in these years too. Returning from Norfolk Island, Ball examined Lord Howe Island (5.9), which lies some 400 miles north-east of Port Jackson, in 31°36'E latitude and 157°E longitude.[2] The return voyages of the convict transports in 1788 also added new information. The *Golden Grove* found an extensive shoal in the vicinity of Lord Howe Island. Captain Sever took the *Lady Penrhyn* to Macao via Tahiti; while Captain Marshall took the *Scarborough* and Captain Gilbert the *Charlotte* along a somewhat less circuitous route, so that they discovered what are now the Marshall and Gilbert Islands as they went (6.2).[3] Then, Lieutenant Shortland took the rest of the transports (*Alexander, Friendship, Prince of Wales, Borrowdale*) north of New Guinea, via Lord Howe Island, New Caledonia,

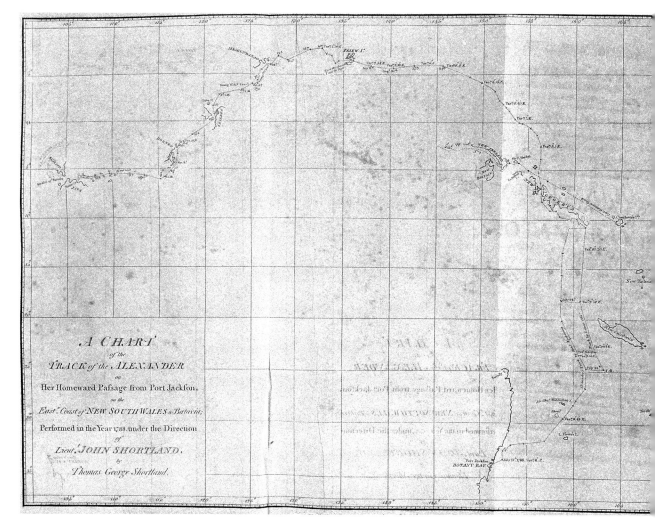

6.2   Thomas Shortland   'A Chart of the Track of the *Alexander* on Her Homeward
      Passage from Port Jackson'   1789

the Solomons (mistaken as a new discovery), the Pelew Islands, and Celebes and
Borneo to Batavia, and thence home.[4]

   In October 1788 Phillip sent Hunter in the *Sirius* to the Cape of Good Hope
for supplies. Despairing of reaching his destination against the westerlies, Hunter
turned east in the south Tasman Sea, to pass under the south island of New
Zealand and across the Pacific 'as much as possible in a parallel between the
tracks of the *Resolution* and *Adventure*; so that if any island lay between the
parallels in which these ships sailed, we might have a chance of falling in with
them'.[5] Passing Cape Horn, he reached Cape Town on the first day of the new
year, after a remarkably quick voyage. He arrived back at Port Jackson on 9 May

210

1789, after narrowly avoiding shipwreck on the south-eastern coast of Van Diemen's Land.[6] In April 1790, when new supplies from England had not yet reached the colony and the *Sirius* had been wrecked on Norfolk Island, Phillip sent Ball in the *Supply* to Batavia. Ball took much the same route as Shortland had, via the Solomons and north of New Guinea. From Batavia, he returned south down the Indian Ocean and round Van Diemen's Land. Soon after the *Waaksamheyd*, the transport hired at Batavia, also followed this route.[7]

Simultaneously, there were some purposeful discoveries of the Australian coast, made during voyages mounted from Europe rather than from Sydney. In 1791, on his way to assert Britain's claim to Nootka Sound and to chart the north-west American coast, George Vancouver examined the southern coast of western Australia, from Cape Leeuwin to the Recherche Archipelago in about 123°E longitude, discovering King George Sound (6.3). He then sailed past Van Diemen's Land for New Zealand.[8] In 1792, sailing in search of the missing Lapérouse, Bruny d'Entrecasteaux repeated and extended Vancouver's survey (6.4). Striking the coast at Cape Leeuwin, the French explorer followed it to 130°E longitude, before turning south for Van Diemen's Land. Sighting its southern coast at 147°E longitude, d'Entrecasteaux reached Recherche (now Storm) Bay and the present Forestier Peninsula (6.5). In this temporary haven 'at the extremity of the globe', the officers found it difficult to express their relief, after 'having been so long driven to and fro in the ocean by the violence of the storms'.[9] From here, d'Entrecasteaux departed for the western Pacific. For the next twelve months, he made broad sweeps across that ocean, past New Caledonia and through the Solomons, to New Ireland and the Admiralty Islands, seeking vainly for signs of his compatriots. After refreshing his crews in the East Indies, he rounded southern Australia again. In December 1792 he was off the south-western coast, which he thought 'had the appearance of the greatest sterility', being in places 'entirely denuded of vegetation'.[10] As a modern scholar has pointed out, this distant, off-shore assessment by d'Entrecasteaux was incorrect, and the area was later to become productive agricultural land. The French navigators 'were judging the lands they saw by colour, and by land form. Like most Europeans they liked their land green, and equated bright green with productivity. The bushes they saw from the decks of their ships in the distance looked very dark green or brown, and they concluded the land was waterless, arid and non-productive'.[11] He reached Recherche Bay once more in January 1793, before continuing his forlorn quest.

D'Entrecasteaux was soon after followed to Storm Bay by a captain in the English East India Company's service. Commanding the *Duke of Clarence* and the *Duchess*, John Hayes sailed from Calcutta for the environs of New Guinea in quest of spices in February 1793, but unfavourable winds led him to take the much longer route south about New Holland. He entered d'Entrecasteaux Channel at the end of April, to chart the estuary of what was to become known as the

6.3 Engraved by John Landseer after John Sykes 'A deserted Indian Village in King George III. Sound, New Holland'

6.4 Charles François Beautemps-Beaupré Leeuwin and Nuyts Lands ('Carte Générale des Terres de Leeuwin et de Nuyts') 1807

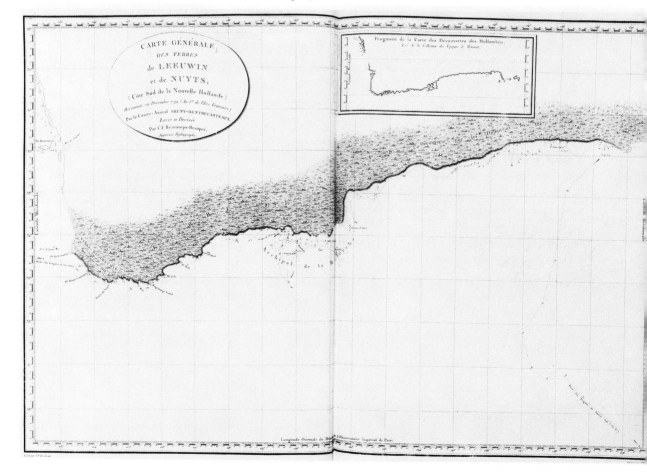

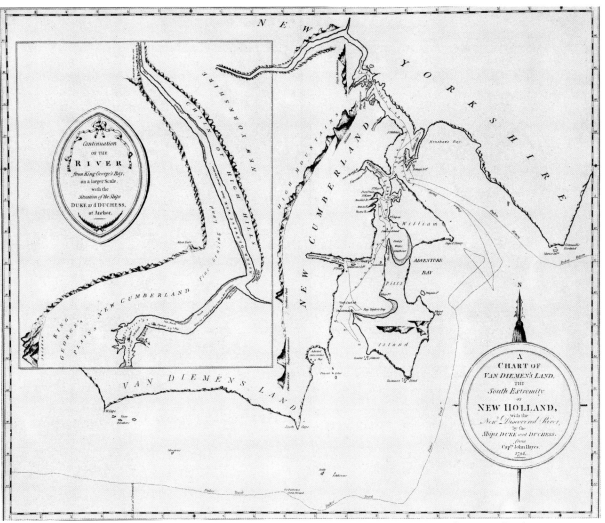

6.5   John Hayes   'A Chart of Van Diemen's Land, the South Extremity of New Holland'
1798

Derwent River during his two months' stay. He then continued on to New
Caledonia, past the Louisiades to New Britain, then through the Moluccas to
Surabaya on Java, which he reached in May 1794. There, he found the remnants
of d'Entrecasteaux's expedition, with whom he compared notes on the Tasmanian
discoveries. Hayes published his 'Chart of Van Diemen's Land' in 1798 (6.5).[12]

   Cape York and Torres Strait also received some incidental attention in these
years. As Hunter was returning to Sydney in May 1789, Bligh was making his
extraordinary passage in the *Bounty's* launch. Reaching the Australian coast in
13°S latitude, he followed it northwards to Cape York (6.6), then proceeded
through the strait to Timor and Batavia.[13] Two years later, in a general way
Edward Edwards repeated this experience when, carrying a number of the
Bounty mutineers, the *Pandora* was wrecked on the Great Barrier Reef in 10°S
latitude. Edwards took survivors in four small boats through Torres Strait to
Kupang in Timor.

213

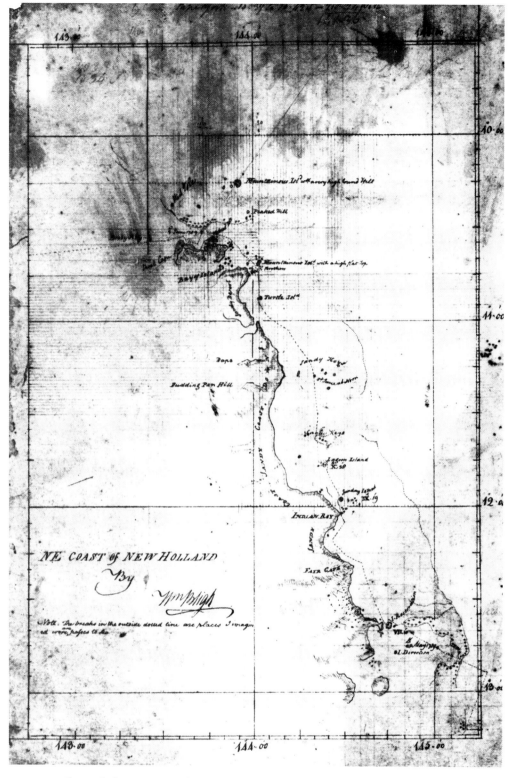

6.6   William Bligh 'NE Coast of New Holland'   1789

214

While the discoveries of these voyages were not often spectacular, and the details were sometimes uncertain, they did have the cumulative effect of establishing the routes linking the infant colony with the great world—with China, the East Indies, the Cape of Good Hope, and ultimately with Rio de Janeiro and Europe. Those interested in sailing Australian seas began to learn how they might, and might not, go—scarcely westwards south of Van Diemen's Land, but with ease eastwards across the Pacific in 40°S latitude; with care, northwards through the shoals of Melanesia to China and the East Indies; and with care again from the East Indies south about Van Diemen's Land to Port Jackson. The *Sirius*'s return voyage from the Cape of Good Hope in 1789 showed the unexpected but real danger of navigating close to the east coast of Van Diemen's Land; the *Pandora*'s loss emphasized the dangers of north-eastern Australia; while the *Guardian*'s striking of an iceberg in the southern Indian Ocean brought home the fact of the inevitable risks attaching to the sailing of such distant seas.

On taking up his governorship in September 1795, John Hunter again attended to the gathering of information about the coasts of New South Wales. To do so, he drew repeatedly on the services of Matthew Flinders and George Bass, two adventurous young men who were respectively the master and surgeon of the *Reliance*. Flinders later wrote of his companion:

I had the happiness to find a man whose ardour for discovery was not to be repressed by any obstacles, nor deterred by danger; and with this friend a determination was formed of completing the examination of the east coast of New South Wales.[14]

The pair began their reconnaissances in October 1795, when they sailed an eight-foot boat, the *Tom Thumb*, from Port Jackson round to Botany Bay and up the Georges River. Then, in March 1796, they coasted to Port Hacking, south of Botany Bay. In August 1796, following reports of sightings of coal, Bass sailed south again, to find seams at various places, including Coalcliff.[15]

Immediately afterwards, events conspired to render these probes preludes to grand discovery, that of the strait separating Van Diemen's Land from the mainland. This, the major discovery of this period, arose from a combination of accidental observation, speculation, and purposeful searching. Tasman's discovery of Van Diemen's Land in 1642 had raised the question of whether it was part of or separate from New Holland.[16] In command of the *Adventure* on Cook's second voyage, Furneaux sighted its southern extremity in March 1773, sailed round into Adventure Bay then up the eastern coast to beyond Flinders Island, perhaps to within sight of the mainland, before turning east to rendezvous with Cook in New Zealand. Though Furneaux was uncertain whether some of his sightings were islands or mainland, his report persuaded Cook that Van Diemen's Land was connected to New Holland.[17]

Still, the question lingered. In 1774, the Duc de Croy asked Kerguelen whether he thought the pair were joined.[18] When the *Sirius* passed eastwards of

Van Diemen's Land in January 1788, the officers noted 'a strong set from between the Schouten Islands and Pt Hicks from which we had a great Sea', circumstances which led them to suspect 'that there may be either a Streight or a deep Gulf' between Van Diemen's Land and New Holland.[19] This was a perception repeated during the *Sirius*'s passage closer to the east coast of the island in April 1789.[20] In 1791 Vancouver, who may have seen records of the First Fleet's voyage, first intended to 'range' the south coast of New Holland in order to 'determine whether it and Van Diemen's Land are joined, which from all information at present extant appears somewhat doubtfull', but he broke off his search too early.[21] D'Entrecasteaux likewise seems to have suspected a strait.[22]

Despite all this speculation, the question was not answered until 1797. In February of that year, the merchantman *Sydney Cove*, sailing from Bengal, was wrecked on one of the Furneaux Islands. Three survivors managed to reach Sydney in May, whereupon Hunter sent Flinders in the *Francis* to rescue those still on Preservation Island. These latter brought with them the information that, during their four months' stay, the winds and currents had set consistently to the east, a point confirmed by Flinders's own observations off the island. These reports encouraged Hunter, who had by then suspected the existence of a strait for some eight years, to send George Bass down the coast in a whaleboat. Bass sailed in December 1797. On his way he found the Shoalhaven River and Twofold Bay, and reached as far west as Westernport. Then, probing directly south, he found 'an open Ocean westwards', with a 'mountainous' sea rolling east. His report inevitably strengthened Hunter's old suspicion—'we have much reason to conclude that there is an open strait through, between the latitude of 39°S and 40°12'S'.[23] The governor then sent Flinders and Bass in the *Norfolk* on the decisive voyage of exploration. From October 1798 until the end of the following January, the pair coasted, probed, and charted. The title of Flinders's manuscript account quietly conveys their achievement:

Narrative of an Expedition in the Colonial sloop *Norfolk*, from Port Jackson, through the Strait which separates Van Diemen's Land from New Holland, and from thence round the South Cape back to Port Jackson, completing the circumnavigation of the former Island, with some remarks on the coasts and harbours.

Among the secondary results were the discoveries of the rivers Tamar (Launceston) and Derwent (Hobart), with their attendant harbours.[24]

Answering a question posed for one hundred and fifty years, and filling an important geographical gap, Bass and Flinders's voyage in the *Norfolk* was a striking achievement. It also had important practical consequences. As the *Sirius*'s near-shipwreck in 1789, the wreck of the *Guardian* later that year, and the wreck of the *Sydney Cove* all showed, the passages to Port Jackson through the depths of the Indian Ocean and south about Van Diemen's Land might be hazardous in the extreme. The confirmation of a strait between New Holland and Van Diemen's Land in 40°S latitude offered the possibility of a route at once

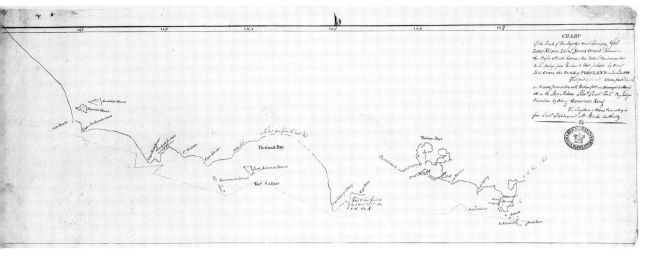

6.7   James Grant and Francis Barrallier   'Chart of the Track of . . . [the] *Lady Nelson*'   1801

6.8   [Anonymous]   'A Chart shewing the Track of the *Harbinger* . . .'   1801

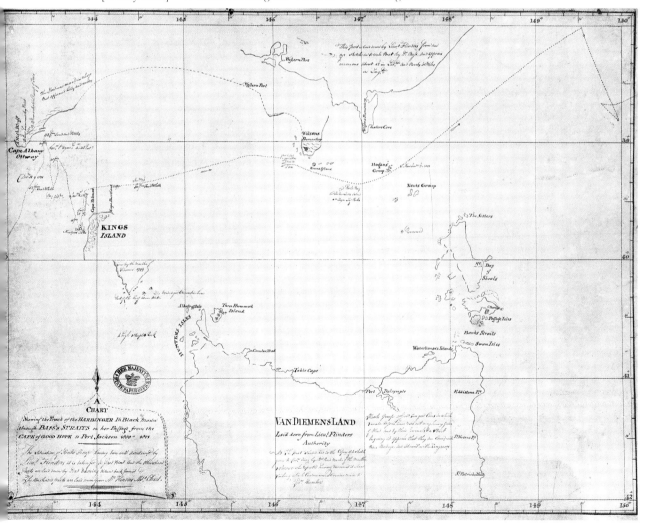

more efficacious because of the consistent westerlies, and much safer because of the lack of icebergs and the absence of a lee shore. These points were taken immediately Flinders's chart was published in London in June 1800, followed by his *Observations*.[25] In the middle of that year, Lieutenant James Grant left England in the *Lady Nelson* for Sydney. He sailed via Bass Strait, charting parts of its northern shore, from the present Cape Otway to Wilson's Promontory as he went (6.7). The next year, he returned to the strait to extend his survey, to be soon followed by Murray. These probes led to the discovery and charting of Port Phillip.[26] At the same time, others followed the new route to Sydney. The first to do so were the captains of the *Margaret* and the *Harbinger*, who arrived from the Cape of Good Hope in January 1801 (6.8). By the end of 1802 the Bass Strait route was the preferred one for ships approaching the New South Wales colony from the west.

Life thereafter took the young explorers along very different paths. After a series of commercial ventures, Bass sailed from Sydney for South America in February 1803, not to be seen again. Flinders, on the other hand, continued to explore the coast of New South Wales, this time north as far as the Glass House Mountains near Brisbane. Gradually, the shape of the continent was filling out (6.9). When Flinders returned to England in 1800 he found that he had established a reputation that would soon bring him more such work.

In March 1802 France and Britain and their allies reached an uneasy peace, which could not mask continuing imperial pretensions. Indeed Napoleon led the way for further French expansion even as he negotiated with the British. In October 1800 he sent Baudin and Freycinet and a party of scientists in the *Géographe* and *Naturaliste* to examine

in detail the *south-west*, *west*, *north-west* and *north* coasts of *New Holland*, some of which are still entirely unknown, while others are known only imperfectly. By combining the work which will be done on these various parts with that of the English navigators on the *east* coast and of d'Entrecasteaux on *Anthony van Diemen's Land*, we shall come to know the entire coastline of this great south land, which, situated not far from the countries of *Asia* where, for three centuries, Europeans have been forming settlements, has seemed until recently to be condemned to a sort of oblivion.[27]

The expedition sailed from Le Havre on 18 October 1800, and after refreshing at Mauritius, sighted Cape Leeuwin on 27 May 1801. Like their predecessors, these explorers were struck by the sterility of the coast. Péron, for example, saw it possessing 'the most afflicting barrenness', being 'covered with unprofitable sand, and having no kind of river, but merely a few simple streams of fresh water'.[28] The ships then coasted northwards, with the explorers surveying as they went. Baudin was at Dampier's Shark Bay at the end of June, and reached Bonaparte Archipelago, north-west of the present Broome, before turning to Kupang for refreshments, where he was joined in September by the *Naturaliste*. From here, he decided to sail south round Van Diemen's Land and up to Sydney. The ships reached d'Entrecasteaux Channel in mid-January 1802, and

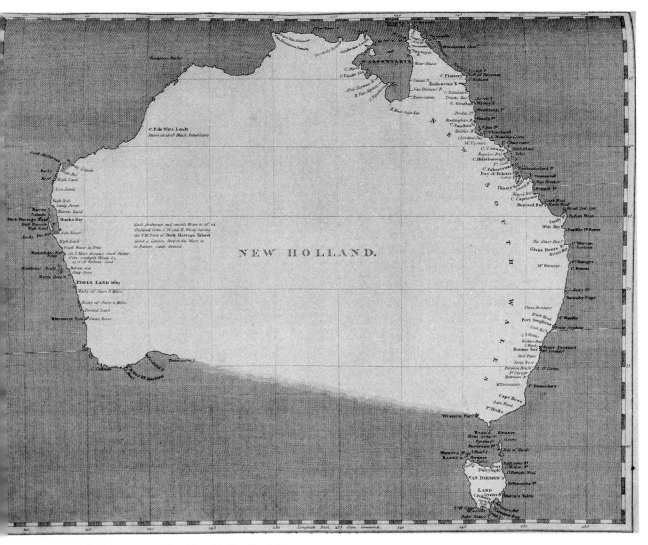

6.9 [Anonymous] 'New Holland' 1802

the officers surveyed north. A storm separated them on 27 March, with Hamelin taking the *Naturaliste* to Sydney, and Baudin coasting the mainland west through Bass Strait, to Encounter Bay, Kangaroo Island, and St Vincent and Spencer Gulfs. He then rounded Van Diemen's Land again, reaching Sydney with his crew scurvy-stricken, on 20 June (6.10).

For the next five months Baudin rested his crews, then sailed again in November for Bass Strait. From King Island, the *Naturaliste* left for France with the natural history collections, while Baudin made his way up to Kupang again. After an abortive sortie to the north-west coast of the continent, he turned for Mauritius, which he reached in mid-August 1803, and where he died a month later.

Alarmed by this renewed French interest in the south land, the British mounted a counter surveying expedition so as to establish a claim to possession

219

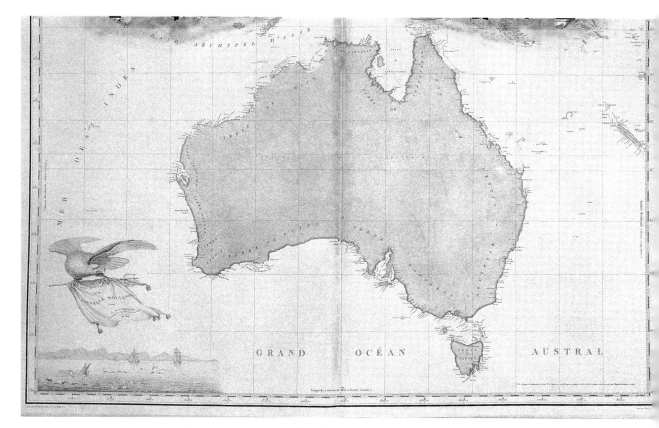

6.10   Louis de Freycinet   New Holland   ('Carte Générale de la Nouvelle Hollande')   1808

of the whole continent. Matthew Flinders received the command.[29] He sailed in the *Investigator* from Spithead on 18 July 1801, and sighted Cape Leeuwin on 7 December. For the next five months he coasted east, surveying constantly. He was at King George Sound in December, in the Great Australian Bight in January 1802, at Nuyts Archipelago and then Spencer Gulf in February and March. On 8 April he met Baudin at what is now called Encounter Bay. From there, he entered Bass Strait, finding and surveying Port Phillip. He reached Sydney on 8 May 1802. (6.11)

Flinders sailed again later in July to continue his surveying northwards, now with the company of the *Lady Nelson*. Progressively the ships pushed up the present Queensland coast to Great Sandy Island, to Port Curtis, then into the waters of the Great Barrier Reef. Sending his escort back to Sydney, Flinders was in the Coral Sea in October, and he passed Cape York on the last day of the month. Through November and December he surveyed the shores of the Gulf of Carpentaria. On 11 February, proceeding west, he passed Cape Arnhem. Six

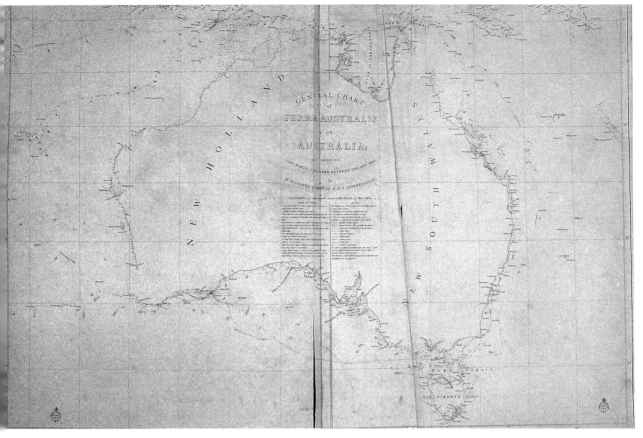

6.11   Matthew Flinders   'General Chart of Terra Australis or Australia'   1814

days later, to their considerable astonishment, the Europeans found a number of Macassan proas gathering bêche-de-mer (6.12), thus establishing for the first time the interesting fact of Asian contact with the continent's northern shore. With the *Investigator*'s condition rapidly deteriorating, Flinders now gave up detailed work, and, touching first at Timor, sailed westwards around the continent for Sydney, which he reached on 9 June 1803.

There, the ship was found too rotten for him to continue his work with it, so he decided to return to England to obtain another. He left Sydney in the *Porpoise* in August 1803, but this vessel struck a reef a week later, and Flinders lost his botanical specimens, and his notes and charts were much damaged. Returning to Sydney in a cutter, he obtained the *Cumberland*, a small schooner of only 29 tons. After succouring the crew of the *Porpoise*, he sailed through Torres Strait, and with his new vessel now much in need of repair, put into Port Louis at Mauritius on 17 December 1803, where he was promptly arrested and

221

his papers seized. And there, to the detriment of his health, he stayed for six long years, until freed by British forces in March 1810.[30]

Bass and Flinders's discovery of Bass Strait, and Flinders's and Baudin's massive surveys of the coast of New Holland and Van Diemen's Land (6.10, 6.11) effectively completed the delineation of the southern continent. (Philip Parker King was to fill in remaining gaps a decade and a half later.) While these seamen were engaged in this great task, the British colonists at Sydney had been consolidating their settlement. In April 1794, Grose reported that almost 3000 acres had been cleared since Phillip's departure. About this time, too, he began to grant land on the rich Hawkesbury River floodplains, and the settlers there soon increased the colony's agricultural production. Those on Norfolk Island made similar progress; and gradually, aided by importations from India and the Cape of Good Hope, the colonists also built up herds and flocks. By the time of Hunter's arrival in September 1795, there were some 2500 colonists on the mainland, who had almost 3000 acres under wheat, and about 200 cattle, 1000 sheep and 1000 goats; and Sydney had developed markedly as a port and a town.

This consolidation of settlement on the Cumberland Plain (6.13) continued under Hunter, who granted more land about the Hawkesbury River, and in the Toongabbie area; and he 'widen'd and repair'd the public roads for the more easy and expeditious travelling between the different districts in the colony'. Agricultural production continued to increase. After the autumn 1796 harvest, the new governor reported with satisfaction that 'the quantity of wheat, public and private, ... may amount to from 35,000 to 40,000 bushels, which will more than ensure us bread for twelve months to come, exclusive of maize, which we continue to issue as part of the weekly ration'. With this increased production, Parramatta (6.14) became an even more important market for the surrounding districts. As more persons built there, Hunter added to the government buildings— a school in 1796; a windmill and a 'strong log-prison' in 1797; a church from late 1798 onwards—and he enlarged Government House.[31] By the end of the decade, the mainland settlement's success was evident. As one observer recorded:

The inconveniences and embarrassments which fettered the growth of this infant Colony, are now daily disappearing. Population rapidly increases, agriculture begins to flourish, and industry is actively employed in many of those subdivisions which seldom prevail but in a long settled country. In short, the present state of the Colony affords every reason to expect that it will soon be able amply to compensate the Mother Country for the expence and trouble of establishing and protecting it.[32]

The situation on Norfolk Island was similar. There, though the population remained more or less static (at about 900 persons), public buildings became more numerous and substantial, and the European presence more striking. King erected brick and stone barracks, houses, storehouses and a school at Sydney Bay, and additional timber buildings (6.15). He built timber houses and a barn and granary at Queensborough; a dam and a watermill in Arthur's Vale; and

222

6.12   Engraved after William Westall   'View of Malay Road, from Pobassoo's Island'   1814

barracks, houses, and a flaxhouse, storehouse, and barn at Phillipsburgh, where he also constructed a 'very strong wharf, 126 feet long' with a 'swinging Crane and capstern' at its end.[33] One observer reported that the wheat harvests were abundant, that

the limes are so exuberant that the Governor from the same tree plucked sixteen pecks of ripe, and left upon it a greater proportion of green fruit. Pomegranates, melons, figs, and sugar-cane are there equally prolific. Though its circumference be merely seven leagues, or twenty-eight miles, it contains 1200 settlers, or reformed farmers, and enjoys a state of cultivation equal to the West India Islands.[34]

This process of consolidation continued during the governorship of Philip Gidley King (1799–1806), as the population grew steadily, as colonists expanded agriculture, and as animals arrived in ever-increasing numbers from India and the Cape of Good Hope. By early 1804 there were 7000 persons in the

223

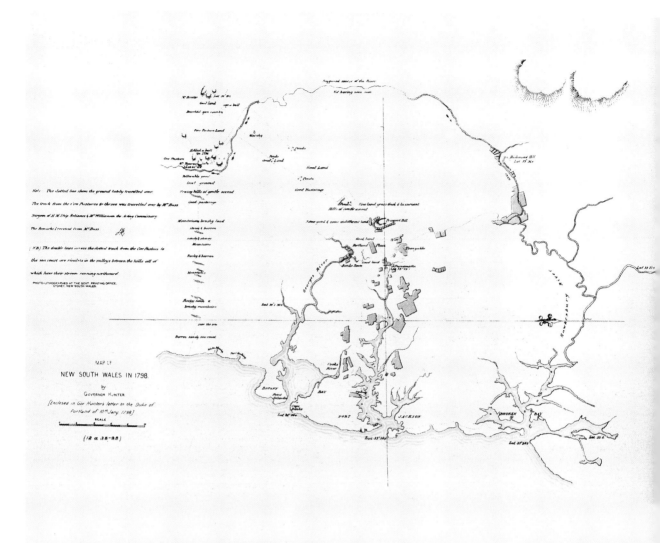

6.13   John Hunter 'Map of New South Wales in 1798'

settlement; there was eleven months' supply of wheat and flour in the government store, and a further 11 000 bushels of wheat and 7000 bushels of maize 'in stacks' on government farms; and King had three years' supply of salted meat.[35] And Sydney (6.20) continued to become even more substantial. King added a wing and extended the verandah of Government House; merchants such as Robert Campbell, Simeon Lord, Henry Kable and James Underwood built boats and erected warehouses; and cottage-lined streets spread outwards over the cove. When Baudin and his officers reached the township in mid-1802, they

224

6.14   Engraved by J. Heath after [Anonymous]   View of Parramatta   1798

admired the 'immense' achievement, finding it difficult to conceive how the British colonists, in the face of all the impediments of the previous fifteen years, had 'so speedily attained to the state of splendour and comfort in which they now find themselves'.[36]

The advent of the French expedition led directly to all but one of the extensions of British settlement of the continent in this period.[37] Just before they sailed again in November 1802, the French officers indiscreetly let slip ideas of establishing a base at Storm Bay, Van Diemen's Land (6.5). Alarmed, Governor King sent a small party to forestall any such move. Simultaneously, the British government sent out from England a party of marines and 450 convicts under David Collins to obtain possession of Port Phillip and control of Bass Strait.

6.15   William Neate Chapman 'View of the town of Sydney, Norfolk Island' 1796

Disappointed with the site he chose on the Mornington Peninsula, Collins shifted his colonists to the Derwent River (Hobart) in February 1804. In October, Colonel Paterson took another group to the Tamar River (Launceston). For some time, these new settlements were only toe-holds on the edge of 'New South Wales', but just as the Sydney one had previously done, they showed the determination of the British to follow discovery with effective occupation, in order to establish possession of the southern continent.

Despite the consolidation of settlement in the Sydney region, however, there was little interior exploration. For all of this period (with the small exception of the outpost at the mouth of the Hunter River), settlement was confined to the Cumberland Plain, that area whose boundaries are Broken Bay in the north, Botany Bay in the south, and the Blue Mountains in the west. Fundamentally, there were two reasons for the lack of examination of the interior. The first was functional. In 1800 and 1810, as in 1788, the Sydney colony was primarily a port at the end of a very long sea route. Once the colonists were able to meet (more or less) their own needs and some of those of incoming ships, and so long as their numbers did not overcrowd their small hinterland, there was little need to probe the continent's vast spaces. The second was practical. For twenty years, the abrupt escarpments of the Blue Mountains (then known as the 'Carmarthen Hills') presented an impenetrable barrier to such probing. A number of people did try to find a way across this section of the Great Dividing Range—for example, a party under Tench in 1789; the ex-convict Matthew Everingham in 1795; Francis Barrallier in 1802; George Caley on various occasions between 1803 and 1806—but, ill-prepared for the rugged terrain, these expeditions always returned defeated. Phillip's report of the first attempt:

after the first day's journey they met with such a constant succession of deep ravines, the sides of which were frequently inaccessible, that they returned, not having been able to proceed more than fifteen miles in five days; when they turned back they supposed themselves to be twelve miles from the foot of the mountains.

stands as a commentary on all. Concerning Caley's 1805 attempt, King went further when he observed that:

As far as respects the extension of agriculture beyond the first range of mountains, that is an idea that must be given up, as the rocks to the west of that range wear the most barren and forbidding aspect, which men, animals, birds, and vegetation has ever been strangers to, a better proof of which may not be adduced than the remark of one of Caley's party in returning, who exclaimed, on seeing two solitary crows, 'That they had lost their way'.[38]

None the less, continued settlement and coastal exploration did lead to a significant increase in knowledge of the continent's attributes. The interested amateurs Paterson and Hunter, and the professionals George Caley and John Lewin, collected large numbers of zoological, botanical and geological specimens for Sir Joseph Banks and other scientists in England.[39] Baudin's expedition resulted in the gathering of some 18 500 zoological specimens, including some 2500 that were new to science; and these were only part of that expedition's richesse. The naturalist Péron recorded that:

Apart from a multitude of cases of minerals, dried plants, shells, fishes, reptiles, and zoophytes preserved in alcohol, of quadrupeds and birds stuffed or dissected, we still had seventy great cases full of plants in their natural state, comprising nearly two hundred different species of useful plants, approximately six hundred types of seeds contained in several thousand small bags and, finally, about a hundred living animals, rare or absolutely new.[40]

A bevy of experts likewise sailed with Flinders: the naturalist Robert Brown, the mineralogist John Allen, the gardener Peter Good, the landscape artist and figure painter William Westall, the draughtsman Ferdinand Bauer. The results of their labours were as spectacular as those of Baudin's party. Brown, for example, collected some 2400 botanical specimens, of which about 2000 were new. And Bauer's drawings are perhaps the finest of all botanical recordings.

These collections were extremely influential in the development of modern science. Antoine Laurent de Jussieu, Professor of Botany at the Muséum d'Histoire Naturelle, considered Baudin's the greatest collection ever to be brought into France; and Sir Joseph Dalton Hooker considered Flinders's voyage, 'as far as botany is concerned, the most important in its result ever undertaken, and hence marks an epoch in the history of that science'. Especially because of Brown's later analytical work, *Prodromus Florae Novae Hollandiae* (1810) de Jussieu's 'natural' system of classification gained in favour over Linnaeus's 'artificial' one; and Brown again did pioneering work in the study of geographical distributions, a subject which Darwin later called 'that almost keystone of the laws of creation'.[41]

The collecting work of these years also produced additional examples of antipodean oddity. There was that curiosity with a lyre-shaped tail, the 'Blue Mountain Pheasant' (*Maemura superba*) (6.16) that imitated a great range of sounds so cleverly; and the New Holland 'sloth' (koala) (6.18), a 'torpid, senseless creature' that one writer found 'wisely intended to fill up one of the great links of the chain of animated nature, and to show the extensive variety of created beings which God has, in his wisdom, constructed'.[42] Other observers, though, found in some of the New Holland creatures disturbing evidence that species might not be fixed. Dr George Shaw thought that, with its 'duck's' bill 'engrafted on the head of a quadruped', the platypus (*Ornithorhynchus anatinus*) (6.17) 'naturally excites the idea of some deceptive preparation by artificial means'. Banks and Lamarck found this and its equally puzzling cousin the spiny anteater (*Echidna*) to constitute a form intermediate between mammal and bird. Banks wrote to Caley in 1803:

Our greatest want here is to be acquainted with the manner in which the duck Bill Animal & the Porcupine Ant Eater which I think is the same genus, breed, their internal structure is so very similar to that of Birds that I do not think it impossible they should lay Eggs or at least as Snakes & some Fish do Hatch Eggs in their Bellies.

'The further we extend our observations', Lamarck concluded a few years later with these animals in mind, 'the more proofs do we acquire that the boundaries of the classes, even apparently most isolated, are not unlikely to be effaced by our new discoveries.'[43] Slowly but surely, the southern continent was giving rise to elements of the evolutionary world view.

The lengthening period of settlement about Port Jackson also brought more detailed knowledge of local Aboriginal culture—of artefacts and weaponry and fighting habits; of relations between the sexes; of childbirth customs; of initiation rites and burial ceremonies; and of tribal punishments. This knowledge led to the perception that Aborigines were not nomadic, that, rather, 'they are divided ... into small families; and each family has a particular place of residence, from which is derived its distinguishing name'.[44] Aboriginal religion, though, remained a mystery. Daniel Paine observed in 1795 that the blacks

do not appear to have any Idea of a Supreme Being having several times questioned Bennelong on that Subject during our passage to Port Jackson they entertain some

6.16   Engraved by Philip Slaeger, 'The Blue Mountain Pheasant of New South Wales' 1814

6.17   Charles-Alexandre Lesueur   Platypus   *?c.* 1802

confused notion of a Wicked Spirit of which they are very much afraid and wear pieces of small Bone or Stick through the lower part of the Nose or Upper lip at times as a Charm to prevent some machinations of this Evil Spirit.[45]

George Cooke observed that

no country has yet been discovered where some traces of religion is not to be found; the writers who had transmitted accounts of [New South Wales] declare, that after the minutest investigation and enquiry, they have not discovered that the natives had any one object of adoration, either the sun, the moon, the stars, any particular animal, or were actuated by any principle that incited them to the practice of what we term moral good, or deter them from the practice of what we call moral evil. They admit that these people have some idea of a future state, but not as bearing any analogy to religion, or in any degree influencing their actions.[46]

The widening range of European contact with the continent also led to the growth of a sense of the diversity of Aboriginal culture. Vancouver's voyage and those of the French to Van Diemen's Land showed striking differences in language, material culture, and dress and ornamentation between the inhabitants

229

of the western, and eastern shores of the continent and Van Diemen's Land (4.20, 4.27, 5.16, 5.18, 6.19). By bringing back details of northern Aborigines, Flinders's voyage broadened this knowledge. The Aborigines about Sydney, observers noted, knocked out a front incisor, those in Van Diemen's Land did not. The southern Aborigines made canoes by tying together the ends of large pieces of bark, whereas the northern ones shaped and burned out tree-trunks or made rafts. Those in the west seemingly did not use canoes. There were important linguistic variations.[47]

Such information bore directly on discussion of one of the most vexing of eighteenth-century puzzles. While it had first arisen with the discovery of the Americas (continents also not allowed for in interpretations of the Biblical scheme of things), the question of whether, especially, the human races constituted a single creation or separate ones progressively gathered prominence as Linnaeus, Buffon, Kant, and Monboddo mulled it over. By the end of the century, opinion in favour of special creations was strengthening. Bound by his commitment to the fixity of species, the great German anatomist Johannes Blumenbach attempted to gainsay the new ideas by arguing that skulls from around the world, including the Australian ones, showed a constant form. Blumenbach's, however, was a rearguard action. Early in the nineteenth century, the Scottish geographer John Pinkerton (in the words of one outraged critic) 'reject[ed] the chronology of the Scriptures, consider[ed] many nations of the earth as aboriginal, and establish[ed] a great Scythian empire in the heart of Asia 3660 years before the Christian aera'. Among Pinkerton's perceptions was that there were 'three or four races', the results of separate creations, in New Holland.[48]

The sheer fact of New Holland also bore one of those elements central to an evolutionary view, that of gradual change through long periods of time. This perception was first developed in terms of the rise and fall of civilizations. As the most recently discovered of the continents, and that presently in the most undeveloped state, New Holland was the logical future site of 'Civilization', then on its relentless shift from Europe to the Americas.[49] However, in the late 1780s this idea took on also a geological aspect, with James Hutton's hypothesis that the process of decay was the first principle of the earth's operation, and that of renovation the second. With the third that the world was always in existence, Hutton presented the idea of a physical world constantly decaying in some places and renovating in others, with the changes emerging only gradually over immense periods of time.[50]

In the context of these perceptions, New Holland became the European future. Sometimes, this perception was put in the older, conventional way, as when the translator of Labillardière's *Voyage* contemplated a time when

the advantages of civilization may..., in the progress of events, be transferred from the Europeans, who have but too little prized them, to those remote countries which they have been so diligently exploring? If so, the period may arrive, when New Zealand may

6.18   John Lewin   Koala   *c.* 1803

6.19   Nicolas-Martin Petit   Ouriaga   1802

6.20 [Anonymous] Sydney *c.* 1800

6.21   William Westall   'View of Sir Edward Pellew's Group, Gulph of Carpentaria'   ?c. 1803

produce her Lockes, her Newtons, and her Montesquieus; and when great nations in the immense region of New Holland, may send their navigators, philosophers, and antiquaries, to contemplate the ruins of *ancient* London and Paris, and to trace the languid remains of the arts and sciences in this quarter of the globe. Who can tell, whether the rudiments of some great future empire may not already exist at Botany Bay?[51]

Sometimes, the perception was put in the newer, geological terms, as when John Pinkerton repeated the speculation that 'the isles of Sunda, the Moluccas, and others in the Indian ocean, are gradually enlarging, and may in time, with Australasia and Polynesia, form a vast new continent; while one or other of the ancient continents will be submerged under the ocean'.[52] Sometimes, both modes of expressing the perception coalesced, as when Banks told Hunter in 1797 that he saw 'the future prospect of empires and dominions which now cannot be disappointed. Who knows but that England may revive in New South Wales when it has sunk in Europe?'[53] The same point was made by Pinkerton, when in his *Modern Geography* (1802) he offered a half-apology for the length of his section on the 'new' continent—'now little known, but which in the year 1900, or 2000, may be found to present such great and singular topics, that a learned and precise pen may dedicate a large volume of geography to this one portion of the globe'.[54]

As these remarks suggest, a sense of the whole continent was emerging. By the mid-1790s geographical writers were identifying 'New Holland' as a continent, and as the 'fifth' or 'sixth' part of the world (depending on whether they counted the Americas as one part or two).[55] George Cooke, for example, drew on the voyages of Cook, Vancouver, and d'Entrecasteaux as well as on the narratives of the New South Wales settlement to suggest (however inadequately) a continental range of geology, climate and flora and fauna.[56] The celebrated naturalist Thomas Pennant in his *Outlines of the Globe* (1800), though he still clung to the old terminology, gave it a continental application. '*New Holland*', he pointed out, 'is in the length from the north point, in Lat. 11° to 46°30' south, about two thousand miles ... This vast tract proves equal in size (according to the estimate of our later navigators) to all *Europe*. I see no reason why it should not be called a fifth continent.'[57] Present now too was a perception of the region's tropical extensions, best conveyed by Flinders's descriptions and Westall's accompanying splendid paintings (6.21).

Even if its interior remained blank, a geographical entity of this size demanded a name. From the time of the Renaissance onwards, a number of variations on the original 'Terra Australis' had been offered, and several alternatives. There was Quirós's 'Australia' (1610); the Dutch 'Nova Hollandia' and its English form 'New Holland'; Charles de Brosses's 'Australasie' (1756) and Pinkerton's 'Australasia' (1802). The late eighteenth-century English suggestion of 'Cookia', after 'our great navigator', rightly found no support.[58] The actual term 'Australia' first appeared in 1625 as a misprint for 'Austrialia'.[59] It was then employed in the English translation (1693) of Gabriel de Foigny's *La Terre Australe Connue*. Callander used it again in his version of de Brosses (1766), as did Alexander Dalrymple in his *Historical Collection* (1770). George Shaw seems to have been the first to give the name specifically to the now-revealed continent, when he wrote of 'The vast Island or rather Continent of Australia, Australasia, or New Holland, which has so lately attracted the particular attention of European navigators and naturalists'.[60] He was followed in this by Matthew Flinders, who in 1804 observed to his brother, 'I call the whole island Australia or Terra Australis' (frontispiece); and who, a few years later, in a paper on the fate of Lapérouse, added: 'I have considered it convenient to unite the two parts [i.e., New Holland and New South Wales] under a common designation which will do justice to the discovery rights of Holland and England, and I have with the object in view had recourse to the name Austral-land or Australia'.[61] Flinders returned to this point in his narrative of his great survey. 'Had I permitted myself any innovation upon the original term [i.e. Terra Australis]', he wrote, 'it would have been to convert it into Australia';[62] and he entitled one of his charts 'Terra Australis or Australia' (6.11). In 1817 this title caught the imagination of Governor Lachlan Macquarie, who thereafter employed Flinders's preferred 'Australia' in his dispatches, in the hope that it would become 'the Name given to this Country in future'.[63] Macquarie's patronage had its effect. By the mid-1820s 'Australia' was coming into general use as the name of the continent, and 'Australians' as that of its inhabitants (at this time, black as well as white).

As he concluded his exploration of the southern reaches of the Pacific Ocean in 1775, Captain James Cook 'flatered' himself that he had put 'a final end . . . to the searching after a Southern Continent, which has at times ingrossed the attention of some of the Maritime Powers for near two Centuries past and the Geographers of all ages'.[64] Cook's explorations, joined to those of the Dutch navigators, also revealed the true southern continent. From the uncertainties of the one slowly emerged the shape of the other, as R. H. Major indicated in 1859 when he called his collection of discovery narratives *Early Voyages to Terra Australis, now called Australia*. Major's title encompasses the dominant theme of this volume also; for it was the search for the mythical Terra Australis which led to the discovery and first settlement of Australia by Europeans. The nature of the quest, with its sequence of failure and disillusionment, achievement and promise, was encapsulated by Pinkerton in 1802. As the geographer discussed possible names for the new discoveries he reminded his readers that one must be found which 'not only implies a continent but the reminiscence that this region supplies the place of the ideal Terra Australis, after which geographers and navigators so long enquired in vain'.[65]

Notes

1 [George III], Instructions to Phillip, 25 April 1787, HRNSW, I, ii, 89.
2 See *The Voyage of Governor Phillip to Botany Bay* [1789], ed. J. J. Auchmuty (Sydney, 1970), p. 50.
3 Ibid., pp. 150–64, 165–74. For a modern account of these and subsequent voyages, see Rhys Richards, 'The Easternmost Route to China and the Robertson Aikman Charts', GC, 8 (April 1986), 54–67, 104–16, 9 (1987), 48–59.
4 See [Phillip], *Voyage*, pp. 129–[49].
5 Hunter, *Historical Journal*, p. 66.
6 Ibid., pp. 61–91. See also Bradley, *Voyage*, pp. 145–62.
7 John Hunter, *An Historical Journal of Events at Sydney and at Sea 1787–1792* [1793], ed. John Bach, (Sydney, 1968), pp. 277–85.
8 George Vancouver, *A Voyage of Discovery to the North Pacific Ocean and Round the World 1791–1795*, ed. W. Kaye Lamb (London, 1984), I, 329–59.
9 M. Labillardière, *Voyage in Search of La Pérouse* (London, 1800), p. 94. See also Hélène Richard, *Le Voyage de d'Entrecasteaux à la Recherche de Lapérouse* (Paris, 1986).
10 Labillardière, *Voyage*, p. 251.
11 Leslie R. Marchant, *France Australe* (Perth, 1982), p. 26.
12 See Hélène Richard, 'L'Expédition de D'Entrecasteaux (1791–1794) et les origines de l'implantation anglaise en Tasmanie', *Revue française d'histoire d'Outre-Mer*, 69 (1982), 289–306.
13 *The Bligh Notebook*, ed. John Bach (Canberra, 1987).
14 Matthew Flinders, *A Voyage to Terra Australis* (London, 1814), I, xcvii.
15 Hunter to Portland, 25 June 1797, HRNSW, III, 237.
16 See above, p. 118.
17 *The Journals of Captain James Cook*, ed. J. C. Beaglehole (Cambridge, 1955–68), II, 163–5, 700.
18 Quoted in L. A. Triebel and J. C. Batt, *The French Exploration of Australia* (Hobart, 1957), p. 9.
19 William Bradley, *A Voyage to New South Wales 1786–1792* (Sydney, 1969), p. 56.
20 Hunter, *Historical Journal*, p. 86.
21 Vancouver to Grenville, 9 August 1791, HRNSW, I, ii, 520; and Vancouver, *Voyage*, I, 346.
22 See Triebel and Batt, *French Exploration*, p. 30.
23 Hunter to Portland, 1 March 1798, HRNSW, III, 363–5.
24 Flinders, 'Narrative . . .', HRNSW, III, 769–818.
25 Matthew Flinders, *Observations on the Coasts of Van Diemen's Land, on Bass's Strait and its Islands, and on part of the coasts of New South Wales* (London, 1801).
26 See King, Instructions to Grant, 5 March 1801, HRNSW, IV, 305–8; and Grant, 'Remarks . . .', ibid., 477–88; King to Murray, 31 October 1801, ibid., 602–4; and other material in this volume.
27 *The Journal of Post Captain Nicolas Baudin*, trans. Christine Cornell (Adelaide, 1974), p. 1. For a recent account of the Baudin expedition see Marchant, *France Australe*, chs 5 and 6.
28 M. F. Péron, *A Voyage of Discovery in the Southern Hemisphere* (London, 1809), p. 285.
29 See the various documents in HRNSW, IV. The details of the survey are based on Flinders, *Voyage*; and see T. M. Perry, 'Matthew Flinders and the Charting of the Australian Coast', *The Globe*, No. 23 (1985), pp. 1–10.
30 The most recent study of Flinders's life and work is Geoffrey Ingleton, *Matthew Flinders, Navigator and Chartmaker* (Guildford, 1986). Older studies are: James D. Mack, *Matthew Flinders, 1774–1814* (Melbourne, 1966); K. A. Austin, *The Voyage of the Investigator* (Adelaide, 1964); S. J. Baker, *My Own Destroyer* (Sydney, 1962); and Ernest Scott, *The Life of Captain Matthew Flinders R.N.* (Sydney, 1914).
31 Hunter to Portland, 28 April 1796 and 10 June 1797, HRNSW, III, 38, 220–1.
32 [A colonist], August 1799, quoted in *Colonial Australia 1788–1840*, ed. Frank Crowley (Melbourne, 1980), p. 92.
33 King, 'Condition of Norfolk Island', 18 October 1796, HRNSW, III, 159–60.
34 [?] to [?], 14 September 1798, ibid., p. 486.
35 King to Hobart, 9 May 1803, 1 March 1804, HRA, IV, 461, 469, 480.
36 Quoted in Ernest Scott, *Terre Napoléon* (London, 1910), p. 196.
37 A small penal settlement was established at the mouth of the Hunter River, seventy miles north of Sydney, in 1801, for the purpose of obtaining coal and lime—see Paterson to King, 25 June 1801, Paterson, 'Journal ', and King to Portland, 21 August 1801, HRNSW, IV, 414–16, 448–53, 476–7.
38 Phillip to Sydney, 13 February 1790, HRNSW, I, ii, 306; and King, report on Caley's expedition, 2 November 1805, HRNSW, V, 726–7. For details of these attempts, see variously: Tench, *Sydney's First Four Years*, pp. 153–5; *The Everingham*

Letterbook, ed. Valerie Ross (Wamberal, 1985); Francis Barrallier, 'Journal of an Expedition . . .', HRNSW, V, 749–825; George Caley, *Reflections on the Colony of New South Wales*, ed. J. E. B. Currey (Melbourne, 1966); Alan E. J. Andrews, 'The Carmarthen Hills and thereabouts', JRAHS, 69 (1983), 1–17.

39 For a survey, see Ann Moyal, *A Bright & Savage Land: Scientists in Colonial Australia* (Sydney, 1986).

40 John Dunmore, *French Explorers in the Pacific* (Oxford, 1969), II, 37–8.

41 See Christine Cornell, *Questions relating to Nicolas Baudin's Australian Expedition 1800–1804* (Adelaide, 1965), p. 53; J. D. Hooker, 'Introduction', *The Botany of the Antarctic Voyage of H.M. Discovery Ships 'Erebus' and 'Terror'* (London, 1847–60), III, cxiv; Darwin to Hooker, [10 February] 1845, *The Life and Letters of Charles Darwin*, ed. Francis Darwin (London, 1887), I, 304.

42 George Perry, quoted in Moyal, *Bright & Savage Land*, p. 42.

43 Shaw, quoted ibid., p. 22; Banks to Caley, 8 April 1803, Mitchell Brabourne Papers, vol. 8; and Lamarck, *Zoological Philosophy* (1809), trans. Hugh Elliot (London, 1914), p. 23.

44 George Cooke, *Modern and Authentic System of Universal Geography* (London, c. 1800), I, 249. (This account is based largely on that of Collins.)

45 Paine, *Journal*, p. 41.

46 Cooke, *System*, I, 249–50.

47 See, variously, Vancouver, *Voyage*, I, 342, 347, and Flinders, *Voyage*, I, lxxxix–xc, xcv, 66, and II, 146. Cooke, *System* I, 241–5, summarized the explorers' observations. N. J. B. Plomley, *The Baudin Expedition and the Tasmanian Aborigines 1802* (Hobart, 1983) offers both original observation and modern commentary.

48 Pinkerton, *Modern Geography*, II, 472; and [anon.], *A Vindication of the Celts* (London, 1803), pp. 4, 8, 137.

49 See Alan Frost, '"As it were another America": English Ideas of the First Settlement in New South Wales at the End of the Eighteenth Century', *Eighteenth Century Studies*, 7 (1974), 255–73.

50 James Hutton, 'Theory of the Earth', *Transactions of the Royal Society of Edinburgh* (1788), and *Theory of the Earth* (1795).

51 Labillardière, *Voyage*, p. vii.

52 Pinkerton, *Modern Geography*, II, 434.

53 Banks to Hunter, 30 March 1797, HRNSW, III, 202.

54 Pinkerton, *Modern Geography*, II, 478.

55 See, for example, *The Edinburgh Magazine*, 1 (1785), 130; Pinkerton, *Modern Geography*, II, 431 and Flinders, *Voyage*, I, iv, and II, 151–76.

56 Cooke, *System*, I, 183–253.

57 Thomas Pennant, *Outlines of the Globe* (London, 1800), IV, 97–8.

58 *Gentleman's Magazine*, 65 (December 1795), p. 1017.

59 Samuel Purchas, *Purchas, His Pilgrimes* (London, 1625), IV, 1423.

60 George Shaw, *Zoology of New Holland* (London, 1794), I, 2.

61 Flinders to Samuel Flinders, 25 August 1804, Flinders Letterbook, Mitchell Safe 1/55; and 'Sur le Banc du Naufrage et sur le Sort de M. de La Pérouse':

> J'ai cru convenable de les réunir sous une dénomination commune, et qui parût étrangère aux droits respectifs de la Hollande et de l'Angleterre quant à la *priorité* de la découverte, et j'ai eu recours, à cet effet, au nom de terre Australe ou Australie. Mais il reste à savoir si ce nom sera adopté par les géographes européens.—in *Annales des Voyages*, II, ed. C. Malte-Brun (Paris, 1810), II, 89–90.

62 Flinders, *Voyage*, I, iii.

63 See HRA, IX, 356, 404, 477, 726.

64 Cook, *Journals*, II, 643.

65 Pinkerton, *Modern Geography*, II, 465n.

Index

239